Economic Causes and Consequences of Defense Expenditures in the Middle East and South Asia

Economic Causes and Consequences of Defense Expenditures in the Middle East and South Asia

Robert E. Looney
and David Winterford

Westview Press
BOULDER • SAN FRANCISCO • OXFORD

This Westview softcover edition is printed on acid-free paper and bound in library-quality, coated covers that carry the highest rating of the National Association of State Textbook Administrators, in consultation with the Association of American Publishers and the Book Manufacturers' Institute.

Copyright © 1995 by Westview Press, Inc.

Published in 1995 in the United States of America by Westview Press, Inc., 5500 Central Avenue, Boulder, Colorado 80301-2877, and in the United Kingdom by Westview Press, 36 Lonsdale Road, Summertown, Oxford OX2 7EW

Library of Congress Cataloging-in-Publication Data
Economic causes and consequences of defense expenditures in the Middle
    East and South Asia / Robert E. Looney and David
    Winterford.
        p.   cm.
    Includes bibliographical references and index.
    ISBN 0-8133-8442-7
    1. War—Economic aspects—Middle East.   2. War— Economic aspects—
South Asia.   3. Military readiness.   4. Middle East—Economic
policy.   5. South Asia—Economic policy.   I. Looney, Robert E.
II. Winterford, David, 1949 –   .
HC415.15.Z9D42   1995
338.4'76233'0954—dc20   94-35985
                                                                                              CIP

Printed and bound in the United States of America

The paper used in this publication meets the requirements
of the American National Standard for Permanence of Paper
for Printed Library Materials Z39.48-1984.

10   9   8   7   6   5   4   3   2   1

Contents

PART THREE
DEFENSE EXPENDITURES IN THE MIDDLE EAST AND
SOUTH ASIA: SUSTAINABILITY AND PROJECTIONS

Tables

PART ONE

Defense Expenditures in the Middle East and South Asia: A Quantitative Analysis

1

Introduction

As growing fiscal problems prompt governments to reorder their spending priorities, it is apparent that decision-makers in the Middle East and South Asia are examining the potential costs and benefits of allocations to the military.

Conventional wisdom has long argued that heavy outlays on defense divert scarce resources from directly productive investment (for example, infrastructure) and human capital formation (for example, education and health). While this view may make intuitive sense, there is evidence that military expenditures do not necessarily reduce overall economic growth in developing countries as a whole.[1] Defense expenditures may in some instances act as an economic stimulus in various ways such as financing heavy industry and the acquisition of advanced technologies, providing employment, and attracting investment.[2]

This study examines the relationship between defense spending and economic performance in the developing world in general, and in nine countries in the Middle East and South Asia in particular–Algeria, Egypt, Iran, Iraq, Israel, Syria, Saudi Arabia, Pakistan and India. It seeks to answer the following questions:

1. Did defense expenditures hinder or aid economic growth in our sample countries during the 1980s?
2. Were the linkages from military expenditures to growth different than in previous time periods?
3. Did defense expenditures impact uniformly or vary by country?

---

1. The literature and debate on this controversial point are examined in-depth for developing countries as a whole in Chapter 4 and for the Middle East and South Asia in particular in Chapter 5. In those chapters we offer a rigorous economic analysis of the impact of defense spending on economic growth.

2. In Chapter 6 we present our detailed economic analysis of the impact of defense expenditures on human capital development in the Middle East and South Asia. In Chapter 7 we analyze its impact on budgetary allocations in the region.

4. If the impact varied by country, what caused the variations and can the differences be depicted by country sub-groupings?
5. What are the individual country patterns and trends in defense and development spending?
6. How do defense expenditures in one country affect those in neighboring states? What arms races exist in the region?
7. Does a causal relationship exist between defense spending and overall economic growth? If it does, in which direction does causation occur? Can we predict the direction and nature of these causal relationships?

Geo-Economics: The Security Context in the Middle East and South Asia

Our study presents a detailed and rigorous quantitative economic assessment, analysis, and interpretation of the impact of defense expenditures in the Middle East and South Asia over the last two decades. However, such an economic analysis needs to be placed within the security context prevailing in the region. In particular, it is useful to discuss briefly the geo-economic and geo-political post-cold war and post-Gulf War security order in the Middle East and South Asia.

Although the end of the cold war has profoundly altered international economic and political relations, it has also revealed that much of the defense spending undertaken by developing countries during the cold war may have had very little to do with superpower-ordered ideological conflicts. The cold war may have been useful to developing countries for obtaining advanced weapons from first and second tier suppliers, however the end of global hostilities does not mean the end of the intra- and inter-state fears and rivalries that have had such a profound influence on regional defense spending. Consequently, it is unwise to expect that more benign security relations at the global level portend drastically reduced military spending at the regional level.

Of course, even in the unlikely event that defense expenditures were markedly slashed, such a reduction would not necessarily result by itself in a major "peace dividend" of increased economic growth in any given nation. Theoretically, the returns on alternative uses of monies devoted to defense may be high.[3] However, realistically such slashing looks very unlikely in the Middle East and South Asia. In any event, there is no assurance that reduced defense budgets would result in higher outlays on social welfare, infrastructure or similar uses.

The region remains beset by a dangerous mixture of ethnic, racial, religious, resource, and territorial conflicts. Moreover, throughout the Middle East and South Asia established authorities increasingly confront the imperatives of fundamentalism and nationalism. Finally, there is no shortage of aspiring regional hegemons eager to fill any power vacuum that may develop in the wake of the collapse of the Soviet Union or in anticipation of a precipitous withdrawal by the United States. Although the 1990-91 Gulf War altered the strategic map of the region, it did not resolve the basic dilemma of national fears, antagonisms, rivalries, and regional conflict.

The Gulf War underlined the elastic nature of regional boundaries. Although Pakistan's involvement with the coalition forces was initially viewed by Western powers through the prism of "deterring aggression," it quickly became apparent that Islam loomed larger at the mass level in Pakistan than any concern with regional power balances, worsening even further Indo-Pakistan relations. India, in turn, with countless of its citizens employed throughout the Middle East and its elites fearful of resurgent Islam at home, finds itself drawn to the Gulf area. New Delhi has quickly determined that its defense forces may need further bolstering in light of India's new post-Gulf and post-cold war security realities.

Renewed hopes exist for the Middle East peace process and an accommodation on the one hand between Israel and the Palestine Liberation Organization and on the other between Israel and its neighbors. Nevertheless both the Gulf War and its aftermath also reveal the continued saliency, indeed vibrancy, of the polarized divide between Israel and much of the Arab world.

Oil remains central to any discussion of defense, security, economics, and sovereignty in the Middle East. Oil is the vital regional strategic and economic resource. We have argued elsewhere that the urgent need for additional oil revenues was a critical part of Saddam Hussein's decision to invade Kuwait.[4] Iraq's mounting irritation over its inability to force Kuwait to accept production cutbacks in order to raise global oil prices set the stage for the invasion and war. Access to, and control of oil has long been a part of the instability and rivalries in the region. Indeed, since the very discovery of the vast Middle Eastern oil resources, oil has been inseparable from any discussion of regional defense planning and resource allocation.

---

3. For example, the Congressional Budget Office calculates that under current resource allocations, if Middle East countries reduced arms imports by one-third, then "the newly available resources could be used to raise living standards in the Middle East. Alternatively, some or all of the extra resources could be invested in that region. Doing that could increase the level of real GDP in major Mideast countries by 2.5 percent or more on average." See Congressional Budget Office, *Limiting Arms Exports to the Middle East* (Washington D.C.: Congressional Budget Office, September 1992) p. xvii. Later in that study it was pointed out that "the full effects might not be realized for 20 or 30 years..." (p. 49).

4. David Winterford and Robert E. Looney, "Gulf Oil: Geo-Economic and Geo-Strategic Realities in the Post-Cold War and Post-Gulf War Era," in M.E. Ahrari and James H. Noyes, eds., *The Persian Gulf After the Cold War* (Westport: Praeger, 1993), pp. 149-171.

Of course, external powers have long been active in attempting to shape the political context of the Middle East and South Asia to meet their ideological, economic, and security goals. Although the imposing military presence of colonial rule long ago yielded to nationalism, enduring ties may still be found in a variety of economic, political, and security arrangements.[5] That these arrangements have found a new life in the post-cold war era signals the abiding importance of the region to others. In turn, regional actors, either as a result of fear, ambition, or concern, have sought increasingly lethal and expensive weapons from western powers and the former eastern bloc.

Lately, some of the more technologically advanced countries in the Middle East and South Asia have concluded co-production or licensing agreements for the local manufacture of weapons. One intent has been to secure a wider range of economic benefits including the transfer of technology and employment creation from the allocation of resources to defense. We now turn to the economic impacts of defense expenditures in the Middle East and South Asia.

Our investigation of the widespread interest in the effects of defense spending begins in Part One with a series of rigorous thematically-oriented quantitative assessments of the economic causes and consequences of defense expenditures. Chapter 2 provides a factor analysis of the patterns of defense expenditures and socio-economic development in the Middle East and South Asia. In Chapter 3 we provide a causality analysis of regional arms races together with an examination of the direction of country causation. In Chapter 4 we undertake an empirical assessment of the macroeconomic impact of defense spending in the Third World. This is followed in Chapter 5 by a specialized focus on the economic consequences of defense spending in our sample of major defense spending nations in the Middle East and South Asia. In Chapter 6 we examine the impact of defense spending on human capital development in the Middle East and South Asia. This is followed in Chapter 7 by an analysis of budgetary priorities and the impact of defense expenditures on budgetary allocations in our sample countries. In Part Two, we present an in-depth assessment of the impact of defense spending in four country-specific chapters (Chapters 8-11) focusing on Iran, Iraq, Saudi Arabia, and Pakistan. In Part Three, our final chapter forecasts future spending patterns and assesses the economically sustainable military expenditure limits for our sample countries in the Middle East and South Asia.

---

5. For example, see the discussion of a free trade arrangement between the European Union (formerly the European Common Market) and six Gulf nations making up the Gulf Cooperation Council in Robert E. Looney and David Winterford, "Patterns of Arab Gulf Exports: Implications for Industrial Diversification of Increased Inter-Arab Trade," *Orient*, 33, 4 (December 1992), pp. 579-597.

2

Patterns of Defense Expenditures and Socio-Economic Development in the Middle East and South Asia: A Factor Analytic Approach

This chapter examines in some detail the manner in which defense expenditures and socio-economic development have evolved in the Middle East and South Asia over the period since the 1973-1974 oil price increases. While the general scope of the analysis is on developing countries, our attention is focused on a sample of seven of the more important nations in the Middle East and South Asia: Algeria, Egypt, Israel, Saudi Arabia, Syria, India and Pakistan. Several questions are addressed in our analysis:

1. What are the country patterns and trends in defense and development spending?
2. Have changes in defense expenditures exhibited any particular pattern with regard to movements in socio-economic development?
3. Do increased levels of defense expenditures curtail expenditures on other government allocations, particularly health and education?

Recent Patterns

In the period following the 1973/74 oil price increases, the region as a whole, and the Middle East in particular, experienced an unprecedented growth in economic output, exports, military spending (Table 2.1), armed forces (Table 2.2) and arms transfers (Table 2.3). Growth in military expenditures and arms transfers, however, decelerated and for many countries was negative over the last few years of the 1980s. Nevertheless, following the Gulf War of 1990-91, those declines did not continue for most of the Gulf states.[1]

TABLE 2.1   Military Expenditures: Shares and Growth (in percentages)

| | World Share | | Average Annual Growth | |
Region	1979	1989	1979-1989	1985-1989
World	100.0	100.0	2.2	-0.4
Developed	81.2	83.8	2.6	0.2
Developing	18.8	16.2	0.3	- 3.1
Region				
Africa	1.8	1.5	-0.7	0.0
East Asia	8.1	8.0	2.0	2.0
Europe, all	56.5	51.7	1.4	0.1
NATO Europe	15.0	14.2	1.4	0.5
Warsaw Pact	39.1	35.3	1.8	-0.1
Other Europe	2.4	2.2	1.2	0.0
Latin America	1.4	1.4	2.6	0.4
Middle East	6.8	5.1	- 1.5	- 8.8
North America	24.0	30.4	4.8	0.1
Oceania	0.6	0.7	3.3	-1.5
South Asia	0.8	1.1	6.4	2.9
Organization				
NATO, all	39.0	44.7	3.6	0.1
Warsaw Pact	39.1	35.3	1.4	-0.1
OPEC	5.6	4.5	- 1.5	- 7.1
OECD	43.7	50.0	3.6	0.3

Source: United States Arms Control and Disarmament Agency, *World Military Expenditures and Arms Transfers, 1990* (Washington, USACDA, November, 1991, reprinted 1992), p. 2.

Several points are worth noting from the data in Tables 2.1-2.3. First, defense expenditures seem remarkably steady in the years covered, even when income is falling. In some cases, they even rise slightly. Second, the figures on expenditures for the last several years covered may be too low. The greatest part of armed forces spending is on salaries and training, rather than equipment purchases. There is little evidence of manpower reductions. Finally, data for defense expenditure in 1989 show that prior to the 1990-91 Gulf War, in many cases—especially for the Gulf States—the proportion spent on defense had begun rising back to levels seen in the mid-1980s. A similar trend, that is, maintenance and often increasing levels of defense spending, is evident in many Middle East states in the early 1990s after the sobering experience of the Gulf War.[2]

----

    1. *The Military Balance 1993-94* (London: Brassey's for the International Institute for Strategic Studies, October 1993) pp. 107-133.
    2. M.E. Ahrari, "Arms Race in the Persian Gulf: The Post-Cold War Dynamics," in M.E. Ahrari and James H. Noyes, eds., *The Persian Gulf After the Cold War* (Westport, CT: Praeger, 1993) pp. 188-192.

TABLE 2.2   Armed Forces: Shares and Growth (in percentages)

Region	World Share		Average Annual Growth	
	1979	*1989*	*1979-1989*	*1985-1989*
World	100.0	100.0	0.8	- 0.3
Developed	37.4	35.5	0.3	- 0.7
Developing	62.6	64.5	1.1	- 0.1
Region				
Africa	4.7	5.9	2.9	0.2
East Asia	31.6	29.8	-0.5	-0.4
Europe, all	34.6	31.7	-0.0	- 1.1
NATO Europe	11.8	11.6	0.6	- 0.2
Warsaw Pact	19.6	17.5	0.1	- 1.6
Other Europe	3.3	2.6	-1.6	-1.9
Latin America	5.6	5.7	1.0	- 4.0
Middle East	7.5	11.3	5.8	7.4
North America	7.9	8.2	1.1	- 0.1
Oceania	0.3	0.3	0.0	-0.2
South Asia	7.8	7.1	1.7	-3.8
Organization				
NATO, all	20.0	19.7	0.8	- 0.2
Warsaw Pact	19.7	18.6	-0.1	- 1.6
OPEC	5.7	8.9	6.0	5.6
OECD	23.3	22.6	0.6	- 0.2

Source: United States Arms Control and Disarmament Agency, *World Military Expenditures and Arms Transfers, 1990* (Washington, USACDA, November, 1991, reprinted 1992), p. 5.

Defense Expenditure/Socio-Economic Associations

The evolution of military and socio-economic expenditures since the 1973/74 oil price increases has produced some interesting patterns. Using data provided by Ruth Leger Sivard, we factor analyzed data on a sample of 110 developing countries over four year intervals: 1974, 1978, 1982 and 1986 (the years for which we have sufficient comparable data). In particular, we are interested in determining: (1) the manner in which defense expenditures have interacted with the process of socio-economic development; (2) whether this interaction has changed over time; (3) differences in these interactions between different country groupings; and most importantly, (4) the evolution of our sample countries with regard to their relative levels of defense expenditure, socio-economic development and the provision of health and educational services.

The variables included in the analysis were:

Military Variables: (a) military expenditures as a share of Gross National Product, (b) military expenditures share in the central government budget, (c) military expenditures per soldier, and (d) armed forces per capita.

TABLE 2.3   Arms Imports: Shares and Growth (in percentages)

Region	World Share		Average Annual Growth	
	1979	1989	1979-1989	1985-1989
World	100.0	100.0	-0.5	-4.1
Developed	16.0	23.6	2.4	-5.6
Developing	84.0	76.4	-1.2	-3.6
Region				
Africa				
East Asia	19.0	8.8	-8.9	-8.2
Europe, all	17.7	11.8	-1.3	- 2.4
NATO Europe	16.9	24.0	1.2	-2.3
Warsaw Pact	6.5	14.0	3.4	13.2
Other Europe	8.1	7.0	-2.4	-17.6
Latin America	2.3	3.0	3.5	3.7
Middle East	6.8	5.6	-1.6	-10.3
North America	32.7	26.6	-1.8	-10.3
Oceania	1.4	3.9	10.2	-1.5
South Asia	0.1	1.7	11.2	- 5.2
Organization	4.5	17.4	11.9	15.2
NATO, all				
Warsaw Pact				
OPEC	7.9	18.0	5.2	8.8
OECD	8.1	7.0	-2.4	-17.6

Source: United States Arms Control and Disarmament Agency, *World Military Expenditures and Arms Transfers, 1990* (Washington, USACDA, November, 1991, reprinted 1992), p. 5.

Nonmilitary, Public Expenditures: (a) educational expenditures per capita, (b) health expenditures per capita, and (c) total (including defense) expenditures share in Gross National Product.

Measures of Socio-Economic Performance: (a) per capita income, (b) percentage of the school age population in school, (c) literacy rate, (d) school age population per teacher, (e) infant mortality, (f) teachers per capita and (g) population per hospital bed.

Two additional variables were added, namely, a regional variable, differentiating the Middle East, North African and South Asian countries;[3] and, a variable depicting the level of violence used by governments against their populations.[4] The former variable was included to determine the manner in which the Middle Eastern, South Asian and North African

---

3. The countries grouped as Middle East/Asian are: Afghanistan, Algeria, Bahrain, Bangladesh, Cyprus, Egypt, India, Iran, Iraq, Israel, Jordan, Kuwait, Lebanon, Libya, Morocco, Nepal, Oman, Pakistan, Qatar, Saudi Arabia, Somalia, Sri Lanka, Sudan, Syria, Tunisia, Turkey, United Arab Emirates, Yemen Arab Republic, and Peoples Democratic Republic of Yemen.

4. This variable has values of 1, 2, and 3 indicating increasing levels of government repression. The data are provided by Sivard, *World Military and Social Expenditures* (Washington: World Priorities) but are only for the years 1982 and 1986.

countries differ from the rest of the developing world. The latter was included to determine to what extent military expenditures were related to internal (as opposed to external) factors.

Factor analysis was used to determine the main groupings of correlated variables for each of the four years under examination.[5] The advantage of this method of analysis lies largely in its ability to derive composite indices, based on a weighted average of variables. For example, countries may vary considerably with regard to their ranking on the military burden as opposed to a ranking based on per capita military expenditures or the share of military expenditures in the budget. By creating a militarization dimension incorporating the various measures of military expenditures, factor analysis allows us to avoid arbitrarily picking one measure of militarization for subsequent analysis. The militarization dimension created by factor analysis should be more indicative of the commitment of national resources to the military than that obtained through reliance on any one single measure.

A representative pattern shows the major dimensions of the data and indicates the manner in which each of the individual variables are correlated with the respective dimensions.[6] For each of the four years examined several different factor analysis were performed.

First the total sample of countries was factor analyzed (Table 2.4). Next, several additional factor analyses were undertaken to determine if any major differences in military expenditures/socio economic performance existed for sub-groupings of countries. Specifically, based on the initial total country results (as in Table 2.4), for each of the years examined, countries were grouped on the basis of factor scores as *high* (factor scores greater than zero) or *low* (factor scores less than zero) in terms of militarization and socio-economic performance.

Additional factor analyses were performed on each of the four sub groupings to determine if their member countries differed significantly from other country groupings with regard to their patterns of military expenditure, public expenditure, and socio-economic performance. For example, countries with high levels of militarization (factor scores greater than zero on Factor 2 in Table 2.4) were factor analyzed to determine if they differed with regard to their patterns of military expenditure/public expenditure per capita from countries with low levels of militarization. Similarly, do countries with high levels of socio-economic performance differ from those with low socio-economic performance with regard to the

---

5. See R.J. Rummel, *Applied Factor Analysis* (Evanston, Illinois: Northwestern University Press, 1970) for a description of this technique.

6. A varimax rotation was used in the analysis. Factors were selected on the basis of having an eigen value greater than one.

TABLE 2.4   Patterns of Government Expenditures and Socio-Economic
Development: Developing Countries, 1974 (varimax rotation
standardized regression coefficients)

Variable	Factor 1 Public Expend/ Capita	Factor 2 Military Expend	Factor 3 Socio-Economic Performance	Factor 4 Region
Educational Expen Cap	0.94*	0.10	0.17	0.01
Per Capita Income	0.91*	0.08	0.16	0.05
Health Expend Cap	0.91*	0.11	0.20	- 0.06
Military Exp / GNP	0.07	0.98*	0.00	- 0.01
Government Exp / GNP	0.14	0.91*	0.05	- 0.14
Military Exp/Budget	- 0.02	0.81*	- 0.06	0.25
Military Exp/Soldier	0.54	0.60*	- 0.11	- 0.20
Armed Forces Capita	0.45	0.50*	0.33	0.21
Sch Age Pop in Sch	0.25	- 0.02	0.86*	- 0.16
Literacy Rate	- 0.04	- 0.05	0.86*	- 0.13
Sch Age Pop / Teach	- 0.20	- 0.08	- 0.79*	0.05
Teachers / Capita	0.54*	0.04	0.72*	- 0.02
Infant Mortality	0.01	0.07	- 0.47	- 0.40
Pop per Hosp Bed	- 0.20	- 0.08	- 0.40	0.72*
Mideast-Asia	0.38	0.42	- 0.06	0.61*
EIGEN VALUES	5.38	3.20	1.69	1.16
Factor Scores				
Egypt	- 0.92	2.74	0.21	0.19
Israel	1.25	4.35	1.44	0.08
Saudi Arabia	2.14	0.98	- 1.38	- 0.23
Syria	- 0.64	1.85	0.75	1.17
India	- 0.42	- 0.01	0.02	1.36
Pakistan	- 0.67	0.92	- 0.65	1.93
Algeria	0.18	- 0.20	- 0.05	0.34

Based on obliquely rotated factor analysis.

Source: Ruth Leger Sivard, *World Military And Social Expenditures* (Washington:
World Priorities), various issues.

manner in which military expenditures are related to public expenditures
per capita?

The resulting country factor scores indicate the relative ranking of each
of the sample countries on each of the main trends in the data (Tables 2.5
and 2.6).[7] Factor scores were also computed for our sample of seven countries relative to those nations in the North African/Middle East/South
Asian region as a whole (Table 2.7).

Several major patterns summarize our sample countries over the 1974-
1986 period.

---

7. A full set of detailed results from the factor analysis are available from the authors
upon request.

TABLE 2.5 Summary: Patterns of Military Expenditure Relative to Socio-Economic Development and Public Expenditures Per Capita (factor scores)

Country	Military Expenditures	Socio-Economic Performance		Public Expenditures	
		Total Country Sample	Military Expenditure Group	Total Country Sample	Military Expenditure Group
1974					
Egypt	2.74	0.21	0.02	- 0.92	- 0.72
Israel	4.35	1.44	1.63	1.25	1.41
Saudi Arabia	0.98	- 1.38	- 1.25	2.14	2.66
Syria	1.85	0.75	0.65	- 0.64	- 0.63
India	- 0.01	0.02	- 0.06	- 0.42	- 0.11
Pakistan	0.92	- 0.65	- 0.64	- 0.67	- 0.94
Algeria	- 0.20	- 0.05	- 0.44	0.18	0.42
1978					
Egypt	1.98	0.04	0.00	- 0.57	- 0.72
Israel	3.93	1.74	1.93	0.40	1.41
Saudi Arabia	1.63	- 1.81	- 1.30	3.83	2.66
Syria	2.63	0.68	0.60	- 0.63	- 0.63
India	- 0.17	- 0.21	- 0.23	- 0.35	- 0.50
Pakistan	0.41	- 0.67	- 0.67	- 0.51	- 0.94
Algeria	- 0.16	- 0.63	- 0.35	0.25	0.83
1982					
Egypt	1.01	- 0.14	- 0.07	- 0.46	- 0.27
Israel	4.11	1.82	1.86	- 0.06	- 0.10
Saudi Arabia	1.02	- 1.44	- 0.92	6.42	4.40
Syria	2.34	0.74	0.61	- 0.66	- 0.78
India	0.07	- 0.50	- 0.61	- 0.18	- 0.37
Pakistan	0.81	- 1.11	- 1.23	- 0.14	- 0.17
Algeria	- 0.04	- 0.05	0.26	0.00	0.32
1986					
Egypt	0.96	0.04	0.00	- 0.35	- 0.78
Israel	2.49	1.04	0.97	1.38	1.42
Saudi Arabia	1.83	- 1.44	- 0.74	4.66	2.68
Syria	2.41	0.74	0.59	- 0.75	- 0.70
India	- 0.05	- 0.29	- 0.20	- 0.20	- 0.02
Pakistan	0.71	- 1.36	- 1.53	- 0.23	- 0.02
Algeria	- 0.41	0.41	0.66	0.55	0.63

1974

In 1974, the beginning of the period covered (Table 2.4), for developing countries as a whole military expenditures were distinct, having little correlation with other measures of socio-economic development. Israel was by far the most militarized of our sample countries followed by Egypt, Syria, Saudi Arabia, and Pakistan. All of these countries were above average (by Third World standards) in terms of military expenditures/armed forces. In contrast, India and Algeria were somewhat below average in terms of their allocations to the military. Also, only Israel, Saudi Arabia,

TABLE 2.6   Summary: Patterns of Military Expenditure Relative to Military
Expenditures and Public Expenditures Per Capita (factor scores)

Country	Military Expenditures	Socio-Economic Performance		Public Expenditures	
		Total Country Sample	Military Expenditure Group	Total Country Sample	Military Expenditure Group
1974					
Egypt	0.21	2.74	2.75	- 0.92	- 1.52
Israel	1.44	4.35	4.73	1.25	0.30
Saudi Arabia	- 1.38	0.98	0.97	2.14	2.07
Syria	0.75	1.85	1.82	- 0.64	0.41
India	0.02	- 0.01	0.04	- 0.42	- 0.22
Pakistan	- 0.65	0.92	1.12	- 0.67	- 0.56
Algeria	- 0.05	- 0.20	- 0.06	0.18	- 0.04
1978					
Egypt	0.04	1.98	1.68	- 0.57	- 0.63
Israel	1.74	3.93	4.18	0.40	0.71
Saudi Arabia	- 1.81	1.63	1.37	3.83	2.67
Syria	0.68	2.63	2.67	- 0.63	- 0.75
India	- 0.21	- 0.17	- 0.25	- 0.35	- 0.28
Pakistan	- 0.67	0.41	0.44	- 0.51	- 0.44
Algeria	- 0.63	- 0.16	- 0.37	0.25	0.41
1982					
Egypt	- 0.14	1.01	1.26	- 0.46	- 0.54
Israel	1.82	4.11	4.08	- 0.06	- 0.02
Saudi Arabia	- 1.44	1.02	0.39	6.42	5.81
Syria	0.74	2.34	2.34	- 0.66	- 0.03
India	- 0.50	0.07	0.05	- 0.18	- 0.31
Pakistan	- 1.11	0.81	0.94	- 0.14	- 0.40
Algeria	0.05	- 0.04	- 0.36	0.00	0.00
1986					
Egypt	0.04	0.96	0.69	- 0.35	- 0.25
Israel	1.04	2.49	2.51	1.38	0.94
Saudi Arabia	- 1.44	1.83	0.50	4.66	5.52
Syria	0.74	2.41	2.21	- 0.75	- 0.56
India	- 0.29	- 0.05	0.46	- 0.20	- 0.60
Pakistan	- 1.36	0.71	0.99	- 0.23	- 0.34
Algeria	0.41	- 0.41	- 0.35	0.55	0.40

and Algeria sustained higher than average levels of non-defense public expenditures. Finally, Saudi Arabia, Pakistan, and Algeria lagged somewhat
below developing countries as a whole in terms of their levels of socio-
economic performance.

In 1974, both the Middle Eastern/South Asian countries and those in
other parts of the developing world had fairly similar patterns of military
expenditure/socio-economic development. However, several significant
differences did occur. First, countries with higher than average military expenditures—Egypt, Israel, Saudi Arabia, Syria and Pakistan—tended to
have increased levels of socio-economic performance associated with

TABLE 2.7   Summary: Evolution of Militarization and Socio-Economic
Performance in the Middle East/South Asian Region, 1974-1986
(factor scores)

Country	Militarization	Socio-Economic Performance	Public Expenditures
1974			
Egypt	1.31	0.35	- 0.87
Israel	2.41	1.77	0.43
Saudi Arabia	0.35	- 0.78	1.30
Syria	0.74	0.43	- 0.90
India	- 0.47	0.01	- 0.64
Pakistan	0.30	- 0.70	- 0.73
Algeria	- 0.69	0.04	- 0.32
1978			
Egypt	0.75	0.29	- 0.75
Israel	2.05	1.75	0.25
Saudi Arabia	0.65	- 0.83	1.21
Syria	1.19	0.58	- 0.34
India	- 0.73	- 0.07	- 0.61
Pakistan	- 0.09	- 0.82	- 0.55
Algeria	- 0.93	0.35	- 0.34
1982			
Egypt	- 0.07	0.19	- 0.42
Israel	1.82	1.86	- 0.35
Saudi Arabia	0.65	- 0.70	3.61
Syria	0.80	0.90	- 0.70
India	- 0.70	- 0.20	- 0.36
Pakistan	0.08	- 1.14	- 0.45
Algeria	- 0.80	0.49	- 0.20
1986			
Egypt	- 0.02	0.12	- 0.41
Israel	1.12	1.33	0.19
Saudi Arabia	1.01	- 0.92	3.41
Syria	1.02	0.81	- 0.83
India	- 0.80	- 0.12	- 0.39
Pakistan	0.19	- 1.44	- 0.47
Algeria	- 1.29	0.77	0.01

Factor scores are relative to the Middle East/South Asian region as a whole.

higher military participation rates (the number of soldiers per 1000 population). Second, countries experiencing lower than average levels of militarization, including India and Algeria, tended to have a positive association between armed forces per capita and military expenditure per soldier and health/education expenditures per capita, rather than with overall increases in socio-economic performance.

This latter phenomenon, associated with the military participation rate in the low militarized countries, also appears to be somewhat stronger for the Middle Eastern/South Asian countries than is the case for countries outside the region. In addition, the regional dimension was also significant in affecting the pattern of public expenditure with the high expenditure Middle East/South Asian countries experiencing greater public expenditures and armed forces per capita than their counterparts in other parts of the developing world. Similarly, the low public expenditure countries in the region had higher levels of militarization than those in other regions.

Finally, in 1974, countries with relatively high levels of socio-economic attainment appeared capable of increasing their military expenditure per soldier and armed forces per capita while at the same time sustaining higher levels of health and educational expenditures. It should be noted, however, that of the sample countries only Israel was above average with respect to this phenomena. India, Syria and Egypt were considerably below the average for developing countries as a whole with regard to this pattern of military participation/expenditure and socio-economic performance. Given their level of socio-economic performance, all of the sample countries had relatively high levels of military expenditure, with Egypt, Israel and Syria considerably above the norm.

For countries with a low level of socio-economic attainment, both military expenditures per capita and armed forces per capita, while also positively associated with health and educational expenditures, were more closely associated with other measures of military expenditures.

1978

By 1978, both Saudi Arabia and Syria had experienced significant increases in their relative degree of militarization. In contrast, both Egypt and Israel suffered a relative decline with regard to this dimension. Several other developments were also of significance. First, in contrast to 1974, military expenditures per soldier increased their degree of association with other types of government expenditures. This pattern was reinforced even further in the Middle East/South Asian region.

Second, countries with relatively high levels of military expenditures in 1978 experienced a fairly close association between their military expenditures (as a share of GNP) and total government expenditures (as a share of GNP). By this time, Egypt, Israel, Saudi Arabia, Syria, and Pakistan all had levels of military expenditure that were high, even relative to the highly militarized group of developing countries.

Third, countries with a high level of military expenditures in the Middle East/South Asian region also had abnormally high levels of military expenditure as a share of the government budget and high levels of armed forces per capita. Among the countries with relatively low levels of defense expenditure, the regional dimension was significant for only armed forces per capita. The regional dimension was also significant for countries characterized as having above average levels of public expenditures per capita. The Middle Eastern/South Asian countries in this group again had relatively high levels of military expenditure and public expenditure per capita. Countries in the Middle East/South Asia region with relatively low levels of public expenditure per capita also tended to have relatively high levels of military expenditures. However, unlike the high expenditure group, the regional dimension was not significant in terms of the level of public expenditure per capita.

Fourth, military expenditure per soldier was highly correlated with other forms of public sector expenditures for the countries experiencing a high level of socio-economic performance. For these countries, the Middle East/South Asian regional dimension was also associated with the military expenditure dimension. Also, at this time, Egypt, Israel, and Syria experienced a high level of military expenditure (relative to other countries with a high level of socio-economic performance).

Finally, for the sample countries with low socio-economic performance, Saudi Arabia's military expenditures were above average and its level of nonmilitary public expenditures considerably above average.

1982

In 1982, the military expenditures per soldier term continued its trend toward closer association with other types of public expenditures. In the Middle East/South Asia region, armed forces per capita continued its trend towards greater association with socio-economic performance, while in countries outside the region this measure of militarization was more closely associated with the general military burden (military expenditures share in GNP).

Several other patterns are worth noting. First, the Middle East and South Asian countries differed from countries in other parts of the world with regard to the manner in which government repression was associated with militarization. Outside the region, repression manifested itself largely in a larger proportion of the central government budget allocated to defense. However, in the Middle East/South Asian countries, no strong correlation existed between repression and allocations to defense.

Second, as in the past, the highly militarized countries tended to have a regional dimension whereby the Middle East/South Asian group had an abnormally high share of military expenditures in the central government budget, together with relatively high levels of military participation (armed forces per 1000 population).

Third, for these countries, military expenditures per soldier continued to be highly correlated with other per capita public allocations.

Fourth, countries with lower than average militarization also had experienced a fairly close association between the military participation rate and overall socio-economic performance.

Fifth, interestingly enough, countries with above average levels of public expenditure per capita tended to have an inverse relationship between repression and the military participation rate and the share of the government budget allocated to defense. It should be noted, however, that of the sample countries only Saudi Arabia was classified in this group in 1982.

Sixth, as noted, in 1982, with the exception of Saudi Arabia, all of the sample countries had relatively low levels of public expenditure per capita. In addition, each of these countries—Egypt, Israel, Syria, India, Pakistan and Algeria—had relatively high levels of military expenditure, compared to similar countries in other parts of the world. Still, for countries of below average public expenditure per capita, Egypt, Israel, Syria and Algeria had above average levels of socio-economic performance.

Finally, in 1982, the regional dimension was prominent in both country groupings based on the level of socio-economic development. That is, military expenditure in each group of countries (high and low) was correlated with the regional dimension. With everything else equal in terms of socio-economic performance, the Middle East and South Asian countries had significantly higher levels of militarization than other parts of the developing world. Repression in the high socio-economic group was inversely correlated with the degree of socio-economic performance, but in the low socio-economic group, repression was not associated with any of the main measures of expenditure/performance.

1986

At the end of the period under consideration, Egypt, Israel, Saudi Arabia, Syria, and Pakistan all continued to have above average levels of militarization. India was slightly below the average for developing countries, while Algeria was considerably below that of the other sample countries. Compared with the beginning of the period (1974), Egypt, Israel, and Pakistan had experienced relative declines in militarization, while Saudi Arabia and Syria had made significant increases in the relative amount of resources allocated to the military. Of the countries with relatively low levels of military expenditure, India and Algeria had slight declines relative to 1974 in their ranking on the basis of relative militarization.

The data also permit other inferences to be drawn. First, at this time, repression in the Middle East/South Asian region was not associated with military or social expenditures. Again, for these countries the military participation rate was fairly closely correlated with the level of socio-economic performance. As in the past, military expenditure per soldier was highly correlated with other forms of public expenditure per capita.

Second, developing countries outside the Middle East/South Asia region tended to increase the share of their budgets allocated to defense as their degree of repression increased. In addition, their rates of military participation tended to be less correlated with socio-economic performance than was the case in the Middle East.

Third, interestingly enough, countries experiencing high levels of militarization at this time had an inverse correlation between repression and their public expenditures per capita. For these countries, the shares of GNP allocated to military expenditure and total government expenditures were fairly strongly correlated to each other and to the regional dimension.

Fourth, of the highly militarized sample countries, Israel and Syria had above average levels of socio-economic performance. Egypt was average, while Saudi Arabia and Pakistan continued to have below average levels of socio-economic performance.

Fifth, in the case of the less militarized countries, repression was, more than in the past, associated with the military burden (the share of GNP allocated to defense) as well as the share of the budget allocated to defense.

Sixth, of the sample countries with above average levels of public expenditure per capita, only Israel had an above average level of socio-economic performance. Saudi Arabia was still considerably below the norm.

Seventh, on the other hand, of the sample countries with relatively low levels of public expenditure per capita, Egypt and Syria had above average levels of social economic performance. All of the sample countries with below average levels of public expenditure had relatively high levels of militarization.

Finally, the regional dimension was still present with regard to countries above and below the average with regard to socio-economic performance. For both groups, the Middle East/South Asian countries had relatively high levels of military expenditure. Again, Algeria was the notable exception in this regard.

The patterns noted above provide insight in to the manner in which the sample countries differ with regard to their patterns of military expenditures, socio-economic development and overall pattern of public expenditures. Clearly, there are a number of similarities between the sample countries, in particular, their generally high levels of military expenditures and their fairly high levels of non-defense expenditures per capita. On the other hand, a number of significant differences exist, particularly with regard to levels of, and movements, in socio-economic performance. Later, in Chapters 4, 5, and 6 and in the country case studies in Part Two of this book, we address in much greater detail the role of military expenditures in accounting for these similarities and differences.

As a prelude to that analysis, it should be emphasized that several trends identified above suggest that the economic effects of military ex-

TABLE 2.8   Summary: Main Correlations Between Government Expenditures
             and Socio-Economic Performance, by Region, 1974-86
             (standardized regression coefficients)

Country Grouping	Military Variable	Factor	
		Socio Economic Performance	Public Expenditures
Total Sample			
1974	Military Exp/Soldier	- 0.11	0.54
1978	Military Exp/Soldier	0.11	0.73
1982	Military Exp/Soldier	0.09	0.84
1986	Military Exp/Soldier	- 0.02	0.84
1974	Armed Forces/Capita	0.33	0.45
1978	Armed Forces/Capita	0.34	0.25
1982	Armed Forces/Capita	0.41	0.15
1986	Armed Forces/Capita	0.33	0.12
Middle East			
1974	Military Exp/Soldier	0.10	0.63
1978	Military Exp/Soldier	- 0.04	0.62
1982	Military Exp/Soldier	- 0.07	0.92
1986	Military Exp/Soldier	0.00	0.93
1974	Armed Forces/Capita	0.10	0.43
1878	Armed Forces/Capita	0.33	0.34
1982	Armed Forces/Capita	0.55	- 0.09
1986	Armed Forces/Capita	0.43	- 0.17
Non-Middle East			
1974	Military Exp/Soldier	- 0.04	0.55
1978	Military Exp/Soldier	0.08	0.17
1982	Military Exp/Soldier	0.06	0.89
1986	Military Exp/Solider	0.11	0.89
1974	Armed Forces/Capita	0.34	0.12
1978	Armed Forces/Capita	0.34	0.39
1982	Armed Forces/Capita	0.42	0.40
1986	Armed Forces/Capita	0.36	0.37

penditures in the sample countries have changed over time. Specifically,
during the period under consideration, several subtle shifts occurred in
the manner in which military expenditures and the military participation
rate were associated with public expenditure per capita. More importantly, similar shifts occurred in the manner in which the military participation
rate impacted on socio-economic performance.

    The data in Tables 2.8 and 2.9 point to several of these nuances. First, for
the total sample of countries, military expenditures per soldier became increasingly associated with non-defense expenditures per capita. At the
same time the military participation rate (armed forces per 1000 population) became less associated with this type of expenditure. Second, the
Middle Eastern countries differed from developing countries in general
with regard to the manner in which the military participation rate affected
socio-economic performance. For developing countries as a whole, the
correlation between military participation and socio-economic perfor-

TABLE 2.9   Summary: Main Correlations Between Government Expenditures and Socio-Economic Performance, by Expenditure Classification, 1974-86 (standardized regression coefficients)

		Factor	
Country Grouping	*Military Variable*	*Socio Economic Performance*	*Public Expenditures*
High Militarization			
1974	Military Exp/Soldier	- 0.22	0.60
1978	Military Exp/Soldier	- 0.18	0.60
1982	Military Exp/Soldier	- 0.14	0.91
1986	Military Exp/Soldier	- 0.04	0.77
1974	Armed Forces/Capita	0.62	0.26
1978	Armed Forces/Capita	0.51	0.33
1982	Armed Forces/Capita	0.60	0.09
1986	Armed Forces/Capita	0.42	0.18
Low Militarization			
1974	Military Exp/Soldier	0.19	0.68
1978	Military Exp/Soldier	0.04	0.81
1982	Military Exp/Soldier	- 0.14	0.91
1986	Military Exp/Solider	0.07	0.91
1974	Armed Forces/Capita	0.05	0.73
1978	Armed Forces/Capita	0.46	0.32
1982	Armed Forces/Capita	0.59	0.34
1986	Armed Forces/Capita	0.58	0.31
High Public Expenditure Per Capita			
1974	Military Exp/Soldier	0.44	0.32
1978	Military Exp/Soldier	0.27	0.34
1982	Military Exp/Soldier	0.19	0.77
1986	Military Exp/Soldier	- 0.11	0.94
1974	Armed Forces/Capita	- 0.33	0.58
1978	Armed Forces/Capita	0.03	0.43
1982	Armed Forces/Capita	0.19	- 0.04
1986	Armed Forces/Capita	0.36	0.00
Low Public Expenditure Per Capita			
1974	Military Exp/Soldier	0.04	0.04
1978	Military Exp/Soldier	0.07	- 0.06
1982	Military Exp/Soldier	0.11	0.19
1986	Military Exp/Solider	0.09	0.16
1974	Armed Forces/Capita	0.49	0.49
1978	Armed Forces/Capita	0.26	0.57
1982	Armed Forces/Capita	0.20	0.64
1986	Armed Forces/Capita	0.18	0.72

mance was fairly constant over time. In contrast, military participation became increasingly positively correlated over time with socio-economic performance. Third, as with developing countries as a whole, the military participation rate in the Middle East/South Asian countries became less associated over time with public non-defense expenditures. Fourth, the reverse was the case for non-Middle Eastern/South Asian countries. For these nations, the relationship between the military participation rate and socio-economic performance was relatively stable. At the same time, these countries experienced a slight positive increase in the association between the military participation rate and public expenditure per capita. Finally, in countries with a high level of militarization, the affect on socio-economic performance of the military participation rate declined over time. On the other hand, this factor increased in importance as a positive factor contributing to improved socio-economic performance in the countries with low levels of militarization. Interestingly enough, the military participation rate was less associated over time with public expenditures in both the high and low military expenditure countries.

Conclusions

The patterns presented here of the military participation rate and socio-economic performance are consistent with those analyzed in depth later in this book.[8] As we indicate there for the Arab world as a whole, human capital development and improvements in literacy have proceeded in a somewhat unique manner. For these countries, improvements in literacy have been much more closely associated with the military participation rate than in other parts of the world. While this relationship appears to be weakening somewhat, it is still a dominant factor in these countries.

Having said this, the reason for this pattern is not completely clear. Are the observed improvements in literacy associated with military participation due to some particular success of Middle Eastern militaries in training recruits, or do they simply reflect deficiencies in the civilian educational systems? Would comparable allocations to conventional schools have produced better progress toward national literacy and skill improvement? While the results presented in this chapter are suggestive, definitive answers to questions of this sort will have to wait until our thematic analyses in Chapters 4, 5 and 6 and our in-depth country analyses in Part Two of the military and educational priorities in Iran, Saudi Arabia, Iraq, and Pakistan.

At this point, it is worthwhile noting that in an earlier study, Erich Weede found that in the 1960s and 1970s, nations with higher skill levels, as indicated by school enrollment ratios, grew faster than others.[9] In addition, he found that nations with better social discipline, as indicated by military participation ratios, also grew faster than others. While these patterns were not found in the analysis presented here, it appears that one important aspect of military participation in the Middle East and South Asia is its potential to contribute to future growth and development. Put

---

8. See below Chapter 6.

9. Erich Weede, "Military Participation Ratios, Human Capital Formation, and Economic Growth: A Cross-National Analysis," *Journal of Political and Military Sociology* 11, 1 (Spring 1983, pp. 11-20.

differently, while the conventional analysis that tends to view military and educational expenditures as competing for resources may be correct, in fact, it may be somewhat beside the point at least as far as the Middle East/ South Asian countries as a whole are concerned. In the longer term, the skills learned and the levels of improved literacy gained in military service may pay high dividends in terms of enabling the labor force to play a more direct role in national economic growth. In Chapter 4 and 5, we explore these connections in much greater depth.

While such beneficial results may offer another perspective on military spending, nevertheless persistent doubts arise concerning the level and rate of increase in military spending in Third World areas. The 1990-91 Gulf War, and a widespread concern with maintaining stability and balance in the post-cold war era, have prompted a new worry over regional "arms races." Consequently, before we begin our extended analysis of the socio-economic impact of defense spending, the next chapter examines from a *quantitative* perspective the existence of, and causation involved in, major arms races in the Middle East and South Asia.

3

Arms Races in the Middle East and South Asia: A Test of Causality

The growth in world military expenditure is one of the key paradoxes of our age. While it is reasonable and prudent for a nation to make provision for security against external threats, one nation's security is likely to be another's insecurity. As a result, particularly in an atmosphere of hostility and suspicion, military expenditure assumes a competitive dynamic such that the security of all nations is diminished. The realization that this process consumes huge quantities of resources that might be used for attaining higher standards of living is only slightly less disquieting.[1]

Certainly, in recent decades, relatively high levels of military expenditures have characterized the budgetary structures of most Middle Eastern and South Asian countries.[2] The basic patterns are fairly well known, and for obvious reasons, there has been an on-going interest among analysts to explain militarization as a whole and to search for variables to explain the level of defense spending of major countries. This latter thrust has focused on factors such as economic conditions, population, size of the country, rivalries, and arms races.

Overall, conventional wisdom stresses regional arms races as the prime culprit in accounting for the staggering military burdens, particularly those accrued by Israel, Egypt, Syria, and to a lesser extent, Pakistan. Unfortunately, most of the analysis in this area has been anecdotal at best. In

---

1. Jean-Christian Lambelet, "The Formal 'Economic' Analysis of Arms Races: What—If Anything—Have We Learned Since Richardson?" *Conflict Management and Peace Science*, 9, 2 (Spring 1986), pp. 1-18.
2. Unless otherwise specified, military expenditure data is from Stockholm International Peace Research Institute, *SIPRI Yearbook*, (New York: Oxford University Press), various issues. Price deflators are from the IMF, *International Financial Statistics Yearbook*, (Washington D.C.: International Monetary Fund) various issues.

addition, many of the empirical studies of militarization are based on models built largely on arbitrary and often unrealistic assumptions concerning the action/reaction patterns of the major participants.[3]

This chapter identifies from a quantitative perspective the existence of, and causation involved in, the major arms races of the Middle East and South Asia. To date, economists have had much less to say about the causes and consequences of arms races, particularly those in the Third World, than might be expected. This relative dearth is surprising in that arms races are about resource allocations in a complex and competitive environment and about the implications such allocations can have for economic structure and performance, the very substance of economics.

Thus, we seek to add to the understanding of the economic dimension of military expenditure through an examination of the interdependence between arms races and economic allocation. Our main aim is to identify the patterns of causation between the major military spenders in the Middle East and South Asia. In this regard, India and Pakistan, with their interdependence from a geographic, economic, political, and social point of view, provide an ideal complementary case study to the Middle East.[4] Based on the analysis in this chapter, several general conclusions are drawn concerning the causes and costs of "arms races" in the Middle East and South Asia.

Determinants of Defense Spending:
A Survey of the Literature

Several studies have attempted to isolate the factors mainly responsible for militarization in the Third World. Of these studies, the most comprehensive is the analysis undertaken by O'Leary and Coplin.[5] They identified seven factors as accounting one way or another for the observed patterns of military expenditures: economic conditions in the country, the role of the military in non-military affairs, internal security needs, reactions to arms purchases by neighbors, budget allocation to service branches in rival states, internal political support, and the age and condition of existing military equipment. The only apparent correlation found by them was between the military budget and arms races and the budget levels in rival states. Apparently, both these factors acted as a "reference point" from which individual countries might set their own budget levels.

---

3. Lambelet, "The Formal 'Economic' Analysis of Arms Races: What—If Anything—Have We Learned Since Richardson?"

4. Manas Chatterji, "A Model of Resolution of Conflict Between India and Pakistan," *Peace Research Society Papers* XII (1969), p. 87.

5. Michael K. O'Leary and William D. Coplin, *Quantitative Techniques in Foreign Policy Analysis and Forecasting* (New York: Praeger Publishers, 1975).

Along similar lines, Hill employed a sample of both developed and developing nations in his attempt to synthesize the various approaches used to examine the determinants of defense spending.[6] Hill was unable to find one "overriding" factor which could explain a large proportion of the variance of defense spending patterns among the sample set. As a result he concluded that "the military spending level of any nation is likely to be a product of a number of separate forces."[7] These "separate forces" include arms races, military alliances, status and rank discrepancies in international systems, military aid, size and wealth of the country, the form of government, the extent of military involvement, internal social friction, and internal political conflict.

In turn, Westing's analysis sought "to present some critical reflections that might prove useful to those concerned with military expenditures and proposals for their reductions·"[8] As a result of his research he found significant correlations between military expenditures for 159 nations and their respective GNP levels, productive land area, and population.

In an important article which related defense spending to economic variables, Ames and Goff examined defense and education expenditures in sixteen South American countries for the twenty year period between 1948 and 1968.[9] They found that political variables were not the major determinants of either education or defense budgets; instead, they concluded that changes in the education and defense budgets were related to the level of available resources.

Maizels and Nissanke examined military spending data for eighty-three countries.[10] They hypothesized that the three main determinants of defense spending are the political framework, military activity, and economic linkages. They believe that the relative importance of each factor is in turn influenced by national, regional or global conflicts or interactions in the individual country. Using multiple regression analysis, they concluded that:

---

6. Kim Quaile Hill, "Domestic Politics, International Linkages, and Military Expenditures," *Studies in Comparative International Development* 13, 1 (Spring 1978) pp. 38-59. This article provides an excellent review of the literature prior to 1978.

7. Hill, "Domestic Politics, International Linkages, and Military Expenditures," p. 53.

8. Arthur H. Westing, "Military Expenditures and their Reduction," *Bulletin of Peace Proposals* 9, (1978), pp. 24-29.

9. Barry Ames and Ed Goff, "Education and Defense Expenditures in Latin America: 1948-68," in *Comparative Public Policy: Issues, Theories and Methods*, ed. Craig Liske, William Loehr, and John McCamant, (New York: John Wiley and Sons, 1975).

10. Alfred Maizels and Machiko K. Nissanke, "The Determinants of Military Expenditures in Developing Countries," *World Development* 14, 9 (Spring 1986) pp. 1125-1140. See also Alfred Maizels and Machiko Nissanke, "The Causes of Military Expenditure in Developing Countries," in Saadat Deger and Robert West, *Defence, Security and Development*, (London: Francis Pinter, 1987) pp. 129-139.

Domestic factors, particularly the need perceived by ruling elites to repress internal opposition groups, and external factors, including relations with the global power blocs and the availability of foreign exchange to purchase arms from abroad, also appear to be major determinants of government decisions in regard to military expenditures.[11]

Harris attempted to measure the effect of military expenditures from domestic economic conditions. In doing so, he examined the budgets over a twenty year period for five ASEAN countries: Indonesia, Malaysia, Philippines, Singapore, and Thailand.[12] He reached three main conclusions. First, defense expenditures in the current year are positively correlated with defense spending and the central budgetary position in the previous year. Second, current defense expenditures have a weak inverse correlation with inflation the previous year. Finally, although current defense budgets are not correlated with the balance of payments in the previous year, the balance of payments affects government revenue which in turn affects defense spending.[13]

In an extension of the Harris paper, Looney and Frederiksen examined the economic determinants of defense expenditures in Latin America. Ten countries were examined using time series data: Argentina, Peru, Mexico, Venezuela, Chile, Paraguay, Uruguay, Colombia, Brazil, and Ecuador.[14] Four alternative models were tested. The independent variables were current and lagged values of GNP, government expenditure, and military expenditures. Looney and Frederiksen found that "a large proportion of variability in defense expenditures can be explained by economic variables; the overall constraint (GDP) and fiscal funding variables...."[15]

In extending Harris's work on the ASEAN countries, Looney and Frederiksen found three basic patterns: "stabilization" (Singapore), "augmentation" (Malaysia), and "distributed lags" (Philippines).[16] All countries increased defense budgets as expected GNP increased. There

---

11. Maizels and Machiko Nissanke, "The Causes of Military Expenditure in Developing Countries," p.137.

12. Geoffrey Harris, "The Determinants of Defence Expenditure in the ASEAN Region," *Journal of Peace Research* 23, 1 (March 1986), pp. 41-49.

13. Harris, "The Determinants of Defence Expenditure in the ASEAN Region," p. 46. For an excellent survey article, see G.T. Harris, "Economic Aspects of Military Expenditure in Developing Countries: A Survey Article," *Contemporary Southeast Asia* 10, 1 (June 1988), pp. 82-102.

14. Robert E. Looney and Peter C. Frederiksen, "Economic Determinants of Latin American Defense Expenditures," *Armed Forces and Society* 14, 4 (Spring 1988), pp. 49-471.

15. Looney and Peter C. Frederiksen, "Economic Determinants of Latin American Defense Expenditures," p. 468.

16. Robert E. Looney and P.C. Frederiksen, "The Economic Determinants of Military Expenditure in Selected East Asian Countries" *Contemporary Southeast Asia* 11, 4 (March 1990), pp. 265-277.

were, however, significant variations between countries as to the timing of increased defense allocations. Specifically, Thailand exhibited a weak stabilization pattern. Indonesia was found to be a special case where resource availability was measured by crude oil production. However, there was a weak augmentation effect as measured by the expected and unexpected rate of inflation.

Clearly, a good case can be made that in the Third World economic variables constrain or at least modify the manner in which defense allocations are undertaken. The slow-down in military expenditures in the Middle East and South Asia during the late 1980s can be traced directly to austerity programs in countries such as Egypt, Israel, Syria, and India. Saudi Arabia's reduced defense expenditures just prior to the outbreak of the 1990-91 Gulf War were also closely related to developments in the international oil markets.

However, in the Middle East and South Asia, factors such as cold war-related financial assistance from the superpowers, and for the Middle East, an abundance of hydrocarbon revenues, undoubtedly buffeted many countries from the economic constraints found in other parts of the world. Hence, the analysis below focuses on arms races *per se*.

Our purpose in this chapter is to identify the patterns of causation between the major military spenders in the Middle East and South Asia. In doing so, we hope to contribute to the literature in two respects. First, as is well known, causality tests are, in general, sensitive to lag lengths. The use of shorter lags than actually existed may distort the causal impact of defense expenditures from one country on those of another. On the other hand, relatively long lags may cause the absence of any causality between defense expenditures and economic growth. Few studies have used an "atheoretical" methodology that allows data themselves to select appropriate lag lengths. Thus, following Hsiao, Akaike's final prediction error (FPE) criterion will be employed to select optimum lag lengths for each variable in each equation.[17]

Alternative Tests for Causation

Several statistical tests are available for addressing the issue at hand. To date, the original and most widely used has been the Granger Test.[18] As we will use it in this chapter and in subsequent chapters, it is worthwhile to examine briefly this statistic test.[19]

17. C. Hsiao, "Causality Tests in Econometrics" *Journal of Economic Dynamics and Control* (1979), pp. 321-346; and C. Hsiao "Autoregressive Modeling and Money Income Causality Detection," *Journal of Monetary Economics* 7 (1981), pp. 85-106.

18. C.W.J. Granger, "Investigating Causal Relations by Econometric Models and Cross-Spectral Methods," *Econometrica* 37, 3 (July 1969), pp. 424-438.

Granger Test

Granger defines causality such that X Granger causes (G-C) Y if Y can be predicted more accurately in the sense of mean square error, with the use of past values of X than without using past X. For example, in assessing the relationship between defense and economic performance (the same basic formulation would also apply to an arms race between the countries), Granger causality can be specified as:

$$(1) \quad DEFA(t) = c + \sum_{i=1}^{p} a(i)DEFA(t-i) + \sum_{j=1}^{q} b(j)DEFB(t-j) + u(t)$$

$$(2) \quad DEFB(t) = c + \sum_{i=1}^{r} d(i) DEFB(t-1) + \sum_{j=1}^{s} e(j)DEFA(t-j) + v(t)$$

Where DEFA is a measure of defense expenditures in country A and DEFB is the corresponding measure for country B; p, q, r and s are lag lengths for each variable in the equation; and, u and v are serially uncorrelated white noise residuals. By assuming that error terms (u, v) are "nice," the specified model is estimated by the ordinary least squares (OLS) method.[20]

Within the framework of unrestricted and restricted models, a joint F-test is commonly used for causal detection. The F-statistic would be calculated by:

$$(3) \quad F = \frac{(RSS(x) - RSS(u)/(df(x) - df(u))}{RSS(u)/df(u)}$$

Where RSS(r) and RSS(u) are the residual sum of squares of restricted and unrestricted models, respectively; and df(r) and df(u) are, respectively, the degrees of freedom in restricted and unrestricted models.

---

19. For a critique of these methods see Charles J. LaCivita and Peter C. Frederiksen, "Defense Spending and Economic Growth: An Alternative Approach to the Causality Issue" *Journal of Development Economics* 35, 1 (January 1991), pp. 117-127. The analysis here follows that undertaken by LaCivita and Frederiksen.

20. If the disturbances of the model were serially correlated, the OLS estimates would be inefficient, although still unbiased, and would distort the causal relations. The existence of serial correlation was checked by using a maximum likelihood correlation for the first-order autocorrelation of the residuals [AR(1)]. The comparison of both OLS and AR(1) results indicated that no significant changes appeared in causal directions. Therefore, we can conclude 'roughly' that serial correlation was not serious in this model.

The Granger test detects causal directions in the following manner. First, unidirectional causality from DEFA to DEFB if the F-test rejects the null hypothesis that past values of DEFA in equation (1) are insignificantly different from zero and if the F-Test cannot reject the null hypothesis that past values of DEFB in equation (2) are insignificantly different from zero. That is, DEFA causes DEFB but DEFB does not cause DEFA. Unidirectional causality runs from DEFB to DEFA if the reverse is true. Second, bi-directional causality runs between DEFA and DEFB if both F-test statistics reject the null hypotheses in equations (1) and (2). Finally, no causality exists between DEFA and DEFB if both null hypotheses cannot be rejected at the conventional significance level.

The results of Granger causality tests depend critically on the choice of lag length. If the chosen lag length is less than the true lag length, the omission of relevant lags can cause bias. If the chosen lag is greater than the true lag length, the inclusion of irrelevant lags cause estimates to be inefficient. While one can chose lag lengths based on preliminary partial autocorrelation methods, there is no *a priori* reason to assume lag lengths equal for all of our sample countries. For example, in a different context, a study of causation between defense expenditures and growth in the Philippines, Frederiksen and LaCivita found no statistical relationship between growth and defense when both variables were entered in the estimating equation with a lag equal to four.[21] When the lag length was changed to two periods, however, it was found that growth caused defense. Since both lag lengths were chosen arbitrarily, one cannot say which is preferred.

To overcome these types of difficulties, Hsiao has developed a systematic method for choosing lag lengths for each variable in an equation. Since we use Hsiao's method in subsequent chapters too, a brief examination of it will further clarify the analysis presented here and later.

The Hsiao Procedure

Hsiao's method combines Granger Causality and Akaike's final prediction error (FPE) defined as the (asymptotic) mean square prediction error, to determine both the optimum lag for each variable and causal relationships.[22] In a paper examining the problems encountered in choosing lag lengths, Thornton and Batten found Hsiao's method to be superior to both arbitrary lag length selection and several other systematic procedures for determining lag length.[23]

---

21. P.C. Frederiksen and C.J. LaCivita, "Defense Spending and Economic Growth: Time Series Evidence on Causality for the Philippines, 1956-1982," *Journal of Philippine Development*, 14 (Second Semester 1987), pp. 354-60.

22. Hsiao, "Autoregressive Modeling and Money-Income Causality Detection," pp. 85-106.

The first step in Hsiao's procedure is to perform a series of autoregressive regressions on the dependent variable. In the first regression, the dependent variable is lagged once. In each succeeding regression, one more lag on the dependent variable is added. That is, we estimate M regressions of the form:

$$
(4) \quad DEF(t) = a + \sum_{i=1}^{m} b(t-1)DEF(t-1) + e(i)
$$

where the values of m range from 1 to M. For each regression, we compute the FPE in the following manner

$$
(5) \quad FPE(m) = \frac{T + m + 1}{T - m - 1} \; ESS(m)/T
$$

where T is the sample size, and FPE(m) and ESS(m) are the final prediction error and the sum of squared errors, respectively.

The optimal lag length, m*, is the lag length which produces the lowest FPE. Once m* has been determined, regressions are estimated with the lags on the other variable added sequentially in the same manner used to determine m*. Thus we estimate four regressions of the form:

$$
(6) \quad DEFA(t) = a + \sum_{i=1}^{m^*} b(t-1)DEAF(t-1) + \sum_{i=1}^{n} c(t-1)DEFB(t-1) + e(i)
$$

with n ranging from one to four. Computing the final prediction error for each regression as:

$$
FPE(m^*,n) = \frac{T + m^* + n + 1}{T - m^* - n - 1} \; ESS(m^*,n)/T
$$

we choose the optimal lag length for D, n* as the lag length which produces the lowest FPE. Using the final prediction error to determine lag length is equivalent to using a series of F tests with variable levels of significance.[24]

---

23. D.L. Thornton and D.S. Batten, "Lag-length Selection and Tests of Granger Causality Between Money and Income," *Journal of Money, Credit and Banking* 17, 2 (May 1985), pp. 164-78.

The first term measures the estimation error and the second term measures the modeling error. The FPE criterion has a certain optimality property that "balances the risk due to bias when a lower order is selected and the risk due to increases in the variance when a higher order is selected."[25] As noted by Judge et al., an intuitive reason for using the FPE criterion is that longer lags increase the first term but decrease the RSS of the second term, and thus the two opposing forces are balanced optimally when their product reaches its minimum.[26]

Again, using the example of defense expenditures in country A and B, four cases are possible: (a) **Defense(A) causes Defense(B)**–occurring when the prediction error for defense expenditures in country B is reduced when defense expenditures in country A is added to the equation. In addition, when defense expenditures in country B are added to the country A defense equation, that equation's final prediction error increases; (b) **Defense(B) causes Defense(A)**–occurring when the prediction error of country B's defense equation increases when defense in country A's defense is added to the equation, and is reduced when country B's defense is added to the regression equation for country A's defense; (c) **Feedback**–occurring when the final prediction error decreases when defense in country A is added to country B's defense equation, and the final prediction error decreases when defense in country B is added to country A's defense equation; and, (d) **No Relationship**–occurs when the final prediction error increases when defense in country A is added to country B's defense equation, and also increases when defense in country B is added to country A's defense equation.

Methodology

Two alternative measures of defense burden were used: (a) constant price defense expenditures and, (b) the defense burden, the share of defense in Gross Domestic Product (GDP).[27] When consistent price deflators were not available the defense expenditure term was specified only in terms of the growth of the defense burden.

Before the tests were performed, one statistical problem needed to be addressed. It is widely known that most economic time series are non-

---

24. Since the F statistic is redundant in this instance they are not reported here. They are, however, available from the authors upon request.

25. Hsiao, "Causality Tests in Econometrics," p. 326.

26. G.G. Judge, W. Hill, H. Griffiths, H. Lutkephol, and T.C. Lee, *Introduction to the Theory and Practice of Econometrics* (New York: John Wiley and Sons, 1982).

27. The data for military expenditures used to carry out the Hsiao tests were compiled from the Stockholm International Peace Research Institute, *SIPRI Yearbook, World Armaments and Disarmament*, various issues.

stationary. As indicated by Judge et al., "stationary is an important property as it guarantees that there are no fundamental changes in the structure of the process that would render prediction difficult or impossible."[28] In order to remove all possible non-stationarities, real defense expenditures and the defense burden were transformed to rates of growth. When these transformed series were regressed on a constant and time, their coefficients on time were insignificantly different from zero for all countries. Similar regressions of the untransformed levels indicated the presence of a trend.

The results for the causality analysis of the regional arms races together with the direction of country causation are presented with the final prediction error (FPE), the coefficient of determination (r^2), together the optimal lag. For simple organizational convenience the results are presented in terms of: (a) Arms races involving Israel (Table 3.1), (b) those involving Saudi Arabia (but not Israel–Table 3.2), (c) other regional arms races (Table 3.3) and, (d) South Asian arms races (Table 3.4). It should be noted that if a country is not listed it is because no statistically significant military expenditure patterns were found vis a vis its neighbors. For example, military expenditures in Libya do not cause or are not affected by those in Israel or neighboring North African countries.

The causality analysis produced several interesting findings, the most significant of which relate to Israel (Table 3.1). Table 3.1 suggests one expected and several surprising findings. First, not very surprisingly, Israel interacts militarily with by far the greatest number of countries in the region. Second, contrary to conventional wisdom, Israel appears to initiate many of the regional arms races. Third, defense expenditures in Israel stimulate (with a one year lag) those in Syria. Syrian defense expenditures do not appear to affect Israeli decisions concerning allocations to the military. Fourth, increases in Israeli defense expenditures cause Egypt to increase (with a three year lag) its defense expenditures. However, increases in Egyptian allocations to the military actually cause a decline in Israeli defense expenditures. Fifth, Israel and Saudi Arabia appear engaged in a mini-arms race, with increases in the defense burden in each country responded to (with a three year lag) by an increase in that of the other.

Again, contrary to conventional wisdom, Saudi Arabian defense expenditures are not passive adjustments to changes in defense allocations in neighboring countries. In addition to its arms race with Israel, Saudi Arabian defense expenditures interact with those in Egypt (Table 3.2).

Several other patterns are also in evidence from Table 3.2. First, while not affected by Iraqi defense expenditures, Saudi Arabian defense expenditures respond to those in Iran (but not vice versa). Second, defense

---

28. Judge, et al. *Introduction to the Theory and Practice of Econometrics*, p. 671

TABLE 3.1   Middle East Arms Races: Israel, Country Causality Tests
(final prediction error)

Dependent Var Independent Var Optimum Lag Sign ()	Israel Def Israel Def	Israel Def Other Def	Other Def Other Def	Other Def Israel Def
Israel/Saudi Arabia (Growth in Defense Expenditures)				
1966-1987	402.62	308.36	650.26	690.37
(Saudi—>Israel)	3 years	3 years	3 years	3 years
	(+)	(+)	(+)	(+)
r²	0.366	0.637	0.320	0.461
Israel/Saudi Arabia (Growth in Defense Burden)				
1966-1987	373.77	349.99	618.99	603.06
(Feedback)	1 year	3 years	4 years	2 years
	(+)	(+)	(-)	(+)
r²	0.133	0.387	0.466	0.573
Israel/Syria (Growth in Defense Expenditures)				
1955-1987	488.84	517.59	937.58	903.78
(Israel—>Syria)	1 year	1 year	1 year	3 years
	(+)	(-)	(-)	(+)
r²	0.162	0.165	0.033	0.225
Israel/Syria (Growth in Defense Burden)				
1966-1987	373.77	401.01	615.42	594.28
(Israel—>Syria)	1 year	1 year	1 year	1 year
	(+)	(-)	(-)	(+)
r²	0.133	0.152	0.086	0.195
Israel/Syria (Growth in Defense Burden)				
1962-1987	329.17	348.65	518.13	491.18
(Israel—>Syria)	1 year	1 year	1 year	1 year
	(+)	(-)	(-)	(+)
r²	0.118	0.136	0.078	0.191
Israel/Egypt (Growth in Defense Expenditures)				
1962-1987	362.96	352.20	609.49	543.18
(Feedback)	3 years	1 year	1 year	4 years
	(+)	(-)	(+)	(+)
r²	0.330	0.340	0.032	0.371

expenditures in Jordan are affected by Saudi allocations to the military (but not vice versa). Third, increases in Syrian defense burdens also stimulate adjustments upward in the Saudi defense burden (but not vice versa). Finally, interestingly, in addition to Saudi Arabia, Iraq's defense expenditures do not appear to be caused by or affect those of its neighbors.

Perhaps the most complex patterns involve Syria and its neighbors (Table 3.3). As Table 3.3 suggests, in addition to affecting allocations to defense in Saudi Arabia, increases in Syrian defense expenditures produce a similar response in Turkey. While increases in Israeli defense expenditures produce a similar adjustment in Syria, those in Egypt do the same, but with a much shorter lag.

The only other major pattern in the Middle East involves Algeria and

TABLE 3.2   Middle East Arms Races: Saudi Arabia, Country Causality Tests
                 (final prediction error)

Dependent Var Independent Var Optimum Lag Sign ()	Saudi Def Saudi Def	Saudi Def Other Def	Other Def Other Def	Other Def Saudi Def
Saudi Arabia/Iran (Growth in Defense Expenditures)				
1966-1985	712.22	701.31	1049.16	1144.18
(Iran—>Saudi)	3 years	1 year	3 years	4 years
	(+)	(+)	(+)	(+)
r^2	0.291	0.372	0.404	0.581
Saudi Arabia/Jordan (Growth in Defense Burden)				
1966-1987	618.99	671.63	518.20	453.94
(Arabia—>Jordan)	4 years	3 years	1 year	1 year
	(-)	(+)	(+)	(+)
r^2	0.466	0.570	0.001	0.202
Saudi Arabia/Egypt (Growth in Defense Burden)				
1966-1987	618.99	601.51	770.95	735.22
(Feedback)	4 years	2 years	1 year	3 years
	(-)	(+)	(+)	(+)
r^2	0.466	0.574	0.101	0.352
Saudi Arabia/Syria (Growth in Defense Burden)				
1966-1987	618.99	510.24	615.42	673.20
(Syria—>Arabia)	3 years	2 years	1 year	1 years
	(-)	(+)	(-)	(+)
r^2	0.466	0.638	0.086	0.088

Morocco, with Algerian defense expenditures affecting Moroccan military expenditures with a two or four year lag depending on whether one looks at the growth in the defense burden or in military expenditures.

Turning to South Asia, the causality analysis produced several interesting findings. Our analysis first examines Pakistan, then India (Table 3.4). In general, Pakistan's defense expenditures have been relatively stable, particularly relative to those in the Middle East. However, several broad trends are apparent. First, during the mid-1950s, defense expenditures decelerated somewhat, following the mobilization after independence. The net result was a contraction in defense as a share of GDP from 6.3 percent in 1953 to 3.7 percent in 1962. Second, beginning in 1963, a fairly rapid expansion took place with rates of growth reaching 9.7% (1963), 13.9% (1964), 60.8% (1965) and 19% (1966). By 1966, the share of defense expenditures in GDP had reached 6.8 percent. Third, the increase in defense expenditures leveled off over the 1967-1977 decade and, as a result, its share of GDP remained about constant, increasing slightly in the early 1970s, but ending at approximately its 1967 level 5.6 percent. Finally, since 1978, defense expenditures have shown a fairly rapid and continuous expansion, averaging 10.7 percent, so that, by 1988, they were 7.2 percent of GDP.

TABLE 3.3   Middle East Arms Races: Syria and Algeria Country Causality Tests (final prediction error)

Dependent Var Independent Var Optimum Lag Sign ()	Syrian Def Syrian Def	Syrian Def Other Def	Other Def Other Def	Other Def Syrian Def
Syria/Turkey (Growth in Defense Burden)				
1962-1986	492.36	516.44	179.31	146.73
(Syria—>Turkey)	1 year	1 year	3 years	2 year
	(-)	(-)	(-)	(+)
r²	0.121	0.150	0.197	0.444
Syria/Egypt (Growth in Defense Expenditures)				
1962-1987	667.50	618.96	609.49	658.66
(Egypt—>Syria)	1 year	2 years	1 year	1 year
	(+)	(+)	(-)	(-)
r²	0.001	0.206	0.032	0.032

Dependent Var Independent Var Optimum Lag Sign ()	Algeria Def Algeria Def	Algeria Def Other Def	Other Def Other Def	Other Def Algeria Def
Algeria/Morocco (Growth in Military Expenditures)				
1967-1986	554.11	576.99	265.64	203.62
(Algeria—>Morocco)	1 year	1 year	1 year	4 years
	(+)	(+)	(+)	(+)
r²	0.002	0.052	0.149	0.571
Algeria/Morocco (Growth in Military Burden)				
1967-1986	562.44	627.86	247.75	144.92
(Algeria—>Morocco)	1 year	1 year	2 years	2 years
	(-)	(+)	(+)	(+)
r²	0.003	0.043	0.212	0.625

While the conventional wisdom holds that Pakistan and India have been engaged in an arms race since partition (1947), there is ample evidence that this pattern has been somewhat one sided, with Indian defense expenditures affecting those in Pakistan, but not vice versa. The decline in defense expenditures which India experienced in the late 1980s has resulted in a similar decrease in Pakistan (defense expenditure share of Gross Domestic Product, see Table 3.4).

During the period as a whole (1955-1987), a pattern existed between changes in the two countries' defense burdens. A conventional arms race, however, did not exist. While increases in Indian defense expenditures elicited a positive Pakistani response, increases in the Pakistani defense burden actually resulted in a mild contraction in Indian defense efforts. Second, during the earlier period (1958-1978), increases in Indian defense spending resulted in a strong, positive response from Pakistan. In general, this response occurred with a two year lag. Finally, during the twenty year period from 1967 through 1987, there was no statistically significant rela-

TABLE 3.4   South Asia Arms Races: India and Pakistan Country Causality Tests
(final prediction error)

Dependent Var Independent Var Optimum Lag Sign ( )	Pakistan Def Pakistan Def	Pakistan Def Indian Def	Indian Def Indian Def	Indian Def Pakistan Def
Pakistan/India (Growth in Defense Burden)				
1958-1987	152.72	113.18	171.30	166.56
(Feedback)	2 years	2 years	1 year	1 year
	(-)	(+)	(+)	(-)
r^2	0.154	0.452	0.042	0.129
1958-1978	229.65	158.46	229.34	231.36
(India—>Pakistan)	2 years	2 years	1 year	1 year
	(-)	(+)	(+)	(-)
r^2	0.158	0.523	0.048	0.128
1967-1987	40.47	41.67	78.46	81.05
(No relationship)	2 years	1 year	1 year	1 year
	(-)	(-)	(-)	(-)
r^2	0.443	0.481	0.041	0.062
Pakistan/India (Growth in Defense Expenditures)				
1958-1987	154.34	85.41	197.82	194.38
(India—>Pakistan)	2 years	3 years	2 years	1 year
	(-)	(+)	(+)	(-)
r^2	0.205	0.641	0.225	0.289
1958-1978	228.40	98.61	287.54	291.40
(India—>Pakistan)	2 years	3 years	2 years	1 year
	(-)	(+)	(+)	(-)
r^2	0.215	0.749	0.241	0.303
1960-1980	224.25	103.96	287.38	284.59
(India—>Pakistan)	2 years	3 years	2 years	1 year
	(-)	(+)	(+)	(-)
r^2	0.213	0.729	0.236	0.314
Pakistan/India (Growth in Defense Expenditures)				
1967-1987	49.73	31.32	63.05	68.00
(India—>Pakistan)	2 years	4 years	2 years	1 year
	(-)	(-)	(+)	(-)
r^2	0.436	0.763	0.266	0.282

tionship between the defense burdens of the two countries.

A similar analysis using military expenditures found more or less the same picture (Table 3.4). During the 1958-87, 1958-78 and 1960-80 periods, Indian defense expenditures stimulated (with a three year lag) a follow-on expansion of Pakistani defense expenditures. However, for the final twenty year period, increases in the rate of growth of Indian defense expenditures actually resulted in a decline in the growth of Pakistani defense expenditures. It is clear, therefore, that the expansion in Pakistani defense expenditures in the mid-to-late 1980s was not simply a response to stepped up Indian militarization.

While it is unlikely that Pakistan's defense expenditures have had an appreciable effect on those of India, it is apparent that changes in defense policy and planning in India have usually arisen from the experience of war and perceptions of continuing hostility on the part of its neighbors. However, the 1970s witnessed a substantial change in the Indian approach to defense planning.[29] This change occurred when domestic political unrest and violence was perceived by the authorities to undermine the security of the nation as much as threats from without. This belief may have existed in the past, but only in more recent years has the security policy-making organization been radically revised to deal with such considerations.

Other changes in Indian defense planning have come about through the gradual broadening and growing sophistication of the Indian economic and technological base.[30] Military self-reliance, at least in certain sectors of Indian defense programs, notably the procurement of weapons for the Indian army and the anticipated use of the country's military industries as major foreign exchange earners, is increasingly becoming a factor affecting the country's defense planning.

Conclusions

The findings presented in this chapter represent a first step in identifying the causal interactions between the major Middle East and South Asian combatants. We recognize that additional work needs to be undertaken to control for factors other than arms races *per se*. In terms of the Middle East, there is always the possibility that defense expenditures in the Middle East may simply reflect Saudi oil revenues and not Saudi defense expenditures, for example, in Jordan or Egypt (both of which receive economic assistance from Saudi Arabia). On the other hand, it is unlikely these considerations would alter the main finding of the analysis presented in this chapter, namely, that suppressing increases in Israeli defense expenditures is the most effective way of reducing militarization in the region.

Turning to South Asia, Pakistan's defense expenditures cannot be said merely to occur in response to Indian militancy. While this may have been true in the early years after independence, there is little evidence that this relationship any longer exists. There is also little evidence that India was forced into a regional arms race (although we did not test for Chinese defense expenditures).

This chapter has been concerned with identifying the existence of, and causation involved in, the major arms races in the Middle East and South Asia. Both the academic literature and the popular media devote consid-

29. Raju G.C. Thomas, "Defense Planning in India," in Stephanie G. Neuman, ed., *Defense Planning in Less-Industrialized States* (Lexington, Mass: Lexington Books, 1984), p. 239.

30. Thomas, "Defense Planning in India," p. 239.

erable attention to "rampant arms spending," especially in the Middle East. Part of this concern stems from the belief that "arms cause war." Another pervasive concern, however, is that defense spending is inherently wasteful and that it involves a diversion of scarce resources from more productive uses. Simply put, a widespread view is that defense spending is a drag on economic growth. Our investigation of this controversial view begins in Chapter 4 with a quantitative assessment of the macroeconomic impact of defense spending in the Third World.

4

Government Expenditures and Third World Economic Growth: The Impact of Defense Expenditures

So far in the 1990s, a slowdown has occurred in defense spending in some developing countries, including a few countries in the Middle East, South Asia, and North Africa. In large part reductions in allocations to the military have been brought on by growing fiscal problems, forcing governments to reorder their spending priorities. Now, in the post-cold war era, it is apparent that for the developing world as a whole (with many notable exceptions), countries are examining the potential benefits of further reducing allocations to the military. Depending on the relative impact of defense spending, shifts in resources may significantly affect the economic performance of these countries.

This chapter examines the likelihood of major "peace dividends" acting as a stimulus to third world economic growth. In doing so, this chapter addresses the following questions:

1. Did defense expenditures hinder or aid developing countries in the 1980s?
2. Were the linkages from military expenditures to growth different than in previous time periods?
3. Did defense expenditures impact uniformly or vary by country?
4. If the impact varied across countries, what country groupings best depict these differences?
5. If they exist, what are the underlying environmental causes of these differences?

The main hypothesis of the analysis in this chapter is that developing countries are likely to show considerable variations with regard to the manner in which defense expenditures affect economic growth. In turn, these variations reflect the underlying economic health of developing countries, and thus their relative ability to minimize potential adverse effects associated with increased defense burdens. Our analysis of the impact on defense expenditures on Third World growth is followed in the next chapter with a detailed examination of the economic consequences of defense expenditures specifically in the Middle East and South Asia.

Literature Survey: The Impact of Defense Expenditures

A body of conventional wisdom has amassed over the years concerning the causes and consequences of Third World militarization. More often than not in the early literature this wisdom has been anecdotal and biased towards the standard "guns versus butter" analogies. Since the modern defense establishment is a heavy consumer of technical and managerial manpower and foreign exchange, resources that are especially scarce in the Third World, the conventional argument is that increased defense burdens should reduce the overall rate of growth.[1]

To test this theory, a rapidly growing body of empirical research has attempted to identify the impact of defense spending on various aspects of economic development and growth. Numerous studies have grown out of this debate. Unfortunately, no consensus has emerged. In the original study, Benoit found strong evidence to suggest that defense spending encouraged the growth of civilian output per capita in less developed countries.[2] On the other hand, Rothschild concluded that increased military expenditures lowered economic growth by reducing exports in fourteen OECD countries during 1956-69.[3] In his examination of 54 developing countries for the sample period 1965-73, Lim found defense spending to be detrimental to economic growth.[4] Deger and Sen,[5] Leontief and Duchin,[6] Faini, Annez and Taylor,[7] Biswas and Ram,[8] and Grobar and

---

1. Excellent critical reviews of this literature are given in Steven Chan, "Military Expenditures and Economic Performance," in United States Arms Control and Disarmament Agency, *World Military Expenditures and Arms Transfers, 1986* (Washington D.C.: USACDA, 1987), pp. 29-38; and Saadat Deger and Robert West, "Introduction: Defense Expenditure, National Security and Economic Development in the Third World," in Saadat Deger and Robert West, *Defense, Security and Development* (London: Francis Pinter, 1987), pp. 1-16.

2. Emile Benoit, "Growth and Defense in Developing Countries," *Economic Development and Cultural Change 26, 2* (January 1978), pp. 271-80.

3. K.W. Rothschild, "Military Expenditure, Exports and Growth," *Kyklos* 30 (1977), pp. 804-13.

4. David Lim, "Another Look at Growth and Defense in Less Developed Countries," *Economic Development and Cultural Change* 31, 2 (January 1983), pp. 377-84.

5. Saadat Deger and Somnath Sen, "Military Expenditure, Spin-off and Economic Development," *Journal of Development Economics* 13, 1-2 (August-October 1983), pp. 67-83.

6. W. Leontief and F. Duchin, *Military Spending: Facts and Figures* (New York: Oxford University Press, 1983).

Porter[9] also found evidence refuting the claim that defense spending stimulates economic growth.

In contrast, research examining the economic impact of Third World military expenditure utilizing various sub-groupings of countries tended to contradict these findings (Table 4.1). Much of this research implicitly argues that in certain economic situations by creating a stable environment it is possible that added defense expenditures may stimulate higher rates of investment, technological progress, technology transfer and hence increased overall growth.[10]

This research has gone through various stages and levels of sophistication. The initial studies were largely based on ordinary least squares regression techniques using Benoit's data set for the 1950-65 period. The original study using this methodology grouped countries on the basis of discriminant analysis with savings and investment used as discriminating variables (Table 4.1), study a). Subsequently, Frederiksen and Looney grouped countries on the basis of discriminant analysis with savings and investment used as discriminating variables.[11] They found that countries with relatively high levels of savings and investment experienced positive impacts on growth, while the impact was statistically insignificant for countries experiencing low levels of savings and investment.

A second study by Frederiksen and Looney also used Benoit's sample countries.[12] However it grouped countries largely on the basis of foreign exchange earnings, import elasticity, and productivity of investment. Again, relatively unconstrained countries experienced positive impacts on growth stemming from defense expenditures, while the relatively foreign exchange constrained countries showed a statistically insignificant but negative impact.

Later, using a different time period, 1965-73, and again grouping developing countries on the basis of their relative savings and investment,

7. R. Faini, P. Annez, and L. Taylor, "Defense Spending, Economic Structure and Growth: Evidence Among Countries and Over time," *Economic Development and Cultural Change* 32, 3 (April l984), pp. 487-98.

8. B. Biswas and R. Ram, "Military Expenditures and Economic Growth in Less Developed Countries: An Augmented Model and Further Evidence," *Economic Development and Cultural Change* 4, 2 (January 1986), pp. 361-72.

9. Lisa M. Grobar and Richard C. Porter, "Benoit Revisited: Defense Spending and Economic Growth in LDCs," *Journal of Conflict Resolution* 33, 2 (June 1989), pp. 318-345.

10. Charles Wolf, "Economic Success, Stability, and the 'Old' International Order," *International Security* 6, 1 (Summer 1981), pp. 75-92.

11. Peter C. Frederiksen and Robert E. Looney, "Defense Expenditures and Growth in Developing Countries," *Journal of Economic Development* (July 1982), pp. 113-126.

12. Peter C. Frederiksen and Robert E. Looney, "Defense Expenditures and Economic Growth in Developing Countries," *Armed Forces and Society* 9, 4 (Summer 1983), pp. 633-646.

TABLE 4.1   Summary of Early Empirical Work on the Impact of Defense
             Expenditures on Growth in the Third World

Classification of Countries	Impact on Growth
Total Sample (a)	positive, but statistically insignificant
Resource Constraint I (b)	
Relatively Constrained	insignificant
Relatively Unconstrained	(+)
Resource Constraint II (c)	
Relatively Constrained	(-)
Relatively Unconstrained	(+)
Resource Constraint III (d)	
Relatively Constrained	insignificant
Relatively Unconstrained	(+)

(+) indicates a positive impact, statistically significant at the 95% interval; (-) indicates a negative impact, statistically significant at the 95% percent interval. Insignificant indicates the defense growth relationship not statistically significant
at the 95% confidence level.

Sources: (a) Emile Benoit, "Growth and Defense in Developing Countries," *Economic Development and Cultural Change* 26, 2 (January 1978), pp. 271-80; (b) Peter
C. Frederiksen and Robert E. Looney, "Defense Expenditures and Growth in Developing Countries," *Journal of Economic Development* (July 1982), pp. 113-126; (c)
Peter C. Frederiksen and Robert E. Looney, "Defense Expenditures and Economic Growth in Developing Countries," *Armed Forces and Society* 9, 4 (Summer 1983),
pp. 633-646; and (d) Peter C. Frederiksen and Robert E. Looney, "Another Look
at the Defense Spending and Development Hypothesis," *Defense Analysis* 1, 3
(September 1985), pp. 205-210.

Frederiksen and Looney found that the relatively unconstrained countries
enjoyed a positive impact from defense expenditures.[13]
    These initial studies examined only the impact of defense expenditures
on growth. More recent analysis in the area has been more sophisticated,
employing more elaborate statistical devices and/or more subtle country
groupings. For example, the studies examining the effects of relative resource constraint (Table 4.2) represent a more elaborate variant of earlier
themes in that they use factor analysis for selecting variables for subsequent discriminant analysis. As before, analysis produced two groups of
Third World countries. This time the grouping reflected total access to foreign resources—exports, external borrowing and similar sources. Again,
countries with abundant foreign exchange derived positive impacts on
growth from military expenditures while that group of countries experiencing foreign exchange shortages found growth unaffected by military
spending.

_____

    13. Peter C. Frederiksen and Robert E. Looney, "Another Look at the Defense Spending
and Development Hypothesis," *Defense Analysis* 1, 3 (September 1985), pp. 205-210.

TABLE 4.2   Summary of Recent Empirical Research on the Macroeconomic
            Impact of Third World Defense Expenditures

	Growth	Debt	Imports	Income Distrib	Investment
Arms Production					
Producers	(+)	(+)	ins	(-)	(+)
Non-producers	(-)	(-)	(+)	ins	(-)
Resource Constraints					
Constrained	(-)	(+)	(-)	na	na
Unconstrained	(+)	(-)	ins	na	na
Regime Type					
Military	(+)	(+)	(+)	(-)	(+)
Civilian	(-)	(-)	(-)	ins	ins
Regime Legitimacy					
High	na	na	na	(-)	(+)
Low	na	na	na	ins	(-)

Sources: *Arms producers/non-producers:* Robert E. Looney and P.C. Frederiksen,
"Impact of Latin American Arms Production on Economic Performance," *Journal
of Social, Political and Economic Studies* 2, 3 (Fall 1987), pp. 309-320; Robert E.
Looney, "Impact of Arms Production on Third World Distribution and Growth
in the Third World," *Economic Development and Cultural Change* 38, 1 (October
1989), pp. 145-154.

Resource constrained/unconstrained: Robert E. Looney and P.C. Frederiksen "Defense Expenditures, External Public Debt, and Growth in Developing Countries,"
Journal of Peace Research 23, 4 (December 1986), pp. 329-338; Robert E. Looney,
"Impact of Military Expenditures on Third World Debt," *Canadian Journal of Development Studies* VII, 1 (1987), pp. 7-26; "Internal and External Factors in Effecting Third World Military Expenditures," *Journal of Peace Research* 26, 1 (February
1989), pp 33-46.

Military/Civilian Regimes: "Political Economy of Third World Military Expenditures: The Impact of the Regime Type on the Defense Allocation Process," *Journal
of Political and Military Sociology* 16, 1 (Spring 1988), pp. 21-30 ; Robert E. Looney
"Defense Budgetary Process in the Third World: Does Regime Type Make A Difference?" *Arms Control* 9 (1988), pp. 186-202; Robert E. Looney "Economic Impact
of Rent Seeking and Military Expenditures in Third World Military and Civilian
Regimes," *American Journal of Economics and Sociology* 48, 1 (January 1989), 11-30.

Legitimacy: "The Role of Military Expenditures in the African Economic Crisis,"
Jerusalem Journal of International Relations 12, 1 (January 1990), pp. 76-101.

Third World countries were divided on the basis of whether or not they
were indigenous producers of at least one major weapon system.[14] It appears that for the 1970-82 period, Third World military producers
experienced positive impacts from military expenditures on growth, in-

---

14. Following the classification of Stephanie Neuman, "International Stratification and
Third World Military Industries," *International Organization* 38, 1 (Winter 1984). pp. 172-173.

vestment, savings, but declines in productivity, while non-producers experienced declines in growth and investment (Table 4.2).

Groupings of Third World countries on the basis of regime type (military or civilian) also produced similar results with military regimes in general obtaining positive impacts from military expenditures (Table 4.2). The same pattern emerged with countries grouped on the basis of the legitimacy of government and threat faced by the regime from internal or external sources (Table 4.3).

In recent years, analysis has branched into more complex issues, and utilized both time series[15] and simultaneous equation models estimated by two-and three-stage least squares regression techniques. These studies introduce the demand for military expenditures into the analysis to allow for feedbacks from the macro-economy to defense. Interestingly enough, the results produced by these techniques tend to confirm the results obtained from simpler, more naive models.[16]

In short, the research summarized above demonstrates a consistent pattern whereby certain groups of Third World countries—usually the more successful economically, the more stable politically, or those engaged in military production, derive positive impacts on investment and growth from military spending. Those countries less successful economically, more politically unstable, or lacking a domestic arms industry fail to derive any positive economic impacts from defense expenditures.

With that having been said, it is important to note that a number of adverse effects may stem from defense expenditures. This is true even in those countries experiencing higher overall rates of growth from increased allocations to defense. In particular, countries with an indigenous arms industry may suffer a deterioration in the distribution of income from added defense expenditures.[17] The same may also occur in military regimes as the authorities shift income from urban consumers to industrial groups.[18]

A major limitation of the studies cited above is that, by their nature, cross-sectional studies are very aggregative so that applying to specific countries is hazardous at best. Obviously they are also incapable of capturing the dynamics associated with time. Lebovic and Ishaq's study of defense spending in the Middle East attempts to overcome these deficien-

---

15. See below Chapters 5 and 6.

16. See Robert E. Looney and David Winterford, "The Environmental Consequences of Third World Military Expenditures and Arms Production: The Latin American Case," *Rivista Internazionale di Scienze Economich e Commerciali* 40, 9, (1993) pp. 769-786; and, Robert E. Looney, "Impact of Arms Production on Income, Distribution and Growth in the Third World," *Economic Development and Cultural Change 38, 1* (October 1989), pp. 145-154.

17. See Chapter 2 above and Looney, "Impact of Arms Production on Income and Distribution and Growth in the Third World."

18. Looney, "Impact of Arms Production on Third World Distribution and Growth."

cies.[19] Using a pooled time-series, cross-sectional analysis on various groupings of Middle Eastern States, they found that higher military spending tended to suppress economic growth in the non-oil states of the Middle East during the 1973-84 period.

However, while Lebovic and Ishaq drew on time series data, they were not able to incorporate the potential effects of lags between the time defense expenditures occur and the period of maximum economic impact. In this regard, Babin has noted that incorporating the time variable into analysis can be critical because some relationships that may exist over time disappear in the short run and vice versa.[20] Clearly, at the national level, development usually requires a series of changes that occur through systems which involve organizations, agencies, economic structures and technological change.[21] Consequently (as Babin concludes) it is not justifiable to assume that a country's defense spending will have an immediate, or even short-term, effect on national economic performance.[22]

Babin's main finding was that while short-run economic impacts of defense expenditure may be nil or even negative, the longer term effect on growth is likely to be positive. Along these lines, Kick and Sharda's analysis suggests that an increase in the military manpower ratio has a significant positive effect on infrastructure and social welfare.[23] This impact occurs with a long (twelve year) lag. Kick and Sharda also found that the relationship over a 12 year period is positive. Militarization, whether measured by expenditures or size of the military, does contribute to development.

Methodology

To overcome some of the limitations of previous cross-sectional studies, the analysis below systematically incorporates various lags between the defense burden and economic growth. The emphasis is on examining the timing movements between these two variables. For this purpose, a small structural model was specified. To correct for any simultaneous equation bias, the model was estimated using a two-stage least squares procedure. In this model, economic growth during the 1980-1987 period was regressed on several measures of military expenditure during the previous

---

19. James Lebovic and Ashafaq Ishaq, "Military Burden, Security Needs, and Economic Growth in the Middle East," *Journal of Conflict Resolution* 31, 1 (March 1987), pp. 106-138.

20. Nehma Babin, "Military Spending, Economic Growth, and the Time Factor," *Armed Forces and Society* 15, 2 (Winter 1989), pp. 249-262.

21. Babin, "Military Spending, Economic Growth and the Time Factor," p. 249.

22. Babin, "Military Spending, Economic Growth and the Time Factor," p. 249.

23. Edward Kick and Bam Dev Sharda, "Third World Militarization and Development," *Journal of Developing Societies* II, 1 (April 1986), pp. 49-67.

decade. Lagged military expenditures were introduced into the model directly (into the growth equation itself) and indirectly (as a determinant of military expenditures in the 1980-1987 period).[24]
Specifically:

$$\qquad\qquad \overset{+}{\ } \quad \overset{?}{\ } \quad \overset{(?)}{\ } \quad \overset{+}{\ }$$
(a)   GDPG = f(GDIG, MEY(MEYo), GCG)

$$\qquad\qquad \overset{+}{\ }$$
(b)   GDIG = f(EX)

$$\qquad\qquad\ \ \ \overset{+}{\ } \qquad\quad \overset{+}{\ } \qquad\quad \overset{+}{\ }$$
(c)   MEY = f(MEYo, MEGo, MIDEAST)

Where:
  GDPG = the average annual growth in Gross Domestic Product, 1980-87
  GDIG = the average annual growth in gross capital formation, 1980-87
  MEY = the average share of military expenditures in GNP, 1980-87
  MEYo = the average share of military expenditures in GNP, 1970-79
  GCG = the average annual growth in government expenditure, 1977-87
  EX = the average annual growth in exports, 1980-87
  MEGo = the average annual growth in military expenditures, 1970-79
  MIDEAST = dummy variable, with values of 1 for Middle East, North
        African countries, and 0, other countries.

Two variants of the model were tested: (a) the military burden was introduced into equation (a) in lagged form (MEYo), and (b) in the current (1980-87) period (MEY). When MEY was included, it was estimated through equation (c) in terms of its previous level, and the growth in military expenditures during the 1980s. Given the higher military burdens in the Middle East, the MIDEAST dummy was also added to improve the estimation. In particular, we were interested in determining whether and to what extent the impact of military expenditures varied by sub-grouping. That is, did growth differ significantly in resource abundant and resource constrained countries with regard to their military burdens?

Results

The first step was to determine if the sub-grouping work for the pre-1980s data sets summarized above (Tables 4.1 and 4.2) extended into the 1980s—that is, did developing countries continue to fall into roughly two

---

24. A sample of sixty-eight countries classified as developing by the World Bank was used in the analysis. Economic data are from The World Bank, *World Development Report, 1989* (New York: Oxford University Press, 1989). Military expenditure futures are from the United States Arms Control and Disarmament Agency, *World Military Expenditures and Arms Transfers, 1988* (Washington: USACDA, June 1989).

groups based on their relative resource endowments and resulting economic performance? For this purpose, our sample of sixty-eight
developing countries[25] was split into two groups—those with real rates of
Gross Domestic Product (GDP) growth (1980-87) higher than the total
sample mean (2.3%), and those with growth rates lower than the sample
mean. The presumption was that the high growth countries possessed resources adequate to enable them to sustain fairly high rates of economic
growth, while the low growth countries were not able to overcome resource scarcity created by poor export markets, high debt burdens, and
similar constraints.

This initial grouping of countries comprised twenty-eight high growth
countries and forty with growth rates below the group mean.[26] Both
groups varied considerably with regard to a number of military expenditure and economic performance indices (Table 4.3).

As Table 4.3 indicates, several patterns are evident in the data. First, the
high growth countries sustained considerably greater rates of growth of
military expenditures during both the 1970-79 and 1980-87 periods. On the
other hand, the lower growth countries had higher rates of growth in the
armed forces during the 1970-79 period and only marginally lower rates of
growth during the 1980s. Second, the military burden (defense expenditures as a percentage of Gross National Product) for both groups of
countries was roughly the same. While for both groups military expenditures averaged around 3.5 percent of GNP, the low growth countries had
a slight increase in this ratio in the 1980s, while the high growth group had
a slight decline. Third, during the 1980s the share of the central government budget accounted for by defense was roughly similar for the two
groups: 13.7% for the low growth countries and 13.4% for the high growth
countries. However, while this figure was roughly the same in the 1970s
for the low growth countries, it was considerably below the 18.7 percent
average for the high growth countries. Finally, a major group difference involved military expenditures per capita, with the low growth countries
spending well over twice the amount as the high growth countries ($110
versus $41). The low growth countries also had more armed forces per
capita as well as nearly twice the share of arms imports in their total import bill.

Several sharp differences also characterized the economic performance
of the two groups of countries. While both groups of countries had roughly similar rates of growth in the 1970s, the high growth countries averaged
5.5% per annum increases in GDP in the 1980s, compared to 0.2% for the

25. Selected on the basis on comparable data across a wide number of military and economic indices.
26. A list of the countries and their classification based on rates of growth in the 1980s is
given in the Growth Group column of Table 4.5.

TABLE 4.3   Profiles of High and Low Growth Developing Economies, 1980-1987: Military Expenditures and Economic Growth

	(means)	
Variable	Growth 1980-87	
Discriminating Variables in Analysis	<2.3%	>2.3%
Military Expenditure Variables		
Growth Military Expenditure 1970-79	4.6	7.7
Growth Military Expenditure 1980-87	0.5	2.9
Growth Armed Forces 1970-79	4.1	3.6
Growth Armed Forces 1980-87	3.4	3.6
Average Military Burden 1970-79	3.5	3.1
Average Military Burden 1980-87	4.1	3.4
Average Share ME in Government Exp 1970-79	13.1	18.7
Average Share ME in Government Exp 1980-87	13.7	13.4
Average Military Exp Per Capita 1980-87	111.0	41.2
Average Forces Per 1000 Pop 1980-87	7.9	5.1
Average % Arms Imports in Total Imports 1980-87	8.2	3.6
Economic Growth Variables		
Growth in Gross National Product 1979-79	4.4	5.5
Growth in Gross National Product 1980-87	0.2	5.1
Growth in Gross Capital Formation 1965-80	7.4	9.2
Growth in Gross Capital Formation 1980-87	- 5.0	1.9
Growth in Private Consumption 1965-80	4.3	5.3
Growth in Private Consumption 1980-87	1.0	4.0
Growth in Government Consumption 1965-80	7.1	6.7
Growth in Government Consumption 1980-87	0.0	4.9
Growth in Imports 1965-1980	4.4	6.1
Growth in Imports 1980-87	- 2.4	2.1
Growth in Exports 1965-80	5.8	6.1
Growth in Exports 1980-87	0.9	6.4
Growth in Government Expenditure 1970-79	8.1	8.4
Growth in Government Expenditure 1980-87	- 0.1	4.0

Source: Military expenditure data from United States Arms Control and Disarmament Agency, *World Military Expenditures and Arms Transfers, 1988* (Washington: USACDA, June 1989). Economic data from World Bank, *World Development Report, 1989* (New York: Oxford University Press, 1989)

low growth countries. Even sharper differences occurred in the relative rates of growth in investment (gross capital formation), and government consumption, imports, exports, and total government expenditures, with the high growth countries averaging significantly higher rates of expansion in each category. In addition, while the high growth countries obtained lower growth rates in each category relative to the 1970s, this fall-off was considerably less than that experienced by the low growth countries. Especially telling is the fact that during the 1980s the low growth countries experienced negative rates of growth in gross capital formation (-5.0 percent per annum), imports (-2.4 percent per annum), and government expenditures (-0.1 percent). The high growth countries experienced positive growth (albeit lower than in the 1970s) in each of these areas.

TABLE 4.4   Profiles of High and Low Growth Developing Economies, 1980-1987:
             Other Economic Differences and Discriminating Factors

Variable Discriminating Variables in Analysis	(means) Growth 1980-87	
	<2.3%	>2.3%
Other Economic		
Inflation 1965-80	58.3	16.0
Inflation 1980-87	19.5	11.3
Terms of Trade 1985 (1980=100)	92.2	93.5
Per Capita Income 1987	1372.0	1191.7
Population 1987	17.8	113.0
Debt Variables		
Long Term Debt (% GNP, 1987)	76.8	53.7
Long Term Debt Service (% GNP, 1987)	5.4	5.9
Long Term Debt (% Exports, 1987)	22.5	24.9
Official Development Assistance (% GNP, 1987)	6.7	4.8
Official Development Assistance (per capita, 1987)	43.7	24.5

Military/Economic Variables Significant in Discriminating Groups	
Variable	Wilks' Lambda F
Growth in Private Consumption, 1980-87	0.521
Growth in Government Consumption, 1980-87	0.410
Growth in Armed Forces, 1980-87	0.382
Growth in Private Consumption 1965-80	0.354
Growth in Gross Capital Formation, 1980-87	0.341
Growth in Government Expenditure 1970-79	0.331
Growth in Imports, 1965-80	0.311
Growth in Military Expenditures, 1970-79	0.289

Table 4.4 compares the two groups of countries in terms of other economic indices. First, the high growth countries experienced relatively low rates of inflation during both the 1970s and 1980s. On the other hand, despite divergent export patterns in the 1980s, both groups of countries had experienced roughly the same deterioration in the terms of trade by 1985. Third, while the low growth countries had on the average higher per capita incomes, they were considerably below that of the high growth countries. Fourth, as one might imagine, the low growth countries had accumulated larger debt burdens (long term debt as a percentage of GNP) by the end of the period under consideration (1987). However, their debt service as a percentage of GNP was roughly similar to that of the high growth countries. Finally, the low growth countries, despite higher per capita incomes, had accumulated relatively large amounts of official development assistance as a share of GNP and on a per capita basis.

Clearly, the high and low growth countries differ in a wide variety of areas, both economic and military. A number of these measures are highly correlated, and it is not obvious which (other than growth itself) are critical (in some sort of statistical sense) for differentiating the two groups of countries. For this purpose, a step-wise discriminant analysis incorporat-

52

TABLE 4.5   Discriminant Analysis: Country Results

Country	Growth Group	Probability In Growth Group	Discriminant Score
Ethiopia	Low	76.4	- 0.149
Zaire	Low	100.0	- 3.975
Malawi	High	99.5	1.874
Tanzania	Low	29.1**	0.488
Upper Volta	High	98.5	1.498
Mali	High	99.9	2.277
Burundi	High	92.3	0.981
Zambia	Low	99.9	- 1.866
Niger	Low	97.9	- 0.975
China	High	100.0	3.071
Somalia	Low	90.7	- 0.489
Togo	Low	96.9	- 0.846
India	High	99.9	2.913
Rwanda	High	98.7	1.552
Benin	High	47.4**	0.182
Central African Republic	Low	70.2	- 0.051
Kenya	High	87.4	0.811
Sudan	Low	100.0	- 2.969
Pakistan	High	99.8	2.159
Haiti	Low	99.4	- 1.385
Nigeria	Low	99.9	- 1.887
Ghana	Low	84.8	- 0.317
Sri Lanka	High	99.9	2.541
Mauritania	Low	97.5	- 0.915
Indonesia	High	100.0	2.734
Liberia	Low	100.0	- 3.117
Senegal	High	94.2	1.076
Bolivia	Low	99.9	- 1.836
Zimbabwe	Low	99.6	- 1.527
Philippines	Low	99.7	- 1.611
Yemen Arab Republic	High	100.0	3.403
Morocco	High	94.3	1.083
Egypt	High	99.9	2.471
Ivory Coast	Low	96.3	- 0.793
Honduras	Low	65.7	0.130
Nicaragua	Low	99.9	- 2.130
Thailand	High	99.4	1.785
El Salvador	Low	98.7	- 1.121
Congo	High	99.4	1.801
Jamaica	Low	100.0	- 2.178
Guatemala	Low	99.9	- 1.859
Cameroon	High	100.0	4.067
Paraguay	Low	66.6	0.002
Ecuador	Low	97.1	- 0.867
Tunisia	High	98.9	1.607
Turkey	High	99.9	2.227
Colombia	High	91.8	0.959
Chile	Low	99.9	- 1.995
Peru	Low	97.6	- 0.922
Mauritius	High	90.1	0.895
Jordan	High	88.2	0.833
Costa Rica	Low	60.9	0.077
Syria	Low	100.0	- 3.476
Mexico	Low	99.8	- 1.784

TABLE 4.5   (continued)

Country	Growth Group	Probability In Growth Group	Discriminant Score
South Africa	Low	95.5	- 0.727
Brazil	High	75.3	0.558
Uruguay	Low	100.0	- 2.770
Argentina	Low	99.8	- 1.703
Yugoslavia	Low	99.9	- 1.466
Algeria	High	100.0	3.278
South Korea	High	100.0	2.579
Gabon	Low	99.8	- 1.683
Portugal	Low	97.1	- 0.873
Venezuela	Low	8.2**	0.958
Greece	Low	90.0	- 0.463
Israel	Low	99.8	- 1.655
Singapore	High	98.4	1.482
Kuwait	Low	0.0**	2.694

ed all of the variables in Tables 4.4 and 4.5. This exercise introduced the variables in a manner so as the variable providing the highest differentiating power was selected first. This procedure continued until it was impossible for an additional variable to make a statistically significant (based on the F-statistic) improvement in the group delineation.

The results of this exercise identified (bottom of Table 4.4) eight variables as statistically significant in splitting the country sample into two groups. In descending order of importance these were: (a) the growth in private consumption, 1980-87; (b) the growth in government consumption, 1980-87; (c) the growth in armed forces, 1980-87; (d) the growth in private consumption 1965-80; (e) growth in gross capital formation, 1980-87; (f) growth in total government expenditure 1979-79; (g) growth in imports 1965-80; and, (h) growth in military expenditures 1970-79.

Using these variables, the analysis classified most countries correctly with a very high probability of correct placement (Table 4.5). The analysis reclassified only one country, the small African country of Benin, from the high to the low group. Similarly, just three countries (Tanzania, Venezuela, and Kuwait) were reclassified from low to high. In the case of the latter two countries, slack oil revenues in the 1980s placed them initially in the low group. However their accumulated reserves obviously enabled them to maintain relatively high rates of investment, government consumption and similar measures.

Interestingly, one of the variables significant in distinguishing the two groups of countries was the growth in military expenditures during the 1970s, with the high growth countries experiencing considerably greater rates of defense expenditures (7.7 percent per annum versus 4.6 percent). Economically, it is apparent that the high growth countries are those having relatively abundant resources, enabling them to finance fairly high

TABLE 4.6   Impact of Military Expenditures on Economic Growth, 1980-87
              (standardized regression coefficients)

Discriminant Score Greater than -4.0 Growth in Income (GNPG)				*Discriminant Score Greater than -1.0* Growth in Income (GNPG)			

(1)
GNPG = 0.62 GDIG+ 0.06 MEY+ 0.35 GCG
     (3.06)   (0.66)   (3.40)
$r^2 = 0.472$; F = 18.50; df = 62
				(4)
				GNPG = 0.72 GDIG+ 0.27 MEY+ 0.28 GCG
				     (3.37) (2.20) (2.24)
				$r^2 = 0.494$; F = 13.67; df = 42			

Country	*Actual*	*Predicted*	*Error*	*Country*	*Actual*	*Predicted*	*Error*
India	4.6	4.5	+ 0.1	India	4.6	4.8	- 0.2
Pakistan	6.6	5.7	+ 0.9	Pakistan	6.6	6.5	+ 0.1
Egypt	6.3	3.6	+ 2.7	Egypt	6.3	5.3	+ 1.0
Algeria	3.8	3.6	+ 0.2	Algeria	3.8	3.8	+ 0.1
Syria	0.3	3.0	- 2.7				
Israel	2.2	3.3	- 1.1				
Discriminant Score Greater than -3.0 Growth in Income (GNPG)				*Discriminant Score Greater than 0.0* Growth in Income (GNPG)			

(2)
GNPG = 0.59 GDIG + 0.13 MEY + 0.35 GCG
     (3.18)   (1.32)   (3.42)
$r^2 = 0.489$; F = 18.85; df = 59
				(5)
				GNPG = 0.76 GDIG + 0.34 MEY + 0.27GCG
				     (3.60) (2.34) (1.91)
				$r^2 = 0.516$; F = 10.68; df = 30			

Country	*Actual*	*Predicted*	*Error*	*Country*	*Actual*	*Predicted*	*Error*
India	4.6	4.4	+ 0.2	India	4.6	5.1	- 0.5
Pakistan	6.6	5.7	+ 0.9	Pakistan	6.6	6.9	- 0.3
Egypt	6.3	3.9	+ 2.4	Egypt	6.3	5.6	+ 0.7
Algeria	3.8	3.5	+ 0.3	Algeria	3.8	4.0	- 0.2
Israel	2.2	4.3	- 2.1				
Discriminant Score Greater than -2.0 Growth in Income (GNPG)				*Discriminant Score Greater than 1.0* Growth in Income (GNPG)			

(3)
GNPG = 0.72 GDIG + 0.15 MEY+ 0.32 GCG
     (3.97)   (1.49)   (3.23)
$r^2 = 0.532$; F = 20.83; df = 55
				(6)
				GNPG = 0.58 GDIG + 0.39 MEY + 0.48 GCG
				     (3.43) (2.60) (3.40)
				$r^2 = 0.622$; F = 9.87; df = 18			

Country	*Actual*	*Predicted*	*Error*	*Country*	*Actual*	*Predicted*	*Error*
India	4.6	4.8	- 0.2	India	4.6	5.1	- 0.5
Pakistan	6.6	6.2	+ 0.4	Pakistan	6.6	7.2	- 0.6
Egypt	6.3	4.4	+ 1.9	Egypt	6.3	6.0	+ 0.3
Algeria	3.8	3.7	+ 0.1	Algeria	3.8	4.0	- 0.2
Israel	2.2	4.7	- 2.5				

Estimated by two stage least squares estimation procedure.

rates of growth in government expenditures and investment.

In terms of the growth equations specified above, a clear picture also emerges. Based on the t-statistic, defense expenditures (MEY, Table 4.6 equation 1) did not affect growth when considering the entire sample[27] of sixty-eight countries. A similar result (not shown here) occurred using lagged military expenditures (MEYo) in the growth equation.[28]

On the other hand, forming sub-groups based on the country discriminant score did produce a number of statistically significant results. Since discriminant scores have a mean of zero, countries with high negative scores are likely to be those with severe resource constraints. Gradually dropping the more resource constrained countries from the analysis systematically improved the statistical significance (and coefficient size) of the military expenditure term.

Thus, dropping three countries (those with discriminate scores less than -3.0) doubled the size of the coefficient (Table 4.6, equation 2) on the military expenditure term (from 0.6 to 0.13). The t test for significance, while still not high enough for a 95 percent confidence level, did improve from 0.66 to 1.32. Dropping four more countries (those with discriminate scores less than -2.0) gradually increased the size of the military expenditure coefficient and its t value (and the overall coefficient of determination, r^2). Finally, a sub group of countries with discriminant scores greater than -1.0 produced statistically significant results, with the size of the military expenditure term increasing to 0.27, and its t value now over the 95 percent confidence level. This pattern continued (Table 4.6, equations 5, and 6) when dropping more of the less resource endowed countries from the analysis. Eliminating countries with discriminant scores less than 1.0 raised the military expenditure coefficient to 0.39, and the overall coefficient of determination to 62.2 percent.

In terms of the Middle East and South Asian countries, several other patterns emerged. First, given their levels of military expenditures, growth rates in India and Pakistan were fairly close to the norm for countries with discriminant scores greater than -1.0. However, gradually confining the analysis to countries with higher discriminant scores, growth rates for India and Pakistan fell further and further short of the group norm. Israel's growth rates fell considerably short of that predicted. That is, given Israel's military burden, its growth rates were considerably below what the model predicted. In contrast Egypt experienced rates of growth considerably above those predicted by the model. Algeria's growth rates fell consistently close to those anticipated by the model. Finally, Syria's growth fell considerably below that predicted by the model.

Clearly, a number of factors affect the productivity of investment, military expenditures and government expenditures in affecting over-all economic growth. The work of Deger indicates that there may be a number of indirect or spinoff type impacts (both positive and negative) stemming from military expenditures.[29] Within the context of the results presented

---

27. For brevity, only the results for equation (a), the growth equation, are presented here. A complete set of results, together the underlying data base are available from the authors upon request.

28. The same holds for the sub-group analysis. Again for brevity only the results using the average military burden during 1980-87 are presented here.

here (Table 4.6) it is safe to assume the difference between the estimated and actual values for the growth equations may represent some of these indirect effects.

To determine the manner in which allocations to defense have contributed to this effect, we regressed several measures of military allocations (together with other types of expenditures) on the error term for each of the equations in Table 4.6.[30] Most of the military expenditure variables covered alternative time periods. For brevity only the period of highest statistical significance appears in the results presented here (Table 4.7). Since theory provides no guidance as to the correct specification of the model, we introduced the expenditure variables in a step-wise regression equation (with expected signs) of the form:

$$+ \qquad ?$$
(d)　ERROR = f(GNPG, EXPENDITURES)

The growth in GNP over the 1980-97 period (GNPG8087) represents a control variable to eliminate any biases stemming from correlations between individual expenditure terms and the overall rate of growth in the 1980s. The results (Table 4.7) again indicate several interesting patterns.

As Table 4.7 suggests, in all of the equations military expenditure terms were statistically significant in explaining the residuals obtained in Table 4.6. Similarly, none of the non-military expenditure terms accounted for fluctuations in the difference between actual and predicted rates of growth.

Second, for country groupings which included many of the low growth countries (and for which military expenditures did not have a direct impact on growth), military expenditures had a negative indirect impact on the residual. That is, increases in arms imports as a share of imports (AIZ) and per-capita military expenditures (MEP), tended to reduce the difference between actual and predicted rates of growth during the 1980s (Table 4.7, equations 1-3).

---

29. See for example Deger and Sen, "Military Expenditure, Spin-off and Economic Development," pp. 67-83.

30. Regressions were step wise, with the order of variables presented in Table 4.6 presented in the order of their selection. In each equation the variables introduced into the regressions were: the growth in military expenditures, 1970-79, 1980-87, 1977-87; the average share of military expenditures in GNP 1970-79, 1974-79; the average share of military expenditures in the central government budget, 1970-79, 1974-79, 1980-87; the average share of arms imports in total imports, 1970-79, 1974-79, 1980-87; growth in armed forces, 1970-79, 1980-87; average military expenditures per capita 1980-87; the growth in government expenditures, 1970-79, 1974-79; growth in GNP, 1970-79, 1965-80; average armed forces per capita 1980-87; and growth in exports 1980-87.

TABLE 4.7 Factors Affecting Expenditure Effectiveness
            (standardized regression coefficients)

Discriminant Score Greater than -4.0
      Actual minus Predicted Value, Equation 1 Table 4.6 (ERROR)
(1) ERROR = 0.51 GNPG8087 - 0.26 AIZ8087 - 0.25 MEP8087
                    (5.20)   (-2.63)   (-2.52)
r^2 = 0.445; F = 16.44; df = 58

Discriminant Score Greater than -3.0
      Actual minus Predicted Value, Equation 2 Table 4.6 (ERROR)
(2) ERROR = 0.53 GNPG8087 - 0.31 MEP8087 - 0.24 AIZ8087
                    (5.20)   (-2.63)   (-2.52)
r^2 = 0.512; F = 19.24; df = 55

Discriminant Score Greater than -2.0
      Actual minus Predicted Value, Equation 3 Table 4.6 (ERROR)
(3) ERROR = 0.41 GNPG8087 - 0.26 AIZ7479 - 0.24 MEP8087
                    (3.50)   (-2.20)   (-2.10)
r^2 = 0.319; F = 7.97; df = 51

Discriminant Score Greater than -1.0
      Actual minus Predicted Value, Equation 4 Table 4.6 (ERROR)
(4) ERROR = 0.71 GNPG8087 - 0.26 MEGE7479
                    (4.54)   (-2.74)
r^2 = 0.347; F = 10.36; df = 39

Discriminant Score Greater than 0.0
      Actual minus Predicted Value, Equation 5 Table 4.6 (ERROR)
(5) ERROR = 0.75 GNPG8087 - 0.48 MEGE7479
                    (3.88)   (-2.48)
r^2 = 0.351; F = 7.55; df = 28

Discriminant Score Greater than 1.0
      Actual minus Predicted Value, Equation 6 Table 4.6 (ERROR)
(6) ERROR = 1.09 GNPG8087 - 0.57 MEGE8087 + 0.43 MEG7079
                    (5.44)   (-3.04)   (2.73)
r^2 = 0.655; F = 10.13 df = 16

Estimated by step-wise ordinary least squares estimation procedure.
GNPG8087=Average annual growth in GNP, 1980-87; AIZ8087=average
share of arms imports in total imports 1980-87; MEP8087 = average military
expenditure per capita, 1980-87; AIZ7479 = average share of arms imports in
total imports 1974-79; MEGE7479 = average share of defense expenditures in
total government budget 1974-79; MEGE8087 = average share of defense expenditures in total government budget, 1980-87; MEG7079 = average annual
growth in military expenditures, 1970-79.

　　Third, for countries deriving positive direct impacts from defense expenditures to growth (Table 4.6, equations 4, 5 and 6), increases in the
average share in military expenditures in the central government budget
(MEGE) tended to have a negative indirect impact on overall economic
growth. (Table 4.7, equations 4, 5 and 6).
　　Fourth, for the first two country groupings (those with discriminant
scores greater than -1.0 and 0), the expenditure term with the highest sta-

tistical significance was increases in the average share of defense in the central government budget in the preceding five year interval (MEGE7479). That is, increases in the proportion of government resources allocated to defense in the late 1970s tended to offset somewhat the positive direct impact of military expenditures on growth in the 1980s.

Finally, this picture changed somewhat for the countries experiencing very high overall growth in the 1980s. For these countries, the negative indirect impact of increases in the share military expenditures in the central government budget during the 1980-87 period (MEGE8087) was offset somewhat by the positive indirect impact of higher rates of growth in defense expenditures in the 1970s (MEG7079).

In short, it appears that for low growth countries military expenditures may have impacted negatively and indirectly on their growth in the 1980s. By preempting scarce foreign exchange, arms imports apparently have diverted resources away from productivity enhancing expenditures. The same applies to domestic resources in the form of increased military expenditures per capita. The result has been lower rates of growth associated with investment and overall increases in government expenditures than might otherwise have been the case.

For the high growth countries a slightly different picture emerges. For these countries, excessive shares of military expenditures in the central government budgets (reflecting the general world wide surge in military expenditures in the late 1970s) appear to have diverted significant resources from areas such as human capital (education and health) and physical capital formation, so that by the 1980s relative deficiencies in these areas were detracting somewhat from the positive direct impact of defense expenditures on growth.

As might have been anticipated, that group of countries with very high rates of growth (discriminant scores over 1.0) and relatively few resource constraints were able to minimize somewhat the negative budgetary effect associated with allocations to defense. For these countries, high rates of growth in defense expenditures in the 1970s carried over into the 1980s in the form of positive indirect effects on growth. Unfortunately it is impossible from the results presented here to determine the nature of this latter indirect effect.

Conclusions

A common view holds that heavy defense expenditures divert scarce resources from productive investment (guns vs. butter) and human capital formation (health and education). Although this view is certainly plausible, it is not at all clear that military expenditures *per se* actually reduce economic growth in developing countries as a whole. Indeed, a counter-argument suggests that defense spending may well provide a stimulus to the economy. That is, defense expenditures may finance heavy industry, the acquisition of more advanced technology, and provide more employment opportunities. Defense spending, or a large military sector, may also attract investment thereby increasing a country's foreign exchange reserves.[31]

The results obtained here are consistent with this dual view of defense expenditures. The findings are also consistent with earlier studies for the periods prior to 1980 (Tables 4.1 and 4.2). For example, Frederiksen and Looney found that defense outlays bear a high opportunity cost, shifting resources from "high growth development projects."[32] This effect may entail a reduction not only in public outlays but in dependent private outlays as well. In their study only countries with buoyant foreign exchange (for example, Saudi Arabia) showed any positive correlation between defense outlays and economic growth; otherwise, the two compete against each other.

Roughly the same picture carried over into the 1980s. During this period, the more abundantly resource endowed countries appear to have derived positive net benefits to growth from increased defense expenditures. On the other hand, there is some evidence that (with a lag) the opportunity costs of defense expenditures have gone up as the share of defense expenditures in the central government's budget passes a certain threshold level. In this situation other types of allocations were likely to become relatively more productive in contributing to longer run growth.

However, a significant note of caution is warranted. As Richards and Waterbury observe:

> We may estimate, counterfactually, the returns on alternative uses of the monies devoted to defense, but practically nowhere in the world is there any assurance that reduced defense budgets would result in increased outlays on say, social welfare or infrastructure. Defense outlays are laden with the symbols and sentiments of national pride and survival. People seem prepared to accept disproportionate public investment in defense. They and their leaders find less justification in using equivalent resources to reduce adult illiteracy or line irrigation ditches.[33]

---

31. Alan Richards and John Waterbury, *A Political Economy of the Middle East: State, Class and Economic Development* (Boulder, CO: Westview Press, 1990), p. 360.

32. Frederiksen and Looney, "Defense Expenditures and Economic Growth in Developing Countries."

33. Richards and Waterbury, *A Political Economy of the Middle East: State, Class and Economic Development*, p. 360.

In other words, in the real world a reduction in defense expenditures would not necessarily in and of itself increase economic growth.

Now we turn to a smaller grouping of countries, our sample of seven Middle Eastern and South Asian nations, to see if the more general Third World patterns we have found pertain to them as well. Specifically, we are interested in examining whether military expenditures in these seven high-profile developing countries have adversely affected physical capital formation, growth, and other aggregate macro measures of their performance.

5

The Economic Consequences of Defense Expenditures in the Middle East and South Asia

Many analysts have argued that the expansion in military expenditures undertaken in the Middle East and South Asia over the last two decades has preempted resources capable of contributing to physical capital formation.[1] As a result, they believe that military expenditures may have tended to frustrate national development programs, especially those of the non-oil exporting countries such as India and Pakistan.

While this view makes intuitive sense, we have argued it is conceivable that military expenditures do not necessarily reduce economic growth in developing countries. Defense expenditures may act as an economic stimulus in such ways as financing heavy industry and the acquisition of advanced technologies, providing employment, and attracting investment.

Since the Middle East has the highest defense burden (defense expenditures as a share of Gross Domestic Product) in the developing world,[2] and India and Pakistan have some of the most pressing development problems in the developing world, it is of some interest to assess the extent to which military expenditures have influenced national efforts at expanding investment. Therefore, the purpose of this chapter is to assess whether military expenditures in seven major defense spenders, Algeria, Egypt, Syria, Israel, and Saudi Arabia in the Middle East, and India and Pakistan in South Asia, have been at the expense of physical capital accumulation

---

1. An excellent example of this view may be found in John Cummings, Hossein Askari, and Michael Skinner, "Military Expenditures and Manpower Requirements in the Arabian Peninsula," *Arab Studies Quarterly* 2, 1 (Winter 1980), pp. 38-49.

2. See United States Arms Control and Disarmament Agency, *World Military Expenditures and Arms Transfers, 1990* (Washington D. C., USACDA, November, 1991, reprinted 1992), p. 18-21.

as well as other macroeconomic aggregates. As a basis of comparison, we undertook a similar analysis using other categories of public expenditures.

The Issue of Causation

As we indicated in the last chapter, several studies have implicitly accepted Benoit's original assertion that "...the direct interaction between growth and defense burdens seems to run primarily from defense burdens to growth rather than vice versa. It seems clear that in the sample countries higher defense burdens simulate growth."[3] While this may well be true, it is simply an assertion and not based on empirical evidence. In fact there is a high likelihood that defense expenditures may simply reflect economic conditions and not be an initiator of economic change. As an extreme case, it is obvious that increased defense expenditures in Saudi Arabia largely reflect improvements in the international oil markets and hence the country's expanded Gross Domestic Product. While defense expenditures might feed back to affect GDP, this impact would be minimal by comparison.

It follows that before drawing any definitive conclusions as to the impact of defense expenditures, one must satisfactorily address the issue of causation. Once again, we turn to the original and most widely used causality test to date, that is, the one developed by Granger.[4]

Based upon the definition of Granger causality,[5] a simple bivariate autoregressive (AR) model for defense and GDP can be specified as follows:

$$(1) \quad GDP(t) = c + \sum_{i=1}^{p} a(i)GDP(t-i) + \sum_{j=1}^{q} b(j)DEF(t-j) + u(t)$$

$$(2) \quad DEF(t) = c + \sum_{i=1}^{r} d(i)DEF(t-1) + \sum_{j=1}^{s} e(j)GDP(t-j) + v(t)$$

Where GDP is the gross domestic product and DEF refers to defense expenditures; p, q, r and s are lag lengths for each variable in the equation; and, u and v are serially uncorrelated white noise residuals. By assuming that error terms (u, v) are "nice" ordinary least squares (OLS) becomes the appropriate estimation method.[6]

---

3. Emile Benoit, "Growth and Defense in Developing Countries," *Economic Development and Cultural Change* 26, 2 (January 1978), p. 276.

4. For an extended discussion of the Granger test see above, Chapter 3.

5. See above, Chapter 3.

6. For additional qualification, see Chapter 3, reference 20.

The Granger test detects causal directions in the following manner: first, unidirectional causality from DEF to GDP if the F-test[7] rejects the null hypothesis that past values of DEF in equation (1) are insignificantly different from zero and if the F-test cannot reject the null hypothesis that past values of GDP in equation (2) are insignificantly different from zero. That is, DEF causes GDP but GDP does not cause DEF. Unidirectional causality runs from GDP to DEF if the reverse is true. Second, bidirectional causality runs between DEF and GDP if both F-test statistics reject the null hypotheses in equations (1) and (2). Finally, no causality exists between DEF and GDP if we can not reject both null hypotheses at the conventional significance level.

Of course, the results of Granger causality tests depend critically on the choice of lag length. Our comments in Chapter 3 concerning the choice of lag lengths applies here as well.[8] Briefly, if the chosen lag length is less than the true lag length, the omission of relevant lags can cause bias. If the chosen lag is greater than the true lag length, the inclusion of irrelevant lags causes estimates to be inefficient. While lag lengths can be chosen on the basis of preliminary partial autocorrelation methods, as indicated in Chapter 3, there is no *a priori* reason to assume lag lengths equal for all of our sample countries. Consequently, once again we adopt the Hsiao procedure to overcome these difficulties.

A detailed discussion of the procedure is provided in Chapter 3.[9] Here, suffice it to indicate that we estimate M regressions of the form:

$$(3) \quad G(t) = a + \sum_{i=1}^{m} b(t\text{-}1)G(t\text{-}1) + e(i)$$

where the values of m range from 1 to M. For each regression, the FPE was computed as indicated in Chapter 3.[10]

The optimal lag length, m*, is the lag length which produces the lowest FPE. Having determined m* additional regressions expand the equation with the lags on the other variable added sequentially in the same manner used to determine m*. Thus we estimate four regressions of the form:

$$(4) \quad G(t) = a + \sum_{i=1}^{m^*} b(t\text{-}1)G(t\text{-}1) + \sum_{i=1}^{n} c(t\text{-}1)D(t\text{-}1) + e(i)$$

---

7. Within the framework of unrestricted and restricted models, a joint F-test is appropriate for causal detection and is determined by the equations given earlier in Chapter 3.

8. See Chapter 3.

9. See Chapter 3.

10. See Chapter 3.

with n ranging from one to four. Computing the final prediction error for each regression was the same as in Chapter 3.[11]

Depending on the value of the final prediction errors, four cases are possible: **(a) Defense causes Growth**—occurring when the prediction error for growth falls when the equation includes defense. In addition when growth is added to the defense equation, the final prediction error increases; (b) **Growth causes Defense**—occurring when the prediction error of growth increases when defense is added to the regression equation for growth, and is reduced when growth is added to the regression equation for defense; (c) **Feedback**—occurring when the final prediction error decreases when defense is added to the growth equation, and the final prediction error decreases when growth is added to the defense equation; and (d) **No Relationship**—occurs when the final prediction error increases when defense is added to the growth equation, and also increases when growth is added to the defense equation.

Methodology

Several conceptual problems remain.[12] First, to overcome the problem that most economic time series are non-stationary, we used the rates of growth of each variable in the estimated equations. Regressing these transformed series on a constant and time produced coefficients that were different from zero for all countries. Similar regressions of the untransformed levels indicated the presence of a trend.

Second, military expenditures may affect the macro economy in a way similar to that associated with other types of public expenditure. If this is the case any adverse affects identified may not be due to military expenditures *per se*, but government expenditures in general. To test for this possibility, we undertook additional regressions using (when available) figures on government consumption and/or public sector capital formation in place of defense expenditures. If the results were significantly different using these other forms of public spending, we concluded that the defense/growth relationship was unique and not simply a reflection of the general nature of public expenditures.

---

11. See Chapter 3.

12. The data for military expenditures used to carry out the Hsiao tests are from the Stockholm International Peace Research Institute, *SIPRI Yearbook, World Armaments and Disarmament*. Annual data on Gross Domestic Product is from various issues of the International Monetary Fund, *International Financial Statistics Yearbook*. When consistent price deflators were not available, we introduced the growth of the defense burden (the share of defense in GDP) in the regression equations.

Finally, investment is only one of many macro aggregates capable of providing insights in to the implications for longer run development. As a basis of comparison, we substituted other macro aggregates such as GDP, inflation, and imports for capital formation.[13]

Results

The results for our five Middle Eastern countries indicate the direction of causation, together with the optimal lag for each macro aggregate (Table 5.1).[14] Strength assessments reflect the size of the regression coefficients together with the relative reduction in the final prediction error of the dependent variable.

The following appear to be the most significant findings for our five Middle Eastern countries.

Algeria

For Algeria, in terms of the defense impact/causality issue, there are five main findings (Table 5.1). First, no statistically significant relationships occur between defense and investment. Second, with regard to other macroeconomic aggregates, causation is from defense to growth. This relationship is positive, with the lag between defense and growth relatively short—one year. However, the final prediction error for growth to defense was only slightly lower than that obtained from the growth to defense regression. Third, perhaps because of their rapid increase in the mid- to late 1970s, Algerian defense expenditures have created inflationary pressures. These pressures occur over time with a lag period of around four years, making budgetary control of inflation difficult. Fourth, while exogenous in terms of their impact on GDP growth and the rate of inflation, defense expenditures themselves also seem to lead the general expansion in government consumption. That is, defense expenditures appear more flexible than other types of government expenditures, expanding and contracting before budgetary changes in other public allocations. This finding suggests that defense is a semi-luxury good, expanding rapidly when extra revenues are available, but cut back during periods of austerity. Finally, defense expenditures also follow general expansions in imports, suggesting that they are largely responsive to the relaxation of foreign exchange constraints.

---

13. These variables are only reported here when a causal relationship was found.

14. Our two South Asian countries, India and Pakistan, are examined separately later in this chapter.

TABLE 5.1   Middle East: Summary of Statistically Significant Direction of
Causation in Country Expenditure Patterns

Causal Relationship	Time Period	Direction of Causation	Optimal Lag (Years) Strength
Algeria			
Defense/Investment	1967-1888	No Relationship	
Defense/GDP	1967-1988	Defense—>GDP(+)	(1) Weak
Defense/Inflation	1967-1988	Defense—>Inf(+)	(4) Strong
Defense/Imports	1967-1987	Imports—>Def(+)	(3) Moderate
Egypt			
Defense/Investment	1965-1988	Defense—>Inv(+)	(4) Strong
Gov Cons/Investment	1970-1987	Gov Cons—>Inv(-)	(1) Moderate
Defense/GDP	1965-1980	Def—>GDP(-)	(1) Moderate
Gov Consumption/GDP	1965-1980	Feedback(-)	(1) Moderate
Defense/Imports	1965-1987	Defense—>Imp(+)	(4) Strong
Gov Consumption/Imp	1965-1987	Defense—>Imp(+)	(4) Weak
Syria			
Defense/Investment	1962-1987	Feedback(+)	(4) Strong
Defense/GDP	1962-1987	Feedback(+)	(4) Strong
Defense/Imports	1962-1987	Feedback(+)	(4) Strong
Israel			
Defense/Investment	1955-1987	Defense—>Inv(+)	(4) Moderate
Defense/GDP	1955-1987	GDP—>Defense(+) GDP—>Gov	(3) Moderate
Government Cons/GDP	1955-1987	Cons(+)	(1) Weak
Saudi Arabia			
Defense/Investment	1965-1988	No Relationship	
Defense/GDP	1965-1988	GDP—>Defense(+)	(3) Strong
Defense/Non-oil GDP	1965-1988	Feedback(+)	(1) Strong
Gov Inves/Non-oil GDP	1965-1988	GDP—>Gov Inv(+) GDP—>Gov	(1) Strong
Gov Cons/Non-Oil GDP	1965-1988	Cons(+)	(2) Weak
Defense/Non-Oil GDP	1970-1988	Defense—>GDP(+) GDP—>Gov	(1) Weak
Gov Con/Non-Oil GDP	1970-1988	Cons(+)	(1) Weak
Gov Inv/Non-Oil GDP	1970-1988	Feedback(+)	(1) Strong

Summary of results obtained from Granger Causality Tests using a Hsiao Procedure to determine the optimal lag. That is, a four year lag indicates that most of
the impact from the expenditures (or GDP) in any one year tends to be distributed over four successive years.

Overall, defense burdens are relatively low in Algeria. If defense does
have an impact on the economy, it is probably slight albeit positive. Excessive defense expenditures may have an inflationary impact, perhaps
because they occur largely in the domestic market, rather than manifesting
themselves in increased imports.

Egypt

For Egypt defense expenditures fluctuated widely, resulting in a corresponding differential impact on the country's leading economic aggregates (Table 5.1). Table 5.1 suggests five main patterns for Egypt.

First, the major difference between defense expenditures and general government current expenditure lies in their respective impacts on real gross capital formation. Increases in the defense burden (the share of defense in GDP) have a strong impact on investment. This impact occurs over a four year period, not only for the period as a whole, but for each of the sub-periods as well. In contrast, changes in government consumption impacted negatively (with a one year lag) on gross capital formation.

Second, if one considers the 1965-87 period as a whole, no statistical pattern occurs between the growth of the defense burden and overall Gross Domestic Product. However, over the earlier 1975-80 period, defense expenditures had a negative impact on real GDP. Finally, the second sub-period, 1970-87, experienced little or no interrelation between defense and the economy as a whole.

Third, to determine if the economic impact of defense expenditures was unique to that category of government allocations, we undertook similar tests using the growth in the share of government consumption in GDP. The main finding here was that government consumption also showed little relationship to GDP over the period as a whole.

Fourth, on the other hand, the impact of government consumption expenditures in the two sub-periods was somewhat different than that of defense. For the 1965 period, government consumption interacted with GDP, tending as with defense to reduce GDP with a one year lag and determined by GDP over the 1970-87 period. From this we can conclude that defense allocations respond to factors other than pure internal economic conditions, while other types of government expenditure are more responsive to changes in the country's underlying economic base.

Finally, both defense and general government consumption expenditures are fairly import-intensive with increases in each leading to a follow-on expansion in imports. However, there is one major difference between the two types of expenditures in that in the 1970-87 period increased imports also facilitated increases in government consumption (but not in defense expenditures). Again, this finding demonstrates the relative reliance of government consumption on the country's underlying resource base.

From these patterns, a general picture emerges whereby defense expenditures in Egypt have a number of positive linkages with the economy as a whole. In particular increased defense expenditures appear to increase the profitability of investment over time, with the ultimate effect being higher rates of investment than would have otherwise been the case. On the other hand, the fairly strong import effect associated with defense expenditures may at times have compounded the country's foreign exchange problems, thus causing a general contraction of the economy. This phenomenon appears to have been present before 1980, but was not a factor in the preceding years, perhaps as a result of military aid from the United States.

These results are suggestive of a Military Keynesianism effect (that is, the use of procurement from local arms industries to stabilize the economy) associated with Egyptian defense expenditures.[15] In fact, similar patterns occur in other Third World arms producers.[16] In situations where governments have used defense expenditures to stabilize the economy, a characteristic pattern is one in which fluctuations in defense allocations offset deviations (positive or negative) in the expansion of the overall economy. That is, when the economy is growing faster than its trend (and overheating occurs) defense expenditures decline to reduce overall demand. Similarly during recessionary periods, defense expenditures expand to increase aggregate demand and thus employment.

Apparently, because of direct links to indigenous arms industries, the multiplier affect associated with defense expenditures is greater than with other types of government procurement. The resulting income and employment multiplier is higher and therefore the preferred way of fine tuning the economy.

Syria

In a comprehensive survey of the Syrian economy, the World Bank noted that the economy averaged around 10 percent real growth over the 1970-82 period.[17] That report argued that the main sources of this growth were government expenditures including military expenditures. In addition, the Bank contends that rapid increases in investment also contributed to that period's rapid economic expansion. From this the Bank concluded that there has been an increasing dependence of the Syrian economy on government expenditures in general and defense expenditures in particular.

This interdependence, whereby expenditures positively affect growth, with growth in turn delineating the amount of resources available for fu-

---

15. Robert E. Looney, "Military Keynesianism in the Third World: An Assessment of Non-Military Motivations for Arms Production," *Journal of Political and Military Sociology* 17, 1 (1989), pp. 43-64.

16. Robert E. Looney and P.C. Frederiksen, "The Economic Determinants of Military Expenditure in Selected East Asian Countries," *Contemporary Southeast Asia* 11, 4 (March 1990), pp. 265-277.

17. The World Bank, *Syria: Recent Economic Developments and Prospects* (Washington: IBRD, Report No. 5563-SYR, May 1986), p. 1.

ture expenditures, is apparent from the causality tests undertaken for the 1962-87 period (Table 5.1). Three main patterns emerge from the data for Syria.

First, increases in the defense burden impacted strongly on investment. This impact occurs over time, averaging four years. In turn, increases in investment provided a short run (one year) stimulus to the defense budget. The same patterns held for defense and GDP.

Second, a fairly strong set of interrelationships occurs between defense and imports, with defense contributing to the country's import burden. In turn, additional imports facilitate an expansion of the country's expenditures on defense.

Third, the same pattern occurs between defense and two other main macroeconomic aggregates, gross fixed capital formation and private consumption (with private consumption probably simply mirroring movements in overall GDP).

From these findings, it is apparent that defense expenditures in Syria have aided that country's economic expansion. However, given the relatively large import effect associated with defense expenditures, other types of public allocations may have been (or at least were potentially) more effective in this regard.

Israel

While Israel's military burden is one of the highest in the world, there is little evidence to indicate any negative impacts on the growth of Gross Domestic Product associated with expanded allocations to the military (Table 5.1). Four main patterns emerge from the data for Israel.

First, defense expenditures appear to have had a generally positive impact on fixed capital formation. That is, increases in defense expenditure have, with a one year lag, stimulated increased rates of investment.

Second, as a basis of comparison, tests using increases in the Government Consumption/GDP ratio indicated a similar pattern with the exception of the 1967-1987 period. During this time, increases in GDP (in contrast to the situation with defense) maintained their positive impact on government consumption. On the other hand, there is little evidence that government consumption (in contrast to defense) was able to stimulate increases in gross capital formation.

Third, for the period as a whole (1955-1987), there is a fairly strong positive relationship from GDP leading to increased defense expenditures (with an average lag structure of three years).

Finally, while this same relationship held for the twenty year period, 1955-75, it appears to have broken down; during the 1967-1987 period there was no statistically significant relationship between the growth in defense expenditures and that of the overall economy.

A similar contrasting pattern with respect to imports exists between defense expenditures and general government consumption. While both categories of expenditures show no relationship with imports over the 1955-75 period, increases in defense expenditures cause increases in imports over the 1967-1987 period. During this time frame, increases in imports permit government consumption to expand.

These import patterns suggest that the impact of defense expenditures on the Israeli economy is fundamentally different from that of other types of government allocation. In addition, this differentiation appears to be increasing with time. In recent years, defense expenditures received a high priority, with non-defense expenditures allowed to expand only when excess resources were available.

The ability of defense expenditures (as opposed to government consumption) to stimulate gross capital formation is consistent with a model of foreign aid developed by McGuire.[18] According to McGuire, foreign aid creates several price and income movements in the recipient country. For Israel, United States aid has created an indirect stimulus to investment via the complementarity between investment and defense. In addition, aid provides significant resources (via tax relief) to the private sector. Subsequently these resources flow into capital formation. "It appears in summary, that a significant fraction of U.S. aid goes to support capital formation in Israel via this diversion of resources."[19] In short, United States military grants to Israel have not only allowed the country to increase military expenditures rapidly in the short run, but perhaps more important, increase them in a way that was not detrimental to investment and economic growth.

Saudi Arabia

While Saudi defense expenditures have in a general sense mirrored developments in the oil sector, the pattern is complex and has altered over time.[20] In particular, there appears to be a structural shift associated with the oil price increases in the early 1970s that sets the 1960-73 period somewhat apart from the latter years. In particular, the impact (on a dollar per dollar basis) of the oil sector on defense was stronger in the earlier period.[21]

---

18. Martin C. McGuire, "Foreign Assistance, Investment, and Defense: A Methodological Study with an Application to Israel, 1960-1979," *Economic Development and Cultural Change* 35, 4 (July 1987), pp. 847-873.

19. McGuire, "Foreign Assistance, Investment, and Defense, p. 867.

20. For a detailed analysis of these patterns see below, Chapter 10. Also see Robert E. Looney, "The Impact of Defense Expenditures on the Saudi Arabian Private Sector, *Journal of Arab Affairs* 7, 1 (Fall 1987), pp. 198-229.

Specifically, for the 1960-85 period as a whole, the short run marginal propensity of the government to spend on defense was 0.03, with a longer run propensity to spend of 0.20. That is, a one billion riyal increase in oil revenues would result in an expansion of allocations to defense of 0.03 billion the same year (in constant prices). Over time (three to five years), the government tended to expand its allocations to defense by 0.20 billion riyals. In contrast, the short and long run propensities to spend oil revenues on defense were respectively: 0.87 and 0.34 for the 1960-73 sub-period; and, 0.16 and 0.03 for the 1973-85 sub-period.

In terms of causality, since oil revenues make up a significant portion of GDP, the results were of no great surprise. Thus the main pattern to emerge from the data is that for the period as a whole (1965-1988), movements in total GDP (at constant prices) tended to induce changes in the Kingdom's allocations to the military. In this sense, defense expenditures in Saudi Arabia are endogenous, affected by economic growth and not vice versa. The average lag was three years, that is, the past three years growth in GDP was the best predictor of the growth in defense expenditure for any one year. Interestingly, except for government consumption, none of the other standard macroeconomic aggregates seem affected by past movements in the country's GDP.[22]

While the relationship between total GDP and defense is fairly intuitive and straightforward, that between defense and non-oil GDP is more complex. Three patterns are worth noting for Saudi Arabia.

First, for the period as a whole (Table 5.1), defense and non-oil economic activity appear closely interrelated, with neither variable being completely exogenous with respect to the other. That is, past movements (an optimal lag of four years) in defense tended to reduce somewhat increases in real non-oil output. On the other hand, increases in non-oil GDP tended (with an optimal lag of one year) to stimulate additional increases in defense expenditures.

Second, over the last eighteen years covered, however, a clear pattern emerged whereby defense expenditures became intertwined with non-oil GDP. This new relationship has involved defense expenditures increasing non-oil GDP with an average lag of two years. In turn, increases in non-oil GDP facilitate (with a one year lag) expanded allocations for defense.

Third, also during this period, the relationship between non-oil GDP and government consumption seems to have changed so that causation began to run largely from GDP to government consumption. One implica-

21. Looney, "The Impact of Defense Expenditures on the Saudi Arabian Private Sector, p. 209.

22. For a detailed analysis of these patterns see below Chapter 10.

tion of this pattern is that defense expenditures have taken on a stronger role relative to government consumption in stimulating non-oil income.

These findings suggest that at least on the aggregate level, for the time period covered by the data, the Saudi Arabian economy did not suffer from the relatively large defense burden assumed by the government. Based on an earlier study,[23] however, several caveats are in order before extrapolating from the analysis of this data to conditions prevailing in the 1990s.

That earlier study found that in general defense expenditures have not had a neutral impact on the pattern of development in Saudi Arabia. In addition, the study concluded that, as with oil revenues, the impacts associated with defense expenditure occur over time. The net effect has been to retard growth in several key sectors, while stimulating expansion of others. Those sectors penalized by defense expenditures include agriculture, manufacturing (other than oil refining), electricity, water and power, and services. It appears that substituting non-defense expenditures for allocations to the military on a riyal for riyal basis would have resulted in rates of growth higher than those actually observed.

On the other hand, several sectors are likely to have benefited from defense expenditures. These include mining, construction, wholesale and retail trade, and the ownership of dwellings. Shifting public sector allocations from defense to non-defense would have reduced the expansion of these sectors relative to the rates of growth actually achieved.

Now we turn to an analysis of the patterns for South Asia, examining first Pakistan then India.

Pakistan

In general, Pakistan's defense expenditures have been relatively stable, particularly relative to those in the Middle East. To understand how Pakistan's defense expenditures have affected the country's pattern of growth, once again causality tests were performed linking defense and various macroeconomic indicators.[24]

In general, defense expenditures in Pakistan have impacted differently than non-defense government allocations. This holds for both the growth in expenditures (Table 5.2) and the growth in expenditure share in GDP (Table 5.3). Over the entire period, 1958-1988, there was no statistically significant relationship between changes in total military expenditures or the military burden and the overall rate of growth of real Gross Domestic

---

23. Looney, "The Impact of Defense Expenditures on the Saudi Arabian Private Sector," pp. 219-220.

24. As a basis of comparison with Chapter 4, time periods were used roughly corresponding to those selected for the Indo-Pakistan arms race analyses.

TABLE 5.2   Pakistan: Causality Between Government Expenditures and Gross Domestic Product, 1958-1988 (final prediction error)

Dependent Var Independent Var Optimum Lag Sign ()	GDP GDP	GDP Expenditures	Expendt Expendt	Expendt GDP
Defense Expenditures/Gross Domestic Product				
1958-1988	23.85	24.76	149.91	158.71
(no relationship)	1 year	2 years	2 years	1 year
	(-)	(-)	(-)	(+)
1958-1978	16.73	15.37	228.40	251.07
(Defense—>GDP)	1 year	2 years	2 years	1 year
	(-)	(-)	(-)	(-)
1968-1988	26.78	29.40	31.67	28.42
(GDP—>defense)	1 year	1 year	1 year	1 year
	(-)	(-)	(+)	(+)
Total Government Expenditures/Gross Domestic Product				
1958-1988	23.85	25.37	142.26	147.86
(no relationship)	1 year	3 years	1 year	2 years
	(-)	(+)	(-)	(+)
1958-1978	16.73	18.23	189.52	205.01
(no relationship)	1 year	1 year	1 year	2 years
	(-)	(-)	(-)	(+)
1968-1988	26.78	28.81	65.35	66.99
(no relationship)	1 year	3 years	1 year	2 years
	(-)	(+)	(-)	(+)
Non-Defense Government Expenditures/Gross Domestic Product				
1958-1988	23.85	25.20	264.70	278.54
(no relationship)	1 year	1 year	1 year	2 years
	(-)	(-)	(-)	(+)
1958-1978	16.73	18.16	334.45	352.24
(no relationship)	1 year	1 year	1 year	2 years
	(-)	(-)	(-)	(+)
1968-1988	26.78	29.31	166.62	172.14
(no relationship)	1 year	1 year	1 year	2 years
	(-)	(+)	(-)	(+)

Product. For the 1958-1978 period, however, both increases in the defense burden and military expenditures impacted negatively on GDP. This effect generally occurred after a one year lag. Finally, for the most recent twenty year period, the relationship between defense and GDP has shifted so that instead of impacting on GDP, defense expenditures have themselves been allowed to expand with the extra resources provided by the country's then steady and rapid economic expansion. It should be noted that this pattern applies to the growth in defense expenditures and not the relationship between the defense burden and GDP. For the latter, there does not appear to be a statistically significant relationship over the last twenty years. In general, government allocations to non-military activities have not had an impact on the aggregate economy, nor have they been affected by changing economic conditions.

TABLE 5.3   Pakistan: Causality Between the Growth in Government Expenditure
Share and Gross Domestic Product, 1958-1988 (final prediction error)

Dependent Var Independent Var Optimum Lag Sign ()	GDP GDP	GDP Expenditures	Expendt Expendt	Expendt GDP
Defense Expenditures/Gross Domestic Product				
1958-1988	23.85	25.45	147.88	156.90
(no relationship)	1 year	1 years	2 years	1 year
	(-)	(-)	(-)	(+)
1958-1978	16.73	16.20	229.65	252.95
(Defense—>GDP)	1 year	2 years	2 years	1 year
	(-)	(-)	(-)	(+)
1968-1988	26.78	28.21	35.94	37.29
(GDP—>defense)	1 year	1 year	1 year	1 year
	(-)	(-)	(+)	(+)
Total Government Expenditures/Gross Domestic Product				
1958-1988	23.85	24.90	93.37	97.65
(no relationship)	1 year	1 year	3 years	2 years
	(-)	(-)	(-)	(+)
1958-1978	16.73	18.21	127.13	140.19
(no relationship)	1 year	1 year	3 years	1 year
	(-)	(-)	(-)	(-)
1968-1988	26.78	28.67	36.81	35.81
(GDP—>GOVEXP)	1 year	1 year	4 years	2 years
	(-)	(-)	(-)	(+)
Non-Defense Government Expenditures/Gross Domestic Product				
1958-1988	23.85	24.79	· 189.70	201.82
(no relationship)	1 year	1 year	1 year	1 year
	(-)	(-)	(-)	(-)
1958-1978	16.73	18.04	240.15	260.17
(no relationship)	1 year	1 year	1 year	2 years
	(-)	(-)	(-)	(+)
1968-1988	26.78	29.31	100.78	117.78
(no relationship)	1 year	1 year	1 year	2 years
	(-)	(-)	(-)	(+)

From these patterns, it appears that Pakistan's defense expenditures
impact on the economy as a whole only during periods when the country
is responding to an Indian military build-up. During normal periods, defense expenditures appear to respond more to changing economic
conditions, rather than to cause economic change. It is also apparent that
the fruits of increased economic growth have tended to be shared more
with defense than with non- military government programs. In a similar
vein, there has been a tendency over time for defense expenditures to lead
in the timing of government allocations. That is, when defense expenditures change, they are followed by a corresponding change in non-defense
allocations. As with the other patterns examined above, this relationship
has changed in recent years (Table 5.4).

TABLE 5.4   Pakistan: Causality Between Defense Expenditures and Government
Expenditures, 1958-88 (final prediction error)

Dependent Var Independent Var Optimum Lag Sign()	Non Defense Non Defense	Non Defense Defense	Defense Defense	Defense Non Defense
Defense Expenditures/Total Government Expenditures				
1958-1988	142.26	94.67	149.91	159.89
(def—>gov exp)	1 year	2 years	2 years	1 year
	(-)	(+)	(-)	(+)
1958-1978	189.52	119.40	228.40	251.84
(def—>gov exp)	1 year	2 years	2 years	1 year
	(-)	(+)	(-)	(-)
1968-1988	65.54	67.65	31.67	34.71
(no relationship)	1 year	1 year	1 year	1 year
	(-)	(+)	(+)	(+)
Defense Expenditures/non Defense Expenditures				
1958-1988	264.70	231.17	149.91	160.01
(defense—>non-def)	1 year	1 year	2 years	1 year
	(-)	(+)	(-)	(+)
1958-1978	334.45	290.09	228.40	251.59
(defense—>non-def)	1 year	1 year	2 years	1 year
	(-)	(+)	(-)	(-)
1968-1988	166.63	180.55	31.68	34.71
(no relationship)	1 year	1 year	2 year	1 year
	(-)	(+)	(-)	(-)

For the period as a whole, changes in defense expenditures tended to precede those of total military expenditures with about a two year lag. For non-defense expenditures, the lag averaged about one year. This pattern was also present in the earlier period (1958-1978). During the more recent period, however, a statistically significant causal relationship has not existed between defense and non-defense allocations. This result is consistent with the pattern found above where, in the last twenty years or so, increased economic growth has gone in large part to defense, but not non-defense categories as a whole.

By the late 1980s, defense expenditure and debt service together accounted for over 70 percent of current expenditures, with debt servicing alone reaching over 35 percent of current expenditures. The role of defense expenditures in compounding the government's debt situation is complex and difficult to identify. Movements in defense and total debt (Table 5.5) show no real relationship over the period from 1958-1978. By the late 1980s, however, both the increase in defense and the defense burden were related to the expansion in debt. However, the pattern was one of increases in debt causing, a year later on average, increases in defense and the defense burden. One possible interpretation of this pattern is that the government contracts for funds before making firm commitments to expanding allocations to defense. That is, increases in defense expenditures

TABLE 5.5   Pakistan: Causality Between Defense Expenditures and Total
            Government Debt, 1958-87 (final prediction error)

Dependent Var Independent Var Optimum Lag Sign ()	Debt Debt	Debt Defense	Defense Defense	Defense Debt
Defense Expenditures\Total Debt				
1958-1987	309.05	321.86	154.34	162.48
(no relationship)	1 years	2 years	2 years	1 year
	(-)	(+)	(-)	(-)
1958-1978	414.21	440.86	228.40	249.83
(no relationship	1 year	1 year	2 years	1 year
	(-)	(+)	(-)	(-)
1967-1987	425.00	458.71	49.73	45.81
(debt—>defense)	1 year	3 years	1 year	1 year
	(-)	(+)	(-)	(-)
Defense Burden/Total Debt				
1958-1987	309.05	315.82	152.72	163.31
(no relationship)	1 years	1 year	2 years	1 year
	(-)	(+)	(-)	(+)
1958-1978	414.21	427.55	229.65	252.51
(no relationship	1 year	1 year	2 years	1 year
	(-)	(+)	(-)	(+)
1967-1987	425.00	446.40	40.47	40.27
(debt—>defense)	1 year	1 year	2 years	1 year
	(-)	(+)	(-)	(-)

are not used by the authorities as the rationale for increased borrowing
needs.

The relationship between non-defense expenditures and debt is much
more straightforward (Table 5.6). For the period as a whole, non-defense
expenditures preceded changes in total government debt by about a year.
Interestingly enough, increases in non-defense expenditures reduced the
expansion in overall debt. That is, increases in non-defense expenditures
had, with a one year lag, a negative impact on the growth in total real government debt. For the period 1967-1987, there was little or no relationship
between non-defense expenditures and the growth in public sector debt.

These contrasting patterns between debt and public sector expenditures can be explained in part by the interaction of Pakistani revenues and
expenditures. Again, defense and non-defense expenditures exhibit dis-
similar patterns (Table 5.7). For the period as a whole, increases in
revenues increased defense expenditures, again after a one year lag. This
pattern also occurred in the 1958-78 period.

Over the period 1968-1988, defense expenditures and revenues became
intertwined, with increased defense expenditures expanding revenues
(with about a four year lag period) and, in turn, augmented revenues increasing defense expenditures, after an average lag of about two years.
Non-defense expenditures have not displayed a causal relationship with

TABLE 5.6   Pakistan: Causality Between Government Expenditures and Total
Government Debt, 1958-87 (final prediction error)

Dependent Var Independent Var Optimum Lag Sign ()	Debt Debt	Debt Expend	Expend Expend	Expend Debt
1958-1987	309.05	300.55	270.00	288.73
(non defense—>debt)	1 year	1 year	1 year	1 years
	(-)	(-)	(-)	(-)
1958-1978	414.21	399.58	334.45	366.65
(non-defense—>debt	1 year	1 year	1 year	1 year
	(-)	(-)	(-)	(-)
1967-1987	425.00	447.55	176.96	194.91
(no relationship)	3 years	1 year	1 year	1 year
	(-)	(-)	(-)	(+)
Total Government Expenditures/Total Debt				
1958-1987	309.05	321.28	145.22	155.22
(no relationship)	1 years	1 year	1 year	1 year
	(-)	(-)	(-)	(-)
1958-1978	414.21	428.52	189.52	207.58
(no relationship)	1 year	1 year	1 year	1 year
	(-)	(-)	(-)	(-)
1967-1987	425.00	458.96	85.27	93.56
(no relationship)	3 years	1 year	1 year	1 year
	(-)	(-)	(-)	(-)

revenues over the period as a whole. However, in the last twenty years or so, they tended to increase revenues, but were not in turn enhanced by revenue expansion. Aggregating both defense and non-defense into total government expenditures apparently blurred the subtle distinctions by individual category to the extent that no statistically causal patterns between this fiscal aggregate and revenues were observed.

The series of debt/expenditure/revenues findings summarized above are suggestive of the general budgetary process in Pakistan. Specifically, during periods when the government feels it must increase allocations to the military to counter increased Indian militarization, the government is forced to allocate a large share of its expanded revenues to the military. Debt is not contracted for this purpose, however, perhaps because of the obvious difficulties of securing commercial funding for this type of activity. During these periods, the government confines its borrowing to support an expanded level of non-defense type activities.

In contrast, during periods when defense expenditures are undertaken for reasons other than an increase in the perceived threat from India, the government apparently has the luxury of exploring alternative sources of financing. In the short run, it expands allocations to the military largely from increased revenues. If the magnitude of defense expenditures outruns the financial capacity of the government, the authorities are then

TABLE 5.7   Pakistan: Causality Between Government Expenditures and
Revenues, 1958-1988 (final prediction error)

Dependent Var Independent Var Optimum Lag Sign ()	Expenditure Expenditure	Expend Revenues	Revenues Revenues	Revenues Expend
Defense Expenditures/Government Revenues				
1958-1988	161.85	167.41	149.91	143.80
(revenues—>def)	1 year	2 years	2 year	1 year
	(-)	(-)	(+)	(+)
1958-1978	243.76	264.44	228.40	223.79
(revenues—>def)	4 years	2 years	1 year	1 year
	(-)	(-)	(-)	(+)
1968-1988	82.82	70.49	31.67	28.53
(feedback)	1 year	4 years	1 year	2 years
	(+)	(+)	(+)	(+)
Non-Defense Expenditures/Government Revenues				
1958-1988	161.85	172.65	264.70	280.57
(no relationship)	1 year	1 year	1 year	1 yea r
	(-)	(+)	(-)	(-)
1958-1978	243.76	268.49	334.45	364.62
(no relationship)	1 year	1 year	1 year	1 year
	(-)	(-)	(-)	(-)
1968-1988	82.82	81.27	166.63	183.35
(non-defense—>rev)	1 year	1 year	1 year	1 year
	(+)	(+)	(-)	(+)
Total Government Expenditures/Government Revenues				
1958-1988	161.85	172.65	142.26	151.80
(no relationship)	1 year	1 year	1 year	1 year
	(-)	(+)	(-)	(+)
1958-1978	243.76	268.48	189.52	208.74
(no relationship)	1 year	2 years	1 year	1 year
	(-)	(-)	(-)	(+)
1968-1988	82.82	85.20	65.54	71.79
(no relationship)	1 year	1 year	1 year	1 year
	(+)	(+)	(-)	(+)

forced to resort to debt financing to complete the defense procurement
process.

India

Unlike Middle Eastern countries or Pakistan, India makes most of its
own military equipment, including tanks and jet fighters, which are domestically produced under license. It produces military goods of such
technological quality that they can be exported for hard currency to many
newly industrializing or less developed nations. In turn, the hard currency
may be used to import more advanced weapons and other military goods.
India's desire to maintain or increase its status in the international defense
community has an undeniable effect on its military budgeting and policy,
in spite of somewhat significant economic constraints.

TABLE 5.8   India: Causality Between Defense Expenditures and Gross Domestic Product, 1957-1987 (final prediction error)

Dependent Var Independent Var Optimum Lag Sign ()	GDP GDP	GDP Defense	Defense Defense	Defense GDP
Defense Expenditures/Gross Domestic Product				
1957-1987	24.76	17.59	200.98	214.40
(defense—>GDP)	2 years	2 years	2 years	1 year
	(-)	(+)	(+)	(+)
1957-1977	22.96	15.00	302.66	307.04
(defense—>GDP)	4 years	1 years	2 years	3 years
	(-)	(+)	(+)	(-)
1967-1987	26.99	19.79	63.06	66.85
(Defense—>GDP)	1 year	2 years	2 years	1 year
	(-)	(+)	(+)	(+)
Defense Burden/Gross Domestic Product				
1957-1987	24.76	16.88	184.73	196.40
(defense—>GDP)	2 years	2 years	1 year	1 year
	(-)	(+)	(+)	(+)
1957-1977	22.96	14.22	254.20	239.31
(feedback)	4 years	1 year	1 year	3 years
	(-)	(+)	(+)	(-)
1967-1987	26.99	20.14	78.47	86.01
(Defense—>GDP)	1 year	1 year	1 year	1 year
	(-)	(+)	(-)	(+)

As with our other cases, causality tests were performed to determine the direction of linkage between Indian defense expenditures and overall economic growth. Has defense simply responded to the greater volume of resources provided by an expanding economy or instead have defense expenditures initiated changes in the country's growth pattern?

For the period as a whole defense impacted on GDP growth rather than vice versa (Table 5.8). This impact has been positive and has occurred with an average lag of approximately two years. The same patterns also characterized two twenty-year sub-periods, 1957-1977 and 1967-1987. In all cases, the impact of defense on growth was positive, with growth not significantly affecting the government's allocations to the military. A minor difference occurred when the defense to growth link occurred with only a one year lag in the earlier period (1957-1977). Fairly similar results were obtained using the defense burden (the share of defense expenditures in GDP). The only difference was seen during the 1957-77 period, where a feedback effect occurred from GDP to defense. This feedback had a average lag of three years and was negative.

A somewhat different pattern occurred using total government expenditures in place of allocations to defense (Table 5.9). A feedback effect occurs with these expenditures whereby they impact positively, with a fairly long lag, on GDP. In turn, GNP growth impacts on total government

TABLE 5.9   India: Causality Between Government Expenditures and Gross Domestic Product, 1957-1987 (final prediction error)

Dependent Var Independent Var Optimum Lag Sign ()	GDP GDP	GDP Expenditures	Expend Expend	Expend GDP
Total Government Expenditures/Gross Domestic Product				
1957-1987	24.76	18.43	107.19	88.47
(feedback)	2 years	4 years	4 years	2 years
	(-)	(+)	(-)	(-)
1957-1977	22.96	14.19	165.90	133.83
(feedback)	4 years	2 years	4 years	1 year
	(-)	(+)	(-)	(-)
1967-1987	26.99	21.17	87.71	81.48
(feedback)	1 year	3 years	1 years	1 year
	(-)	(+)	(+)	(-)
Government Consumption/Gross Domestic Product				
1957-1987	24.76	16.91	62.51	55.51
(feedback)	2 years	1 years	2 years	1 year
	(-)	(+)	(-)	(-)
1957-1977	22.96	12.19	89.49	78.84
(feedback)	4 years	3 years	2 years	1 year
	(-)	(+)	(-)	(-)
1967-1987	26.99	16.85	51.44	38.77
(feedback)	1 year	1 year	1 year	2 years
	(-)	(+)	(-)	(-)

expenditures with a shorter negative lag. Similar patterns occurred using government consumption, although here, as one might imagine, the lags were shorter.

These findings are consistent with those obtained by other researchers. Ward et. al.,[25] have developed a formal model of the economy whereby the impact of defense expenditures over the period 1950 to 1987 has been examined within the context of a Mintz-Huang neo-classical growth model. In this model, defense impacts directly on both growth and investment. In addition to government expenditures, both military and non-military, economic growth is also a function of the growth in investment, and increases in labor productivity.

Their main findings are that investment and government spending each have a positive impact on growth. Separating government spending into military and non-military, they found that both had a direct, strong and positive effect on economic growth in the short run. In addition, they concluded that non-military expenditures had about a one third greater impact on GDP than military expenditures.

---

25. Michael D. Ward, et al., "Economic Growth, Investment, and Military Spending in India, 1948-1988," Working Paper, Research Program On Political and Economic Change, Institute of Behavioral Science University of Colorado (March 15, 1990), pp. 20-29.

The Ward model links new investment to production and government spending—both military and nonmilitary—as well as to the depreciating level of capital stock. This formulation has the advantage of allowing one to determine the manner in which military expenditures influence investment, and in the longer run, growth in GDP. Their findings indicate that private consumption in India drives down investment, government spending (both military and nonmilitary) is associated with higher levels of investment, and the capital stock increases investment levels. It is especially interesting that the beneficial impact of government spending is split between military and non-military spending. These findings suggest that the short run multiplier of military spending is positive in India, with the spin-off effect providing enhanced economic growth in the longer run.

Indian defense expenditures appear to have a beneficial impact on growth and investment in spite of the fact that historically they have been a very heavy user of foreign exchange. For example, Terhal's analysis of the 1950-72 period concluded that the total foreign exchange requirements for defense were equivalent in value to nearly half of the Indian imports of machinery and equipment.[26] Terhal found that during the 1960-70 decade, the level of these foreign exchange requirements oscillated between eight percent and forty-two percent of the deficit on the balance of payments, with an average of about twenty percent.[27]

This apparent paradox, the positive impact of defense expenditures on growth and investment and the diversion of foreign exchange from non-defense activities, can be reconciled in part by examining the dynamics of government expenditures and public indebtedness. Using the Granger test to determine the causal direction of government expenditures and public sector debt, it was found that defense expenditures appear to have played a direct role in increasing the country's foreign currency denominated debt (Table 5.10). This finding holds whether one uses growth in defense expenditure or the change in the country's defense burden. For the 1957-87 period as a whole, increases in defense preceded increases in foreign currency debt with an average lag of about three years.

In contrast, while causation was also from defense expenditures and the defense burden to rupee-denominated debt, the impact was negative. That is, increases in defense expenditure tended to reduce rupee denominated debt. The average length of the lag between defense and debt was about four years. A considerably different relationship has developed between total government expenditures and the government's debt. Here, Granger causality tests indicated that foreign currency denominated debt has pre-

26. Peter Terhal, "Foreign Exchange Costs of the Indian Military, 1950-1972," *Journal of Peace Research* XIX, 3 (1982), pp. 251-260.
27. Terhal, "Foreign Exchange Costs of the Indian Military, 1950-1972," p. 256.

TABLE 5.10 India: Causality Between Expenditures and Government Debt, 1957-
1987 (final prediction error)

Dependent Var Independent Var Optimum Lag Sign ()	Debt Debt	Debt Defense	Defense Defense	Defense Debt
Defense Burden/Foreign Currency Denominated Debt				
1957-1987	267.74	202.76	184.73	195.06
(defense—>DEBT)	4 years	3 years	1 year	2 years
	(+)	(+)	(+)	(-)
Defense Expenditures/Foreign Currency Denominated Debt				
1957-1987	267.74	164.84	200.98	214.55
(defense—>DEBT)	4 years	3 years	2 years	1 year
	(+)	(+)	(+)	(-)
Total Government Expenditures/Foreign Currency Denominated Debt				
1957-1987	267.74	280.65	107.19	103.76
(DEBT—>GOVEXP)	4 years	2 years	4 years	2 years
	(+)	(-)	(-)	(-)
Gross Capital Formation/Foreign Currency Denominated Debt				
1957-1987	267.74	287.87	36.78	38.81
(no relationship)	4 years	1 year	2 years	1 year
	(+)	(+)	(-)	(-)
Defense Burden/Domestic Currency Denominated Debt				
1957-1987	59.82	55.81	184.73	185.29
(defense—>DEBT)	1 year	4 years	1 year	2 years
	(+)	(-)	(+)	(+)
Defense Expenditures/Domestic Currency Denominated Debt				
1957-1987	59.82	54.85	200.98	212.56
(defense—>DEBT)	4 years	4 years	2 years	1 year
	(+)	(-)	(+)	(-)
Total Government Expenditures/Domestic Currency Denominated Debt				
1957-1987	59.82	61.47	107.19	89.41
(DEBT—>GOVEXP)	1 year	1 year	4 years	2 years
	(+)	(+)	(-)	(+)
Gross Capital Formation/Foreign Currency Denominated Debt				
1957-1987	59.82	60.74	36.78	39.16
(no relationship)	4 years	1 year	2 years	1 year
	(+)	(+)	(-)	(-)

ceded government expenditures. Specifically, movements in this type of
debt have tended to lead changes in government expenditures by about
two years. In addition, the impact on total government expenditures has
been negative. Rupee denominated debt has also tended to cause changes
in total government expenditures but, in contrast to foreign currency denominated debt, the impact has been positive. In addition, the lag between
changes in rupee debt and total government expenditures has been fairly
short, averaging about one year. As a basis of comparison, Granger tests
were also performed on the growth in real gross capital formation (invest-

ment) and debt. No relationship was found with either foreign currency denominated debt or rupee denominated debt.

These findings support the notion that government spending is a high priority for Indian development planners, so long as revenues can be generated fast enough to keep the so-called debt trap from overtaking macroeconomic conditions. The high priority given defense spending allows the military to finance its acquisitions with foreign denominated debt. Through this mechanism, defense expenditures are financed without necessarily preempting the country's foreign exchange earnings from other types of development activity. The impact of defense expenditures on growth can therefore remain positive through short run direct Keynesian demand linkages, and longer run supply side spinoff-type effects.

Non-defense expenditures can also have a positive impact on growth because, while their foreign currency denominated debt financing appears constrained, the government allows a safety valve through domestically denominated debt. Perhaps in a manner similar to Pakistan's military expenditures, the government is willing to borrow domestically to cover revenue shortfalls, and thus complete the expenditure cycle for non-defense development projects. Apparently to avoid inflationary pressures, a ceiling linked to defense expenditures is placed on domestically denominated debt. Rapid defense expenditures, with a four year lag time, are seen as a signal to the government to restrict domestically denominated debt. There are apparently limits on how far the government will go in expanding its foreign currency denominated debt to finance military expenditures.

In fact, India's recent history of military expenditures is related to its development in several interesting ways. For many years, India's primary supplier was the former Soviet Union because of the Soviets' acceptance of Indian rupees as an exchange currency and the existence of a barter system of payments. For two reasons, this situation was enhanced for the Soviets during the 1980s as India experienced inflation, leading to a decline in India's balance of payments position. First, the Indian military was already familiar with Soviet equipment such as the MiG-29 fighter jet. Additionally, the shortage of hard currency in the country meant that exchange in any medium besides the rupee would involve great difficulties with any purchase package proposed by Western European nations or the United States.[28]

Summing up, the analysis for South Asia suggests that the negative impact of defense on Pakistan's economy may have stemmed from an overreaction to Indian defense expenditures. The net result was to com-

---

28. Ward et al., "Economic Growth, Investment, and Military Spending in India, 1948-1988," p. 17.

press military allocations into too narrow a time frame to allow for an efficient transfer from the civilian sector. This is also evidenced by the fact that debt has been contracted to cover unanticipated overruns in the defense budget. In addition, Pakistan's lack of a sizable defense industry sector negated the possibility of any positive military Keynesianism effects that could have provided a short run stimulus to the economy.

In contrast, India appears to have had much better control over its allocations to defense. As Chapter 3 indicated, there is little evidence that India was forced into a regional arms race (although we did not test for Chinese defense expenditures), and until quite recently, Indian defense spending has not really grown much faster than the economy as a whole. These factors may have allowed India's sizable defense industry sector to benefit from military Keynesianism effects while at the same time remaining below the level consistent with efficient resource absorption. In short, even with three potentially hostile borders and then wavering international partnerships,[29] India has managed to provide for its national defense at a cost that does not appear to have markedly impeded its economic progress and may, in fact, have aided the development of the industrial sector.

Conclusions

For the most part, cross sectional studies have implicitly assumed that causation runs from defense to investment and/or growth. The seven country case studies examined in this chapter provide evidence that is somewhat at odds with this view. While there is little evidence supporting the alternative position that investment or growth causes defense, many countries have developed fairly elaborate feed-back mechanisms whereby defense impacts on investment and growth and in turn is affected by that growth. In addition, aside from Pakistan, there is little evidence that defense hurts investment or growth. However, there is ample support for the position that the relationship between defense and investment or growth varies considerably among countries and that the lag structures also differ greatly.

We now turn from the broader question of the consequences of defense spending for economic growth to examining impacts on specific public policy sectors. In refining our analysis, our interest is quite focused: in the next chapter we investigate whether military expenditures in the Middle East and South Asia, and in particular in our sample of seven countries, Algeria, Egypt, Israel, Syria, Saudi Arabia, Pakistan and India, have been

---

29. In the early 1990s India's main international partner, the Soviet Union, collapsed leaving India bereft of its long time global partner.

at the expense of national human resource development. The ability of a nation to adjust its economy to the realities of the post-cold war global economy may depend largely on investments made in the social services available to, and the skill levels and health of, its population. Have defense expenditures preempted this type of investment?

6

Defense Expenditures and Human Capital Development in the Middle East and South Asia

The ability of developing countries to adapt to changing, and for many more austere, economic environments in the 1990s, will depend in large part on how effectively they took advantage of any relatively abundant revenue years to increase the education and skills of their domestic workforces.

Stephanie Neuman has argued in her analysis of the pre-revolutionary Iranian situation that some of the skills taught by the military can provide just such benefits to the civil sector.[1] She points out, however, a question still remains as to:

> ...how one would distinguish between the military and the civilian costs and benefits. What is the net balance over the long and short term? Furthermore, how are the skill levels related to the kinds of military technology imported? Does more technology demand higher skills and, therefore, indirectly upgrade the educational level of the country? Instead, does it draw away needed skilled manpower from the civilian sector?[2]

Given the available data, we can not directly address the issues posed by Neuman. However, it is still possible to determine whether and to what extent military expenditures have retarded the overall allocation of resources to education and health in the developing world. Specifically, the purpose of this chapter is to address whether military expenditures in the region in general, and in particular in our sample of seven cases, Algeria, Egypt, Israel, Syria, Saudi Arabia, Pakistan and India, have been at the ex-

1. Stephanie Neuman, "Security, Military Expenditures and Socioeconomic Development: Reflections on Iran," *Orbis* 22 (Fall 1978), pp. 569-594.

2. Neuman, "Security, Military Expenditures and Socioeconomic Development," p. 589.

pense of national human resource development. Based on this analysis several implications are drawn as to the development of human capital in the Middle East and South Asia.

Recent Expenditure Patterns

Human capital accumulation can be stimulated in developing countries through public education expenditure, as well as government spending on health and other social services. Clearly, governments are by far the most important agencies in this area and can do much more than private enterprises could ever hope to achieve.

Government initiative in this area has expanded in recent years (Tables 6.1 and 6.2), with our sample countries as a whole increasing their educational expenditures as a percentage of GNP from 3.91 in 1974 to 5.73 in 1986 (Table 6.1). The corresponding figures for non-Middle East/South Asian countries were 3.44 percent and 4.04 percent respectively. Our sample countries' educational commitment is also somewhat higher than that of other countries in the region. For these countries, educational expenditures as a share of GNP increased from 3.08 percent in 1974 to 4.56 percent by 1986.

These differences are more dramatic when viewed in per capita terms. Here, our sample countries increased their educational expenditures per capita from around $60 in 1974 to over $200 by 1986. The corresponding figures for non-Middle East/South Asian countries were $22.12 and $67.90 respectively.

There is considerably less variation in the pattern of health expenditures. In this expenditure category, our sample countries increased their health expenditures as a percentage of GNP from 1.19 percent in 1974 to 1.61 by 1986. Corresponding figures for the non-Middle East/South Asian countries were 1.42 and 1.91 respectively. Still, on a per-capita basis our sample countries did show dramatic increases in their allocations to health. For these countries health expenditures per capita increased form $18.07 in 1974 to $66.93 in 1986, compared with $10.56 and $38.52 for the non-Middle East/South Asian countries.

As might be expected, our sample countries tended to have the heaviest military burden (military expenditures as a percent of Gross National Product) and per capita military expenditures. In fact, the military burden of this group of countries in 1986 was over three times that of the non-Middle East/South Asian countries.

Interestingly enough, high military burdens were not necessarily reflected in high rates of growth in military expenditures over the twelve year period, 1974-86. In fact, during this interval the military burden decreased at an average annual rate of 0.8 percent (Table 6.2). By comparison

TABLE 6.1   Human Resource and Military Expenditures in Middle East-South Asian and non-Middle East-South Asian Developing Countries 1974-1984 (means)

Year	Sample Middle East/ South Asian (# countries)	Non-Sample Middle East/ South Asian (# countries)	Total Middle East/South Asian (# countries)	Non-Middle East/South Asian (# countries)
Military Expenditures (percentage of GNP)				
1974	12.19 (7)	6.10 (22)	7.57 (29)	2.34 (74)
1978	10.72 (7)	6.88 (21)	7.84 (28)	2.80 (80)
1982	10.38 (7)	9.27 (21)	9.55 (28)	3.19 (77)
1986	11.08 (7)	9.85 (20)	10.17 (27)	3.29 (79)
($ per capita)				
1974	237.23 (7)	117.54 (22)	146.43 (29)	16.06 (74)
1978	304.80 (7)	213.57 (22)	235.29 (29)	34.34 (80)
1982	605.86 (7)	431.12 (22)	473.30 (29)	59.04 (77)
1986	435.87 (7)	310.12 (22)	365.71 (29)	56.17 (79)
Educational Expenditures (percentage of GNP)				
1974	3.91 (7)	3.08 (22)	3.28 (29)	3.44 (76)
1978	5.37 (7)	3.82 (21)	4.21 (28)	4.28 (80)
1982	4.88 (7)	3.96 (21)	4.19 (28)	4.34 (80)
1986	5.73 (7)	4.56 (20)	4.86 (27)	4.04 (79)
($ per capita)				
1974	60.36 (7)	68.41 (22)	66.47 (29)	22.12 (74)
1978	145.35 (7)	180.70 (21)	171.86 (28)	44.73 (80)
1982	230.44 (7)	173.72 (22)	187.41 (29)	72.26 (77)
1986	206.32 (7)	169.47 (20)	179.02 (27)	67.90 (79)
Health Expenditures (percentage of GNP)				
1974	1.19 (7)	1.25 (22)	1.23 (29)	1.42 (76)
1978	1.38 (7)	1.37 (21)	1.37 (28)	1.75 (79)
1982	1.93 (7)	1.51 (18)	1.63 (28)	1.90 (78)
1986	1.61 (7)	1.52 (19)	1.54 (27)	1.91 (79)
($ per capita)				
1974	18.07 (7)	29.05 (22)	26.40 (29)	10.56 (76)
1978	40.77 (7)	60.25 (21)	55.38 (28)	21.85 (79)
1982	112.02 (7)	73.56 (19)	83.92 (26)	38.23 (78)
1986	66.93 (7)	65.04 (19)	65.55 (26)	38.22 (79)

Source: Ruth Leger Sivard, *World Military and Social Expenditures* (Washington: World Priorities), various issues.

that of the other regional Middle East/South Asian countries increased by 4.07 per annum, while that of the non-Middle East/South Asian countries increased by 2.88 percent per annum. Similar patterns also occurred with regard to per capita military expenditures, with our sample countries' military expenditures per capita increasing at an average annual rate of 5.2 percent per annum, compared with 8.42 and 11.00 percent for the non-sample Middle East/South Asian countries and non-Middle East/South Asian countries respectively.

TABLE 6.2   Human Resource and Military Expenditures in Middle East-South
            Asian and non-Middle East-South Asian Developing Countries
            1974-1984 (average annual rates of growth)

Years	Sample Middle East/ South Asian (# countries)	Non-Sample Middle East/ South Asian (# countries)	Total Middle East/South Asian (# countries)	Non-Middle East/South Asian (# countries)
Military Expenditures (percentage of GNP)				
1974/78	- 3.16 (7)	3.05 (22)	0.88 (29)	4.59 (74)
1978/82	- 0.80 (7)	7.74 (21)	5.06 (28)	3.31 (80)
1982/86	1.64 (7)	1.53 (21)	1.59 (28)	0.77 (77)
1974/86	- 0.80 (7)	4.07 (20)	2.49 (27)	2.88 (79)
($ per capita)				
1974/78	6.47 (7)	16.10 (22)	12.58 (29)	20.92 (74)
1978/82	18.73 (7)	19.20 (22)	19.09 (29)	14.51 (80)
1982/86	- 7.90 (7)	- 7.91 (22)	- 7.91 (29)	- 1.24 (77)
1974/86	5.20 (7)	8.42 (22)	7.92 (29)	11.00 (79)
Educational Expenditures (percentage of GNP)				
1974/78	8.25 (7)	5.53 (22)	6.44 (29)	5.61 (76)
1978/82	- 2.36 (7)	0.90 (21)	- 0.12 (28)	0.35 (80)
1982/86	4.19 (7)	3.59 (21)	3.78 (28)	- 1.77 (80)
1974/86	3.24 (7)	3.32 (20)	3.33 (27)	1.34 (79)
($ per capita)				
1974/78	24.57 (7)	27.49 (22)	26.80 (29)	19.25 (74)
1978/82	12.21 (7)	- 0.98 (21)	2.19 (28)	12.74 (80)
1982/86	- 2.75 (7)	- 0.61 (22)	- 1.14 (29)	- 1.54 (77)
1974/86	10.78 (7)	7.85 (20)	8.61 (27)	9.80 (79)
Health Expenditures (percentage of GNP)				
1974/78	3.77 (7)	2.32 (22)	2.73 (29)	5.36 (76)
1978/82	8.74 (7)	2.46 (21)	4.44 (28)	2.08 (79)
1982/86	- 4.43 (7)	0.17 (18)	- 1.41 (28)	0.13 (78)
1974/86	2.55 (7)	1.64 (19)	1.89 (27)	2.50 (79)
($ per capita)				
1974/78	22.56 (7)	20.01 (22)	20.34 (29)	19.94 (76)
1978/82	28.75 (7)	5.12 (21)	10.95 (28)	15.01 (79)
1982/86	-12.08 (7)	- 3.03 (19)	- 5.99 (26)	- 0.01 (78)
1974/86	11.52 (7)	6.95 (19)	7.89 (26)	11.31 (79)

Source: Ruth Leger Sivard, *World Military and Social Expenditures* (Washington:
World Priorities), various issues.

Another pattern of significance involves the relative expansion of educational and health expenditures. In this regard our sample countries
experienced average annual increases in education expenditures as a share
of GNP of 3.24 percent per annum over the 1974-86 period. Comparable
figures for the non-sample Middle East/South Asian and the non-Middle
East/South Asian counties were 3.32 and 1.34. In other words, our sample
countries expanded their human capital development slightly below that
of the other regional countries, but considerably faster than other parts of

the developing world. With regard to health expenditures as a share of GNP, our sample counties expanded allocations in this area considerably faster than other countries in the region and slightly above that achieved by the non-Middle East/South Asian nations. The same was also true of health expenditures per capita.

In short, concurrent with rapid economic growth in our sample countries, there has been an acceleration in military spending, but at a slightly lower rate than the overall expansion of the economy. Still, the absolute levels of military expenditure dwarf other parts of the world. In large part, defense expenditures have been financed by oil revenues and by military aid and grants from the major industrial country arms suppliers. Lebovic and Ishaq have noted that while absolute regional military spending has been phenomenal, the military also controlled a greater percentage of the central government budget in the Middle East, and twice as much of the national output, as in other developing countries or in the world as a whole.[3]

Middle Eastern defense accounted for one third of the military spending of developing countries and almost one-half of world arms imports. During the 1973-1982 period, the average annual economic growth rate for individual Middle Eastern states was about 6.0%, while military expenditures grew by approximately 13.0 percent per year. Although military expenditure levels vary greatly across countries, in a great majority of the countries the growth rate of military spending outpaced economic growth. This indicates a striking trend in the region toward higher military burdens (military expenditures as a ratio of GDP).[4]

While these trends seem to have slackened in the post 1982 period, the fact still remains that military expenditures may represent a considerable burden in terms of foregone allocations to other types of activities. For example, despite the relative affluence of a number of our sample countries, the rate of expansion (1974-86) of educational expenditures on a per-capita basis was only slightly above the average of the non-Middle East/South Asian countries, and below that of the other regional economies.

Looking at the impact of military expenditures from a different perspective, that of labor scarcity, Cummings, Askari and Skinner, note that labor shortages in the Gulf States created by expanded military expenditures may be a far greater long term impediment to growth in the region than any effects associated with the diversion of capital or foreign exchange to military activities.[5] In a somewhat similar manner, Mousad found that in the early-to-mid 1980s a ten percent reduction in the military spending ra-

---

3. James Lebovic and Ashafaq Ishaq, "Military Burden, Security Needs, and Economic Growth in the Middle East," *Journal of Conflict Resolution* 31, 1 (March 1987), p. 107.

4. Lebovic and Ishaq, "Military Burden, Security Needs, and Economic Growth in the Middle East," p. 107.

tio (percentage of GNP), or a decrease of around of $12.9 billion, would increase education expenditure by around $8.1 billion per year.[6]

Along these lines, Deger estimated that a 15 percent reduction in the share of military spending ratio, that is, from 6.3 percent of GDP to 5.4 percent (approximately 13 billion dollars in absolute terms) would increase the education expenditure ratio to 2.93 percent of national output.[7] These estimates were made for developing countries as a whole, with no distinction made between countries that were resource abundant or resource constrained, labor abundant or labor scarce.

In the remainder of this chapter we seek to extend several strands of the analysis surveyed above. Specifically, we are interested in determining whether and to what extent military expenditures have affected human capital development in our sample countries and the region as a whole. Finally, are the linkages between military expenditures, human capital development, and allocations to health in the region, fundamentally different than those in other parts of the world? If they are, in what manner?

Framework for Analysis

The main measurable variables pertain to allocations to defense, government expenditures and public education that may generate human capital. The latter is proxied by the ratio of public education expenditure as a proportion of GDP. Following Deger, we assume that public education spending as a proportion of the national product is a crucial determinant of human capital formation (MEY).[8] If this ratio falls, the rate of growth of human capital will probably also fall. As Lebovic and Ishaq have noted, one of the difficulties with previous studies was their lack of clarity as to whether the military burden acted in some way as a statistical proxy for government expenditures.[9] To avoid this problem, total government expenditures were included in the analysis as a control variable, with the share of military expenditures lagged. Specifically, because government

5. John Thomas Cummings, Hossin G. Askari and Michael Skinner, "Military Expenditures and Manpower Requirements in the Arabian Peninsula," *Arab Studies Quarterly* 2, 1 (Winter 1980), pp. 38-49.

6. Mohammed Raief Mousad, "Human Resources, Government Education Expenditure and the Military Burden in Less Developed Countries: With Special Reference to Arab Countries," *Bulletin of Arab Research and Studies* (Number 11, 1984), pp. 35-55.

7. Saadat Deger, "Human Resources, Government Education Expenditure, and the Military Burden in Less Developed Countries," *Journal of Developing Areas* 20, 1 (October 1985), pp. 37-48.

8. Deger, "Human Resources, Government Education Expenditure, and the Military Burden in Less Developed Countries," pp. 42-43.

9. Lebovic and Ishaq, "Military Burden, Security Needs, and Economic Growth in the Middle East," p. 110.

expenditures usually go up across the board, including military expenditures in the current year would capture this spurious budgetary element. To eliminate this effect, lagged military expenditures (MEYo) were included in the regression equation. The share of military expenditures in GNP in 1986 was then lagged on the residuals of the estimated education equation (see below, equation a) to determine whether, and to what extent, military expenditures retarded the potential allocations to human capital.

There is considerable continuity in the provision of health and educational expenditures, with the proportion of national resources allocated to each changing only gradually over time. To control for this factor, the percentage of human resources allocated to education at an earlier period was introduced into the regression equation. For this purpose 1982 was selected since this date represents the beginning of the current phase of relatively slack oil markets, and international debt problems, both of which have resulted in austerity in many parts of the developing world.

The literature is unclear as to whether health and educational expenditures are substitutes or complements. Certainly, a logical case could be made for either position. In addition, in many developing countries, the military is intimately involved in the provision of education and health services, particularly in rural areas, so that these three expenditure categories may be correlated. To avoid this problem government expenditures were specified as being a function of their level in a base period (again, 1982), together with total government expenditures.

Preliminary regressions indicated that the share of government expenditures in GNP was highly correlated with military expenditure per soldier. As one might imagine, expenditures per soldier tend to be closely correlated with per capita income.

Finally, several regional variables were introduced to determine whether our sample countries and/or the Middle East/South Asian region as a whole varied significantly from developing countries in general in the provision of health and educational services.[10]

In sum, the model with expected signs used for examining the impact of military expenditures on human resource development, was of the form:[11]

---

10. For countries included in the Middle East/South Asian region see Chapter 2, reference 3 on p. 10.

11. Data was taken from Ruth Leger Sivard, *World Military and Social Expenditures* (Washington: World Priorities) various issues. The original sample of developing countries consisted of 109 nations. Because of missing observations on several countries the usual sample size was around 90 countries. The Arab countries consisted of the twenty members of the Arab Monetary Fund: Jordan, UAE, Bahrain, Tunisia, Algeria, Saudi Arabia, Sudan, Syria, Somalia, Iraq, Oman, Qatar, Kuwait, Lebanon, Libya, Egypt, Morocco, Mauritania, Yemen Arab Republic and the Peoples Democratic Republic of Yemen. Because of missing observations, Lebanon, Qatar, and Mauritania were absent from most of the regressions.

$$
\begin{array}{lll}
& + \qquad ? \qquad + \\
\text{(a)} & \text{EDY} = f(\text{GEY, MEYo, EDYo}) \\
& + \qquad + \\
\text{(b)} & \text{GEY} = f(\text{GEYo, MEAF}) \\
& + \qquad + \\
\text{(c)} & \text{MEAF} = f(\text{YP, MEAFo})
\end{array}
$$

Where:

   EDY = the percentage of GNP allocated to education (1986)

   MEYo = the percentage of GNP allocated to defense (1982)

   EDYo = the percentage of GNP allocated to education (1982)

   GEY = the percentage of GNP allocated to government expenditures (1986)

   GEYo = the percentage of GNP allocated to government expenditures (1982)

   MEAF = military expenditures per soldier (1986)

   MEAFo = military expenditures per soldier (1982)

   YP = per capita income (1986).

Results

The estimated model produced[12] several interesting patterns (Tables 6.3 and 6.4).[13] First, for the total country sample,[14] lagged military expenditures had a negative impact on the proportion of national resources allocated to education (Table 3, equation 1). Second, the model predicted education expenditures in the sample countries fairly well. As may have been anticipated, Israel, Saudi Arabia, and Algeria's commitment to education was somewhat higher than the norm, with Syria and Pakistan, slightly below the norm. Third, regressing the current share of GNP allocated to defense, along with several regional variables[15] on the residual (from equation 1), it appears that the Middle East/South Asia region in general, and our sample countries in particular, had better rates of educational attainment than that experienced in other parts of the world (Table 6.3, equation 1'). Finally, and more importantly, military expenditures sig-

---

12. For brevity, only the results for equation (a) are presented here. The full model and results are available from the authors upon request.

13. Sivard, *World Military and Social Expenditures, 1989* and *World Military and Social Expenditures, 1985*.

14. The original sample consisted of 110 developing countries. Because of missing observations only ninety-three of these were used in the analysis.

15. The regional dummy variables used were (a) SAMPLE with values of 2 for the seven countries under consideration and 1 for all other developing countries; and SAMPLERG with values of 3 for the sample countries, 2 for other countries in the Middle East/South Asia Region and 1 for all others.

TABLE 6.3   Defense Expenditures and Allocations to Education, 1986
(standardized regression coefficients)

Total Sample				*Non-Middle East/South Asian Countries*		
(1)				(3)		
EDY = 0.86 GEY + 0.38 EDYo - 0.42 MEYo				EDY = 0.46 GEY + 0.53 EDYo - 0.10 MEYo		
(4.66)	(4.71)	(-2.93)		(2.62)	(5.11)	(-0.88)
$r^2 = 0.652$; F = 56.21: df = 90				$r^2 = 0.689$; F = 48.73: df = 66		
Residuals	*Actual*	*Predicted*	*Error*	(3') ERROR = - 0.24 MEY		
Egypt	4.8	4.7	0.1		(-2.32)	
Israel	7.3	6.7	0.6	$r^2 = 0.068$; F = 5.41; df = 74		
Saudi				*High Military Expenditure Countries*		
Arabia	10.6	9.6	1.0	*(ME > 5.04% GNP)*		
				(4)		
Syria	5.7	6.1	- 0.4	EDY = 0.94 GEY + 0.33 EDYo - 0.42 MEYo		
India	3.4	3.3	0.1		(3.26)	(2.43)	(-2.00)
Pakistan	2.2	2.6	- 0.4	$r^2 = 0.607$; F = 13.93: df = 27		
Algeria	6.1	4.7	1.4			
(1') ERROR = - 0.43 MEY + 0.29 SREGIONX				*Residuals*	*Actual*	*Predicted*
	(-3.95)	(2.66)		Egypt	4.8	4.4
$r^2 = 0.140$; F = 8.07; df = 99				Israel	7.3	6.6
Middle East/South Asian Countries				Saudi		
				Arabia	10.6	9.6
(2)						
EDY = 1.40 GEY + 0.28 EDYo - 0.89 MEYo				Syria	5.7	5.8
(3.54)	(1.57)	(-2.47)		Pakistan	2.2	2.3
$r^2 = 0.615$; F = 10.67: df = 20						
				(4')		
Residuals	*Actual*	*Predicted*	*Error*	ERROR = - 0.52 MEY + 0.33 SAMPLE		
Egypt	4.8	5.0	0.2		(-3.23)	(2.05)
Israel	7.3	5.8	1.5	$r^2 = 0.282$; F = 5.89; df = 30		
Saudi				*Low Military Expenditure Countries*		
Arabia	10.6	10.8	- 0.2	*(ME< 5.04% GNP)*		
				(5)		
Syria	5.7	6.0	- 0.3	EDY = 0.34 GEY + 0.49 EDYo + 0.08 MEYo		
India	3.4	3.4	0.0		(2.43)	(4.59)	(0.83)
Pakistan	2.2	2.5	- 0.3	$r^2 = 0.675$; F = 51.67: df = 59		
Algeria	6.1	5.1	1.0			
(2') ERROR = - 0.42 MEY				*Residuals*	*Actual*	*Predicted*
	(-2.25)			India	3.4	3.5
$r^2 = 0.175$; F = 5.08; df = 24				Algeria	6.1	4.5

Estimated with a two-stage least squares estimation procedure. See text for a definition of the variables.

nificantly reduce the difference between the actual level of educational expenditures, and that predicted by the model. That is, increased military expenditures apparently have a retarding effect on budgetary allocations to human capital, offsetting to a certain degree the inclination of our sample countries to fund education at levels above the developing country norm.

Because the Middle East/South Asian countries appear *ceteris paribus* more willing that other parts of the developing world to fund educational expenditures, this group of countries was examined in a separate set of regressions. In general countries in this region do not have as much continuity in their educational allocations as other parts of the world as shown by the lack of statistical significance on the lagged share of education in GNP (Table 6.3, equation 2). For these countries, military expenditures have a strong and negative impact on the proportion of funds allocated to human capital development (the size of the standardized coefficient of the lagged military expenditure term is approximately twice that for the developing world as a whole). As evidenced by the analysis of residuals, military expenditures also appear to depress the *ceteris paribus* propensity of the Middle East/South Asian countries to allocate funds to education (the negative sign on MEY, Table 6.3, equation 2').

Finally, as a basis of comparison, education in the non-Middle East/South Asian countries as a group did not experience adverse effects stemming from increased commitments to defense (the lack of statistical significance of the military expenditure term, MEY_0, Table 6.3, equation 3). In addition, military expenditures were not significant (not shown here) in explaining the difference between the actual and expected level of education for this group of countries.

An obvious question at this point is whether or not there is something unusual about the countries in the Middle East/South Asia region *per se* with regard to their budgetary patterns. Given the fact that this region as a whole allocates a proportionately high amount of GNP to defense, the negative impact observed may simply reflect the fact that for all countries there may be a threshold past which military expenditures come at the expense of social expenditures. That is, defense and education/health may not compete for funds as long as defense expenditures remain relatively low, the tax base being large enough to support both. Once a certain level of defense expenditures are reached however, the government may be unable to fund a wide spectrum of non-defense allocations. Under these circumstances defense may simply have a higher priority, and receives funding at the expense of other programs.

To test this hypothesis, our sample countries were split into two groups, those with a military burden higher than the norm (5.04 percent of GNP in 1986) and those lower than the norm. Estimating the model produced results similar in many respects to those found for the regional sub-groups. First, education suffers in countries with high military burdens. For these countries, this effect operates directly with a lag (Table 6.3, equation 4) and also, indirectly through reducing the propensity for funding human capital development (Table 6.3, equation 4'). Second, the sample countries (in this case Egypt, Israel, Saudi Arabia, Syria and Pakistan) were somewhat

TABLE 6.4   Defense Expenditures and Allocations to Health, 1986 (standardized regression coefficients)

Total Country Sample

(1)
HEY = 0.50 GEY + 0.72 HEYo - 0.43 MEYo
         (4.85)   (8.82)   (-4.09)
r^2 = 0.602; F = 45.34: df = 90

Residuals	Actual	Predicted	Error
Egypt	1.0	3.2	
Israel	2.1	1.8	
Saudi Arabia	4.0	4.4	
Syria	0.8	0.6	
India	0.9	1.0	
Pakistan	0.2	0.1	
Algeria	2.2	1.5	

Middle East/South Asian Countries

(2)
HEY = 1.06 GEY + 0.95 HEYo - 1.07 MEYo
         (3.06)   (2.33)   (-2.55)
r^2 = 0.492; F = 6.47: df = 20

Residuals	Actual	Predicted
Egypt	1.0	4.0
Israel	2.1	1.6
Saudi Arabia	4.0	4.6
Syria	0.8	0.2
India	0.9	0.9
Pakistan	0.2	0.0
Algeria	2.2	1.5

Non-Middle East/South Asian Countries

(3)
HEY = 0.31 GEY + 0.70 HEYo - 0.14 MEYo
         (5.54)   (9.47)   (-1.35)
r^2 = 0.772; F = 74.75: df = 66
(3') ERROR = - 0.24 MEY
                    (-2.32)
r^2 = 0.068; F = 5.41; df = 74

High Military Expenditure Countries
(ME > 5.04% GNP)

(4)
HEY = 0.67 GEY + 0.52 HEYo - 0.52 MEYo
         (4.97)   (1.45)   (-2.60)
r^2 = 0.567; F = 11.80: df = 27

Residuals	Actual	Predicted
Egypt	1.0	3.3
Israel	2.1	1.9
Saudi Arabia	4.0	4.5
Syria	0.8	0.9
Pakistan	0.2	0.2

(4') ERROR = - 0.56 MEY + 0.37 SAMPLE
                     (-3.31)   (2.17)
r^2 = 0.291; F = 5.95; df = 29

Low Military Expenditure Countries
(ME< 5.04% GNP)

(5)
HEY = 0.14 GEY + 0.92 HEYo - 0.22 MEYo
         (0.83)   (6.44)   (-2.24)
r^2 = 0.800; F = 78.78: df = 59

Residuals	Actual	Predicted	Error
India	0.9	0.9	
Algeria	2.2	1.7	1.5

r^2 = 0.05 F = 4.16; df = 67

Estimated with a two-stage lease squares estimation procedure. See text for a definition of the variables

unique in that their inclination to fund education was greater than that of other highly militarized countries (Table 6.3, equation 4'). Finally, as with the non-Middle East/South Asian countries, defense expenditures did not come at the expense of allocations to education in the group of countries with low defense burdens.

While suggestive, the above results are not conclusive in pinpointing the underlying cause—regional or budgetary constraint—of the negative trade-off between defense and education. However it does appear (for whatever reason) that the Middle East/South Asia region in general, and our sample countries in particular, are more willing to fund education (given a level of military expenditures) than countries outside the region. This propensity offsets somewhat the generally negative impacts of defense on education in these countries.

Health expenditures present a similar picture, with several notable exceptions (Table 6.4). First, in general there is more continuity over time in health expenditures in the Middle East/South Asia countries, with health expenditures in 1982 significant in predicting 1986 values. Second, while military expenditures have a negative impact on allocations to health in the Middle East, this effect is only indirect (Table 6.4, equation 2) with the differences between actual and anticipated levels of health expenditures not affected by the current military burden. Third, although not affecting educational expenditures directly, non-Middle East countries with high levels of defense tended to suppress their commitments to health programs (Table 6.4, equation 3'). Finally, as with the case of education, the sample countries (given their levels of military expenditures) were more included to increase health expenditures (Table 6.4, equation 4').

Again the general pattern is one whereby excessive military burdens appear funded in part by cutbacks to non-defense programs.

Conclusions

While it might seem intuitively obvious that reducing military expenditures would accelerate human capital development and hence increase a country's long run growth prospects, the results presented above indicate that this view is too simplistic. Admittedly, this possibility undoubtedly holds validity for countries with especially high military burdens, and/or those in the Middle East/South Asia region, but it does not appear to be an accurate description of the process by which resources are allocated in the Third World in general.

Based on the results presented above, we can only speculate as to the mechanisms linking military expenditures and human capital formation in the Middle East/South Asian countries. While military expenditures do appear to retard human capital development in the region, the fact remains that levels of educational expenditures in the region are still high by Third World standards (Table 6.1). In addition, these countries also appear more inclined *ceteris paribus* to fund educational programs.

What may be happening is that governments in the region are subsidizing education of increased numbers of civilians during periods of stepped up military expenditures with the understanding that upon completion of training those individuals will serve some time in the military. This strategy would allow the military to absorb the large volume of sophisticated weapons flowing into the region while at the same time not requiring drastic increases in the numbers of foreign military advisers.

This interpretation is consistent with the results obtained above. Given the fairly high correlation between military expenditures and government revenues in the region,[16] allocations to both defense and education could increase fairly rapidly without either category experiencing significant changes in its share of the budget. Because of the low skill levels of the local populations in these countries, it is unlikely that rapid increases in military expenditures per soldier and in the number of soldiers per capita could be absorbed without accelerated training programs both within and outside the military.

Turning now to budgetary matters, in recent years, many countries in the Middle East and South Asia have been forced to introduce austerity programs. Such measures must entail choices about which sectors of public policy will receive augmented or reduced allocations of resources. However, despite the central nature of this process, little is known about how these governments set priorities for their shrinking revenues between major expenditure categories. Consequently, we now examine the specific relationship between defense spending and budgetary allocations in the Middle East and South Asia. This is followed by four country-focused chapters which offer an in-depth analysis for each of these prominent countries of defense spending and budgetary trade-offs in public expenditures.

16. Robert E. Looney, "The Impact of Defense Expenditures on the Saudi Arabian Private Sector," *Journal of Arab Affairs* 7, 1 (Fall 1987), pp. 198-229.

7

The Budgetary Impact of Defense Expenditures in the Middle East and South Asia

In the aftermath of the 1990-91 Gulf War, defense spending has increased in many countries in the Middle East, North Africa, and elsewhere. This expansion has occurred even though a number of these countries face growing fiscal problems and pressing social and economic difficulties. Depending on the relative impact of defense spending, shifts in resources may significantly affect economic performance, as well as democratization, in these countries.

This chapter examines the relationship between defense spending and budgetary allocations in twelve countries in the Middle East, North Africa/Mediterranean, and South Asia. These countries include four of the countries we have examined in detail in the other thematic chapters of this book (Egypt, Israel, Syria, and Pakistan),[1] one additional country whose budgetary priorities we examine in more depth in Part Two (Iran), and seven countries from the Gulf area and North Africa which serve as useful points of comparison (Bahrain, Cyprus, Jordan, Malta, Morocco, Oman, and Tunisia).

In recent years, many of these countries have been forced to introduce austerity programs. However, despite its importance, little is known about how these governments set priorities for their shrinking revenues between major expenditure categories. Do expenditures on certain categories vary systematically with unanticipated changes in the budgetary deficit? Do

---

1. Saudi Arabia was not included with this group in the present chapter because its data is not strictly compatible with that of the other countries examined. Riyadh does not publish its budget in the International Monetary Fund, *Government Finance Statistics Yearbook*. The country's budget published in the Saudi Arabian Monetary Agency's *Annual Report* includes some categories not used by the International Monetary Fund. See Chapter 10 below for our detailed examination of Saudi budget priorities.

they vary with military expenditures? If they do, which sectors gain or lose? Do these patterns provide insights in to the manner in which a government established budgetary priorities during this period?

More formally, this chapter addresses the following questions:

1. What are the country patterns in defense expenditures, budgetary allocations, and arms imports?
2. Does a causal budgetary trade-off exist between defense spending and these budgetary categories? If it does, what are the magnitudes of this trade-off? Is the trade-off modified by budgetary conditions such as deficits?
3. Do the trade-offs vary over time. Are the patterns found in the long run significantly different from those experienced in the short term?
4. Do the budgetary patterns involving defense vary by country group, that is, countries with high versus low defense burdens (defined in terms of the share of Gross National Product devoted to military expenditures)?

Survey of the Trade-off Literature

On the surface, budgetary trade-offs between allocations to defense and socio/economic programs would seem to be straight forward. That is, a given budgetary increase in military expenditure will crowd out an equivalent amount of all other spending, and these programs will be reduced according to their proportion of the total. However, recent research has shown that this view of the budgetary process is simplistic and does not conform with the manner in which governments often chose to prioritize expenditures.[2]

A related issue, and one of significant relevance for the many of the Middle Eastern and South Asian countries facing austerity programs, is the manner in which austerity-driven budgetary cuts are allocated. Anecdotal evidence suggests that officials often follow rather ad hoc rules for making large contractions in a short time, cutting new rather than ongoing projects, new rather than present employment, and materials and travel expenses rather than personnel; and favoring ministries that are politically powerful, or reducing those that have expanded most rapidly in the past.[3]

Operationally, several methods have been used to establish whether trade-offs exist.[4] First, using cross-section data, it should be possible to dis-

---

2. See for example, Saadat Deger, "Human Resources, Government Education Expenditure and the Military Burden in Less Developed Countries," *Journal of Developing Areas* 20, 1 (October 1985), pp. 37-48.

3. N. Caiden and A. Wildavsky, *Planning and Budgeting in Poor Countries* (New York: John Wiley, 1974).

cern whether relatively big spenders on the military are relatively small spenders in areas such as education and health (and vice versa). In their study Harris, Kelly and Pranowo presented several pertinent findings.[5] First, based on one year's data (1983), they found that countries that allocate relatively high proportions of their central government expenditure (CGE) to defense do not commonly allocate relatively low proportions to education and health (and the converse applies). Second, defense expenditure has a low vulnerability during times of overall CGE cuts, but so do health and education expenditures. If anything, defense is more vulnerable than the other two, particularly in low income countries. Third, during times of CGE expansion, defense expenditure in low income countries expands at a rate comparable with education and somewhat more than health. In middle income countries, health expenditures increase more proportionally than defense and education. Finally, for 12 Asian countries between 1967 and 1983, multiple regression analysis confirmed that trade-offs between defense expenditure and education/health were rare.

Another method to establish whether trade-offs exist, again following Harris, is to examine the effect of central government expenditure increases or cutbacks on, say, defense, health, and education allocations.[6] If a trade-off existed, it might be expected that defense expenditure would gain relative to other expenditure categories during years of CGE cutbacks.

As to the choice of which sectors to cut back, it is often felt that some sectors are more "vulnerable" than others. The defense sector, in particular, is usually considered difficult to reduce, while social sectors, such as health, education and rural development, are considered vulnerable. The alleged vulnerability of the social sector in developing countries is evident in World Bank documents:

> In the difficult past few years, budgetary crises have often meant that social services were cut back, in the process unraveling carefully designed programs.[7]

Since many human development programs are publicly funded, they are especially vulnerable when growth is threatened and budgets are under pressure. The recurrent costs of social programs, especially salary cuts, tended to

---

4. The following draws heavily on G.T. Harris, "Economic Aspects of Military Expenditures in Developing Countries: A Survey Article," *Contemporary Southeast Asia* 10, 1 (June 1988), pp. 95-96.

5. Geoffrey Harris, Mark Kelly and Pranowo, "Trade-offs Between Defense and Education/Health Expenditures in Developing Countries," *Journal of Peace Research* 25, 2 (June 1988), pp. 165-177.

6. Harris, "Economic Aspects of Military Expenditures in Developing Countries."

7. The World Bank, *IDA in Retrospect* (Washington D.C.: World Bank, 1983), p. 52.

make them a permanent and, therefore, vulnerable part of Government budgets.[8]

'Quick Fix' relief through disproportionate cutbacks—in, for example, education or rural development—may well have negative consequences for the
entire economy.[9]

Many member countries have had to reduce and reorient investment programs to curtail recurrent expenditure and to delay the completion of high
priority development projects. Programs in health, education and other social sectors have been particularly vulnerable.[10]

In the crisis situations confronting African governments, education, training
and health programs are continuously in danger of becoming the residual
legatees of both resources and attention by policy makers.[11]

In the first comprehensive study of relative vulnerability Kicks and
Kubisch examined 37 cases of budgetary reductions.[12] These were defined
as occurring in countries where real expenditure declined in one or more
years. According to Hicks and Kubisch, a sector was defined as:

Well protected, if expenditure on it was reduced by less than the percentage
reduction in total expenditures.

Vulnerable, if its percentage of reduction exceeded the average.[13]

In brief, a simple ratio of percentage change in each sector's expenditure relative to total spending served as the measure of vulnerability.
Where the ratio had a greater value than one, it suggested that the sector
was highly vulnerable; a value between zero and one indicated low vulnerability, with less than proportional reduction in the relative sector. A
negative value indicated that, despite overall expenditure reductions, the
sector was allowed to expand.

Hicks and Kubisch's main findings indicated that the countries examined experienced an average decline of 13 percent in real government

---

8. The World Bank, *World Development Report, 1981* (New York: Oxford University Press,
1981), pp. 97-98.

9. The World Bank, *Focus on Poverty, 1983* (Washington D.C.: World Bank, 1983), p. 5.

10. The World Bank, *World Bank Program on Special Assistance to Member Countries* (Washington D.C.: World Bank, 1984), p. 1.

11. The World Bank, *Sub-Saharan Africa: Progress Report on Development Prospects and Programs* (Washington D.C.: World Bank, 1983), p. 30.

12. Norman Hicks and Anne Kubisch, "Cutting Government Expenditure in LDCs," *Finance and Development* 21, 3 (September 1984), pp. 37-40.

13. Hicks and Kubisch, "Cutting Government Expenditure in LDCs," p. 38.

expenditure. Associated with this decline was a contraction of only five percent in the social sectors (producing a vulnerability index of 0.4). By contrast, the index was 0.6 for the administrative/defense sectors and over one percent for production and infrastructure. In short, the various social sectors were less vulnerable to cuts than defense and administration, which in turn were considerably less vulnerable than production and infrastructure—contrary to the generally accepted view.[14]

The fact that social sectors and defense were both relatively protected suggests that there were high political costs associated with reducing them. On the other hand, countries appeared to have been more willing to cut spending on infrastructure and production which, of course, are likely to have adverse implications for longer term growth, but few early, direct, and immediate costs.

This picture was confirmed by McKinlay who found that there was no evidence that Third World military expenditures are responsive to government financial constraints of a short or long term variety.[15] He concluded that "In this respect, then, we infer that military expenditure has a life largely independent of central financial constraints, indicative therefore on its part of a substantial degree of autonomy."[16]

Regarding budgetary priorities, McKinlay found that while a substantial commitment was made by Third World countries to the growth and expansion of education and health expenditure, that commitment was not nearly as high as in the area of military expenditure. In this respect military expenditure was generally taken to be a higher priority. McKinlay found also that Third World countries as a whole move their education and health expenditures in a much narrower band than their allocations to defense. He found that military expenditure had a greater independence or autonomy of movement. Further, the greater harmony or synchronization between budget size and education/health expenditures could not be explained in terms of the size of education/health as opposed to military expenditures. From this he concluded:

> We are inclined to the argument that the lower level of synchronization of military expenditure with the budget is a reflection of the greater independence of military expenditure. Third World governments are more inclined to move education and health expenditures in line with overall budget expansions and contractions. This leads us to infer that education-health expenditure is a rather more stable component of general government expenditure than military expenditure, which though of course ultimately

---

14. Hicks and Kubisch, "Cutting Government Expenditure in LDCs," p. 38.

15. Robert McKinlay, *Third World Military Expenditure: Determinants and Implications* (London: Frances Pinter, 1989).

16. McKinlay, *Third World Military Expenditure: Determinants and Implications*, p. 35.

entirely constrained by budget expenditure does show greater freedom or latitude in its movement.... Although military expenditures do seem to attract some special priority and enjoy a greater degree of autonomy, our conclusion suggests that military expenditure is not detrimental to education or health expenditures.[17]

Along these lines, De Masi and Lorie found that military spending in developing countries has tended to exhibit resilience during adjustment programs that have emphasized fiscal tightening, particularly in cases were the program levels of expenditure were below average.[18] The authors warn however that:

In adjustment programs that were accompanied by fiscal accommodation, the evidence suggests that the non-military sector tends to be given priority in the allocation of additional resources. Both the scarcity and uncertain quality of data, however, mean that the above conclusions must be interpreted with great caution.[19]

In a related study Harris and Kusi found that in the African context countries involved with the International Monetary Fund (IMF) were more likely to cut defense expenditures than those who were not undergoing the Fund's stabilization programs.[20] They suggest that "Possibly the economic weakness which drove some countries to the IMF also caused them to cut military expenditures."[21]

As well, based on data between 1950 and 1983, it appears that in Venezuela defense expenditure was reduced by far less than overall CGE in the six years when overall real CGE fell.[22]

Finally, in their examination of defense/education trade-offs in the Third World, Hess and Mullan found several pertinent patterns.[23] First, an increase of 1 percent in the average annual growth rate in per capita real GNP from 1960 to 1982 was associated with an increase of from 0.5 to 0.8 percent in the military burden. Second, significant political violence since 1960 was associated with an increase between 1.8 to 2.8 percent in the mil-

17. McKinlay, *Third World Military Expenditure: Determinants and Implications*, p. 37.

18. Paula de Masi and Henri Lorie, "How Resilient are Military Expenditures?" *International Monetary Fund Staff Papers* (March 1989), pp. 130-165.

19. De Masi and Lorie, "How Resilient are Military Expenditures?" p. 159.

20. Geoff Harris and Newman Kusi, "The Impact of the IMF on Government Expenditures: A Study of African LDCs," *Journal of International Development* (1992), pp. 73-85.

21. Harris and Kusi, "The Impact of the IMF on Government Expenditures," p. 73.

22. Robert E. Looney, "Austerity and Military Expenditure in Developing Countries: The Case of Venezuela," *Socio-Economic Planning Sciences* 20, 3 (1986), pp. 161-64.

23. Peter Hess and Brendan Mullan, "The Military Burden and Public Education Expenditures in Contemporary Developing Nations: Is There a Trade-off? *Journal of Developing Areas* 22, 4 (July 1988) pp. 497-514.

itary burden. Third, North African and Middle Eastern nations spent significantly more of GNP on the military (from 2.5 to 4.6 percent more). Fourth, a rise of 1 percent in the military burden was associated with an increase of from 0.2 to 0.4 percent in the share of GNP going for public expenditures in education. Fifth, military controlled governments spent 0.7 to 0.8 percent less of GNP on public education. Lastly, mineral rich nations used 0.8 to 0.9 percent more of GNP for public expenditures on education.

Once again following Harris, a third method of examining budgetary trade-offs involves the use of time series data.[24] For example, education expenditure as a proportion of CGE (as the dependent variable) could be regressed against other variables including defense expenditure as a proportion of CGE. A significant negative coefficient would provide support for the view that a trade-off existed, that is, it "suggests that a rise (fall) in the defense expenditure causes a fall (rise) in the education expenditure variable."[25]

Using this method several studies have come up with rather inconclusive results. Verner examined 18 Latin American countries between 1948 and 1979.[26] Harris et al. examined twelve Asian countries between 1967 and 1982.[27] In neither case was there evidence of important trade-offs between education/health and defense expenditure. Of the 24 possible trade-offs between defense/education and defense/health for the twelve Asian countries only four negative trade-offs were identified. Of the remaining, twenty-nine had positive relationships and eleven indicated no relationship.[28]

This same general pattern appears to exist in the UAE where Looney found that defense has not expanded its share of the budget at the expense of education.[29] Instead, the observed decline in the educational share of the budget in recent years appears to be more related to general budgetary considerations than any explicit set of priorities involving defense.

Looney broadened the analysis to include budgetary trade-offs between defense and all other budgetary categories.[30] He found in the case

---

24. Harris, "Economic Aspects of Military Expenditure in Developing Countries."

25. Harris, "Economic Aspects of Military Expenditure in Developing Countries," p. 96.

26. Joel Verner, "Budgetary Trade-offs between Education and Defense in Latin America: A Research Note," *Journal of Developing Areas* 18, 1 (October 1983), pp. 77-92.

27. Harris, Kelley and Pranowo, "Trade-offs Between Defense and Education/Health Expenditures in Developing Countries."

28. Harris, Kelley and Pranowo, "Trade-offs Between Defense and Education/Health Expenditures in Developing Countries." p. 96.

29. Robert E. Looney, "Human Capital Development in the UAE: An Analysis of Budgetary Conflicts in an Era of Relative Austerity," *Public Budgeting and Financial Management* (1992).

30. Robert E. Looney, "Military Expenditures in Latin America: Patterns of Budgetary Trade-offs," *Journal of Economic Development* (July 1986), pp. 69-103.

of Latin American countries (roughly over the period 1970-1983) that those
countries with negative trade-offs appear to have them for all the social expenditures—public services, education and social security welfare. Thus,
with the exception of a positive trade-off in Chile between defense and
health, all the statistically significant trade-offs for Venezuela, Brazil, Argentina, Chile, Ecuador, Dominican Republic, Mexico, Peru, and El
Salvador were negative between this category of government expenditures and defense. He also found that with the exception of a negative
trade-off for Costa Rica between defense and health, Bolivia, Paraguay,
Uruguay and Costa Rica all had positive trade-offs between defense and
public services, education, health and social security, welfare. Lastly, he
found that countries that tended to have negative trade-offs between defense and social services (public services, education, health, social
security-welfare) tended (with the exception of Chile) to have a positive
trade-off with economic services.

A closer examination of the Latin American countries reveals that (leaving out El Salvador because of its civil war during most of this period) they
fall into two general groups: (1) Venezuela, Brazil, Argentina, Chile, Ecuador, Dominican Republic, Mexico and Peru; and (2) Bolivia, Paraguay,
Uruguay and Costa Rica. Each group has one common element—whether
or not it was an arms producer. Countries that experienced negative trade-
offs between defense expenditures and social welfare expenditures tended
to be the arms producers. Those countries that experienced positive relationships between defense and social expenditures tended to be the non-
arms producers.

This finding is suggestive of some modification of the Hicks-Kubisch
thesis. Apparently, there is pressure on the governments of arms producing industries to maintain and expand supporting economic facilities and
infrastructure as defense expenditures (and the local industrial component) increase.

A recent examination of Saudi Arabian[31] budgetary priorities estimated
a model of the form:[32]

SHARE = [DEFENSE(?), AFS(+), UFS(?)]

Where:
    SHARE = the share of government expenditures budgeted for major
                categories of expenditure

---

31. For reasons indicated in reference 1, Saudi Arabia is not generally included in the
present chapter. See Chapter 10 below for our analysis of Saudi budgeting priorities.

32. Robert E. Looney, "Deducing Budgetary Priorities in Saudi Arabia: The Impact of Defense Expenditures on Allocations to Socio-Economic Programs," *Public Budgeting and Financial Management* (1992), pp. 311-326.

AFS = the actual fiscal surplus (as a share of government expenditures) during the current budgetary year

UFS = the unexpected fiscal surplus (as a share of government expenditures) during the current budgetary year. The unexpected fiscal surplus was defined as the difference between actual revenues and expenditures and budgeted revenues and expenditures.

This formulation facilitated the direct trade-off between defense expenditures and other budgetary categories, while at the same time controlling for any possible austerity affects associated with the government's short run fiscal position.

This analysis reached five main findings. First, in the Saudi Arabian context, defense expenditures appear to be quite complementary with increased allocations to human resource development. In fact, of the various government budgetary categories, the link to human resource development was the strongest associated with defense expenditures. Second, defense expenditures were also complementary with allocations to health. Third, the major negative budgetary trade-offs involving defense were concentrated in the economic areas: (a) transportation and communications, (b) economic resource development and, to a much lesser extent, (c) infrastructure. Fourth, defense expenditures also tended to come at the expense of a number of administrative allocations including payments to municipalities, and subsidies for government lending institutions. Finally, on the other hand, areas such as general administration and the direct government subsidies program (largely agriculture) did not suffer a reduction in their relative share of the government budget stemming from the government's commitment to high levels of military expenditure.

From these patterns it was concluded that while defense has retained its leading share of the budget during a period of relative fiscal austerity, the country does not appear to have fallen into a guns versus education dilemma. In fact, the two types of expenditure appear to compliment each other in the minds of the Saudi budgetary authorities. Of comparative interest, while not as complementary, in Iran education and defense do not appear to have competed for resources either during the same period.[33]

An examination of budgetary trade-offs in Pakistan found that economic services as a whole were adversely affected by military expenditures.[34] These expenditures were also retarded somewhat by the overall government debt. However they were not significantly affected by the government's fiscal (budgetary deficits) position.

---

33. See Chapter 8 below for our analysis of Iran's budgetary priorities.
34. See Chapter 11 below for our analysis of Pakistan's budgetary priorities.

A much different pattern characterized the administrative social categories of Pakistan's budget. When these categories were affected by increased shares of the budget allocated to defense, it was in a positive manner. Specifically, public services, social security, welfare and housing, and recreation and religious activities, all had increases in their budgetary shares simultaneously with defense. Education appeared little affected by defense and the debt, while the other major budgetary category, health, received a high budgetary priority. This was evidenced by a high correlation of its share and increased public sector deficits.

Summing up these recent studies, Hicks and Kubisch found that when faced with difficult choices in reducing public expenditures, governments consider a wide range of factors, including political and economic costs, present versus future consumption and the potential impact on employment, distribution and welfare. Their empirical results suggest that when governments in developing countries implement austerity programs, they do not apply across-the-board reductions in expenditures. Generally, capital expenditures are reduced more than recurrent expenditures. Within both capital and current budgets, the social and administrative/defense sectors appear to be relatively protected, while infrastructure and production absorb disproportionately larger reductions. The novel finding of that study was that social sectors do not appear to be highly vulnerable to expenditure reductions in times of austerity.

Subsequent to Hicks and Kubisch's study several additional patterns have been identified. Without necessarily making a distinction as to current versus capital expenditures, these studies suggest that countries tend to make selective cuts in non-defense categories, focusing either on social or economic programs. These patterns are further modified by the manner in which countries choose to selectively fund high priority sectors through running larger fiscal deficits.

This pattern was found to be present in several arms producing countries where a fairly close link exists between the government budget deficit, public consumption, and military expenditures. These countries show defense expenditures linked to budgetary deficits, that is, defense expenditures rise with government deficits. Other expenditures may be cut back during periods of high deficits. With surpluses, defense expenditures, everything else equal, tend to decline in percentage terms.[35]

In the next section of this chapter we attempt to identify the differential budgetary effect in our sample of countries from the Middle East, North Africa, and South Asia. That is, do sub-groups of countries tend to respond differently and selectively in cutting economic or social programs as defense expenditures increase their share of the central government budget?

---

35. Looney, "Military Expenditures in Latin America," p. 101.

If they do, what are the common characteristics of these groups of countries? How are these patterns of budgetary trade-offs modified by the willingness or unwillingness to run higher fiscal deficits?

Patterns of Defense Expenditures in the Middle East and South Asia

Before a rigorous budgetary analysis can be undertaken for our sample of countries, there should be some sense as to the relative amounts of resources devoted to the military in each country. Unfortunately, there is no consensus on the best measure of the economic burden imposed by defense expenditures. Instead, most analysts rely on several alternate measures, each providing a certain insight as to the relative amount of national resources preempted by the sector.

Using these measures for our sample countries several patterns quickly emerge (Table 7.1). First, the four standard measures of relative defense effort, namely, (a) defense expenditures share of GDP, (b) defense share of the central government budget, (c) armed forces per 1000 of population and, (d) arms imports share of total imports, roughly divides the sample into two groups of countries. The first group are those with relatively high levels of defense expenditure, that is, Egypt, Syria, Jordan, Oman, Israel, and Iran; and the second group are those with significantly lower allocations to the military, namely Pakistan, Malta, Morocco, Tunisia, Cyprus, and Bahrain. Second, these patterns are not completely unambiguous however, with Pakistan and Morocco having relatively high shares of defense in their budgets, Iran having a relatively low percentage of armed forces in the population (with Cyprus a relatively high percentage) and Oman and Israel having relatively low shares of arms imports in total imports. The last pattern of interest is that countries with high shares of defense in their budgets also tend to have large shares of public expenditures in total income. However, Iran and Syria (with low shares) and Malta and Syria (with relatively high shares) are borderline in this regard.

While these measures of defense expenditure roughly divide the sample countries into two groups, there are still gray areas where classification is somewhat subjective. One way of resolving this issue is to use factor analysis to identify the main trend in militarization. In turn, the relative factor scores on this dimension provide a means of unambiguously ranking countries in terms of their patterns of defense expenditures.[36] Besides the military variables noted above, a number of economic performance,

---

36. For a general survey of this method see R.J. Rummel, *Applied Factor Analysis* (Evanston, Illinois: Northwestern University Press, 1970). SPSS was used for the actual computations. See *SPSS/PC+ Statistics 4.0* (Chicago, Illinois: SPSS Inc., 1990) for a description of the program and interpretation of generated output.

TABLE 7.1   Indicators of Defense Expenditures (percentages)

Country	Defense Expenditures Share of GDP		Defense Expenditures Share of Budget		Public Expenditures Share of GDP		Armed Forces per 1000 Population		Arms Imports Share of Total Imports	
	1972-1979	1980-1989	1972-1979	1980-1989	1972-1979	1980-1989	1972-1979	1980-1989	1972-1979	1980-1989
Egypt	23.68	11.02	44.91	19.13	52.71	57.61	10.80	9.62	25.36	14.28
Syria	14.04	16.36	35.94	43.37	39.06	37.72	24.34	35.39	62.96	54.37
Jordan	30.75	17.08	59.90	36.61	51.34	46.65	27.25	35.91	10.70	19.44
Oman	36.69	23.54	44.96	44.77	72.70	52.60	14.10	18.23	8.15	5.76
Israel	28.55	19.69	40.94	26.91	69.74	73.17	47.46	48.46	12.50	7.86
Iran	11.59	6.73	29.36	20.70	39.46	32.53	10.21	7.79	16.40	14.38
Average	24.21	15.74	42.67	31.92	54.17	50.05	22.36	25.90	22.67	19.35
Pakistan	5.88	6.44	28.14	26.10	20.88	24.67	6.68	5.77	8.78	7.51
Malta	1.18	1.00	2.61	2.53	45.21	39.52	14.58	2.90	0.01	0.00
Morocco	4.63	6.75	14.25	20.73	32.46	32.56	4.24	6.90	6.03	5.51
Tunisia	1.90	3.50	5.70	8.76	33.33	39.95	3.60	4.87	1.38	2.94
Cyprus	1.92	1.30	7.22	4.40	26.31	19.51	23.11	20.52	0.00	1.70
Bahrain	4.21	5.12	10.52	14.30	30.10	39.91	11.73	7.20	0.10	2.31
Average	3.29	4.02	11.41	12.80	31.38	32.69	10.66	8.03	2.73	3.33

Figures are the average value over the indicated period.

Source: USACDA, *World Military Expenditures and Arms Transfers* (Washington D.C.: United States Arms Control and Disarmament Agency), various issues.

TABLE 7.2   Factor Analysis: Developing Country Patterns of Military
Expenditures, Growth and External Debt (factor loadings)

Variable	Factor 1 Debt Arms Imports	Factor 2 Growth	Factor 3 Public Spending Debt	Factor 4 Military Spending	Factor 5 Debt Service
Debt/Exports 1989	0.888*	-0.190	0.011	0.063	0.167
Res Bal/GDP 1989	-0.803*	-0.266	0.052	0.034	0.173
Savings /GDP 1989	-0.798*	0.193	-0.013	0.277	0.064
Arms Imp 1980-89	0.775*	0.008	0.056	0.395	0.063
Arms Imp 1972-89	0.771*	0.032	0.138	0.412	0.038
GDP growth 80-89	0.038	0.899*	-0.026	0.246	-0.063
Import growth 80-89	-0.078	0.862*	0.080	0.059	-0.065
Priv Cons 80-89	0.041	0.790*	0.162	0.049	0.157
Investment 80-89	0.052	0.757*	-0.336	0.040	-0.231
Invest /GDP 1989	-0.287	0.547*	-0.078	0.363	-0.106
Govt Cons 80-89	0.186	0.540*	-0.227	0.110	-0.219
Govt Exp/GNP 80-89	-0.158	0.060	0.847*	0.004	-0.063
Govt Exp/GDP 72-79	-0.010	-0.001	0.831*	0.251	-0.079
Debt / GDP 1980	0.383	-0.069	0.687*	0.128	0.267
Debt / GDP 1989	0.489	-0.316	0.629*	0.065	0.210
Exports / GDP 89	-0.469	0.050	0.620*	-0.128	-0.232
Govt Cons/GDP 89	0.134	-0.029	0.556*	-0.261	-0.221
Av Milx / GE 72-79	0.082	0.299	-0.087	0.865*	-0.049
Av Milx / GE 8089	0.075	0.057	-0.287	0.818*	-0.073
Milx / GNP 80-89	0.077	0.162	0.379	0.802*	-0.046
Milx / GNP 72-79	0.121	0.219	0.336	0.787*	-0.036
Interest/ Exp 80	-0.212	-0.012	-0.025	-0.021	0.900*
Debt Serv /Exp 80	-0.199	-0.044	0.006	0.060	0.877*
Debt Exp / 89	0.436	0.085	0.084	0.108	0.737*
Interest/ Exp 89	0.076	-0.155	-0.089	-0.097	0.710*
Eigen Values	5.470	5.140	3.464	3.299	2.138

Based on oblique factor rotation. * = loadings over 0.50. For a description of the program and its interpretation, see *SPSS/PC + Statistics 4.0* (Chicago: SPSS Inc., 1990).

debt, and structural parameters were added to the factor analysis to determine if military variables were systematically associated with other standard economic indices.[37]

Several preliminary runs suggested that armed forces per population did not add significantly to the factor patterns as to warrant inclusion. The final factor pattern identified five major trends:[38] (1) debt/arms imports, (2) economic growth, (3) general public spending/debt, (4) defense spending and (5) debt servicing (Table 7.2).[39] Arms imports are more highly

---

37. Economic variables were taken from The World Bank, *World Development Report, 1991* (New York: Oxford University Press, 1991). Several earlier issues of the *Report* were also used.

38. The initial sample of countries were those classified in *World Development Report* as non-high income industrial countries. The original sample was comprised of 98 countries. This was subsequently reduced to 62 countries due to missing observations.

39. Factors were selected on the basis of their Eigen Values being greater than two.

114

TABLE 7.3 Developing Country Rankings: Military Expenditures, Growth and External Debt (factor loadings)

Country	Factor 1 Debt Arms Imports	Factor 2 Growth	Factor 3 Public Spending Debt	Factor 4 Military Spending	Factor 5 Debt Service
Tanzania	2.10	0.05	0.01	-0.13	0.05
Somalia	5.63	-0.49	0.17	0.88	-0.26
Malawi	0.61	0.28	0.49	-0.85	0.85
Burundi	1.31	0.84	-0.76	-0.42	-0.29
Madagascar	0.93	-0.82	-0.80	-0.24	1.32
Nigeria	-0.70	-2.72	-0.57	0.59	-0.84
Zaire	0.12	-0.10	-0.20	-0.09	0.00
Mali	1.02	0.98	-0.42	-0.20	-0.69
Niger	0.31	-1.32	-0.65	-0.98	0.21
Upper Volta	0.75	0.60	-1.49	-0.26	-1.38
Rwanda	0.63	0.38	-1.31	-0.64	-1.14
India	0.50	1.06	-1.14	0.40	-0.29
China	-0.91	2.15	-0.78	2.03	-1.32
Haiti	0.13	-1.24	-1.04	-0.48	-1.35
Kenya	0.11	0.61	0.29	-0.53	0.45
Pakistan	0.67	1.21	-0.42	1.13	-0.13
CAR	0.61	-0.23	-0.35	-0.92	-1.32
Ghana	0.33	0.16	-0.86	-1.18	0.07
Togo	0.16	0.21	1.20	-0.74	-0.41
Zambia	0.25	-1.11	1.44	0.87	0.00
Sri Lanka	0.07	0.84	0.27	-0.97	-0.60
Indonesia	-0.69	0.75	-0.63	0.18	0.00
Mauritania	0.44	-0.50	2.35	1.18	0.32
Bolivia	0.26	-1.10	-0.34	0.25	1.60
Egypt	1.13	0.68	2.40	3.68	0.06
Senegal	0.16	0.29	0.15	-0.69	0.45
Zimbabwe	-0.27	-0.39	0.36	0.48	-1.53
Philippines	-0.36	-0.34	-0.63	-0.09	1.12
Ivory Coast	0.00	-0.43	1.35	-1.12	1.18
Dominican Rep	-0.42	0.27	-0.78	-0.46	-0.23
Morocco	0.16	0.60	0.46	0.72	1.10
Papua New Guinea	0.04	0.37	1.03	-1.44	-0.61
Honduras	0.20	-0.03	-0.10	-0.44	-0.17
Guatemala	0.05	-1.59	-1.67	-0.15	-1.17
Congo	0.11	-0.15	2.37	-0.06	-0.06
Cameroon	-0.06	0.07	-0.72	-0.57	-0.44
Peru	-0.22	-1.14	-0.57	1.81	0.80
Ecuador	-0.03	-0.46	-0.52	0.58	1.37
Paraguay	-0.34	0.01	-1.12	-0.07	-0.42
El Salvador	0.32	-0.57	-1.31	0.33	-1.19
Colombia	-0.42	0.31	-1.09	-0.54	0.77
Thailand	-0.73	1.74	-0.51	0.38	-0.28
Jamaica	-0.48	0.10	1.42	-1.11	0.00
Tunisia	-0.40	0.29	1.04	-0.58	-0.59
Turkey	-0.11	1.24	-0.22	0.62	1.33
Panama	-0.22	-1.30	1.81	-0.91	-1.16
Chile	-0.76	-0.18	0.18	0.58	1.30
Costa Rica	-0.18	0.72	0.38	-1.34	0.58

TABLE 7.3   (continued)

Country	Factor 1 Debt Arms Imports	Factor 2 Growth	Factor 3 Public Spending Debt	Factor 4 Military Spending	Factor 5 Debt Service
Mauritius	-0.60	2.03	0.59	-1.83	-1.09
Mexico	-0.48	-0.29	-0.61	-1.00	2.54
Argentina	-0.12	-1.41	-0.35	0.64	1.74
Malaysia	-1.39	0.72	1.07	0.24	-1.26
Algeria	-0.18	0.26	0.25	-0.04	1.08
Venezuela	-1.05	-0.50	0.13	-0.30	0.94
Brazil	-0.68	0.65	-0.64	-0.71	2.77
Hungary	-1.06	-0.17	1.25	0.92	-0.11
Uruguay	-0.61	-0.97	-0.30	-0.14	0.10
Yugoslavia	-1.80	-0.98	-1.72	3.03	-0.62
Gabon	-0.97	-0.61	1.48	-0.23	-0.92
Trinidad	-1.17	-2.57	0.51	-0.45	-1.73
Portugal	-0.68	1.06	0.65	0.01	-0.28

Source: Derived from analysis in Table 7.2.

associated with the pattern of debt/exports than with the actual defense expenditure ratios. The military dimension indicated that countries with relatively high shares of defense expenditures in the central government budget also experience high military burdens (the share of defense in Gross National Product).

The country factor scores on each dimension have a mean of zero, with countries above the mean having higher than average rates of militarization (Table 7.3). On this basis, our sample of developing countries was split into two groups—those with factor scores on the military dimension greater than zero and those with negative scores. Using these initial groupings and the same set of military and economic variables applied to the factor analysis (Table 7.2), discriminant analysis was performed to identify the overall environment characterizing each group of countries.[40]

The discriminant results produced two distinct groupings with most countries classified with a probability grater than 90% (Table 7.4). As might be expected, the first discriminating variables introduced by the program into the analysis were military related—the share of defense in the central government budget, the military burden, and the share of arms imports in total imports. However, as the program attempted to delineate the two groups of countries, the defense share of the budget and the arms

---

40. See *SPSS/PC+ Advanced Statistics 4.0* for a description of the program used for computations. A previous use of this methodology in a similar context is given in Robert E. Looney and Peter C. Frederiksen, "Defense Expenditures, External Public Debt and Growth in Developing Countries," *Journal of Peace Research* 23, 4 (December 1986), pp. 329-337.

TABLE 7.4 Relative Militarization: Country Groupings

Country	Discriminant Score	Initial Classification	Probability of Group Placement	
			Low	High
Mozambique	3.38	-	0.0	100.0
Tanzania	-1.59	low	99.7	0.3
Somalia	1.28	high	5.3	94.7
Malawi	-2.37	low	100.0	0.0
Burundi	-0.48	low	92.8	7.2
Sierra Leone	-2.62	-	100.0	0.0
Madagascar	-0.09	low	79.7	20.3
Nigeria	-0.01	high*	75.2	24.8
Zaire	-1.61	low	99.8	0.2
Mali	-0.20	low	84.5	15.5
Niger	-2.54	low	100.0	0.0
Upper Volta	-1.46	low	99.6	0.4
Rwanda	-1.55	low	99.7	0.3
India	1.42	high	3.6	96.4
China	1.67	high	1.7	98.3
Haiti	-1.15	low	99.0	1.0
Kenya	-0.38	low	90.4	9.6
Pakistan	1.84	high	1.0	99.0
Benin	0.21	-	60.6	39.4
CAR	-1.76	low	99.8	0.2
Ghana	-1.67	low	99.8	0.2
Togo	-1.04	low	98.7	1.3
Zambia	2.12	high	0.4	9.6
Sri Lanka	-2.35	low	100.0	0.0
Lesotho	-5.34	-	100.0	0.0
Indonesia	0.44	high	42.8	57.2
Mauritania	2.22	high	0.3	96.7
Bolivia	0.74	high	23.0	77.0
Egypt	4.79	high	0.0	100.0
Senegal	-0.83	low	97.5	2.5
Zimbabwe	1.48	high	3.0	97.0
Philippines	-0.31	low	88.5	11.5
Ivory Coast	-1.28	low	99.3	0.7
Dominican Rep	-0.70	low	96.2	3.8
Morocco	2.30	high	2.4	99.8
Papua	-2.70	low	100.0	0.0
Honduras	-0.51	low	93.5	6.5
Guatemala	-0.77	low	97.0	3.0
Congo	0.57	low	33.3	66.7
Syria	17.78	-	0.0	100.0
Cameroon	-1.34	low	99.5	0.5
Peru	3.51	high	0.0	100.0
Ecuador	2.03	high	0.5	99.5
Paraguay	-0.13	low	81.4	18.6
El Salvador	1.38	high	4.0	96.0
Colombia	-0.25	low	86.7	13.3
Thailand	1.71	high	1.5	98.5
Jamaica	-2.40	low	100.0	0.0
Tunisia	-0.52	low	93.6	6.4
Turkey	1.85	high	1.0	99.0
Botswana	-1.67	-	99.8	0.2
Panama	-2.49	low	100.0	0.0

TABLE 7.4   (continued)

Country	Discriminant Score	Initial Classification	Probability of Group Placement Low	High
Chile	1.39	high	3.8	96.2
Costa Rica	-1.95	low	99.9	0.1
Mauritius	-1.80	low	99.9	0.1
Mexico	-2.12	low	100.0	0.0
Argentina	2.11	high	0.4	99.6
Malaysia	2.05	high	0.5	99.5
Algeria	0.82	low	18.9	81.1
Bulgaria	8.41	-	0.0	100.0
Venezuela	-0.84	low	97.5	2.5
South Africa	0.13	-	66.1	33.9
Brazil	-2.55	low	100.0	0.0
Hungary	2.07	high	0.5	99.5
Uruguay	-0.46	low	92.4	7.6
Yugoslavia	3.90	high	0.0	100.0
Gabon	-0.59	low	94.8	5.2
Trinidad	-1.91	low	100.0	0.0
Czechoslovakia	3.64	-	0.0	100.0
Portugal	0.01	high*	74.0	26.0
South Korea	3.07	high	0.0	100.0
Greece	1.14	-	8.1	91.9
Ireland	-1.89	-	99.9	0.1
Spain	-1.38	-	99.5	0.5
Israel	10.07	-	0.0	100.0
Singapore	6.15	-	0.0	100.0

* = misclassified from original factor analysis. Discriminant analysis based on variables used in factor analysis. Variables statistically significant (with Wilks' Lambda in parenthesis) in forming the discriminant function (in order of importance) were: [1] military expenditures/GNP 1980-89 (0.530); [2] savings / GDP 1989 (0.402); [3] growth in government consumption 1980-89 (0.383); [4] arms imports share of total imports 1980-90 (0.356); [5] government expenditures share of GNP 1972-1979 (0.321); [6] Government consumption GDP, 1989 (0.312); [7] exports share in GDP 1989 (0.306); and, [8] external debt / GNP 1989 (0.299)(37).

import variables were replaced by economic variables. On this basis several countries were reclassified—Congo and Algeria were moved to the high group and Nigeria and Portugal placed in the low group.[41]

As Table 7.5 indicates, the two groups of countries formed by the discriminant analysis vary in a number of important ways. First, not very surprisingly, the high group has relatively high levels of defense in the central government budget, in terms of GNP, and arms imports in total imports. Second, the high defense group of countries experienced more rapid

41. While initially included in the discriminant function, the share of military expenditures in the government budget 1980-89, and the share of arms imports in total imports 1980-89, were subsequently removed from the discriminant function and replaced with economic variables.

TABLE 7.5   Country Characteristics: High and Low Defense Spenders (means)

	Low	High	Total
	Defense Expenditure Group		
Military Expenditures			
Av Budgetary Share 72-79	8.4	19.5	12.7
Av Budgetary Share 80-89	8.5	20.0	13.0
Av Share of GNP 72-79	1.8	5.3	3.2
Av Share of GNP 80-89	2.0	4.9	3.1
Av Arms Imports/Total Imp 72-79	1.7	6.6	3.6
Av Arms Imports/total Imp 80-89	2.4	5.8	3.7
Growth In:			
GDP 1980-1989	2.0	3.3	2.5
GDP 1970-1980	4.4	5.0	4.7
Investment 1989-90	-0.5	0.4	-0.1
Investment 1970-1980	6.5	5.9	6.3
Government Consumption 1980-89	2.6	2.7	2.6
Government Consumption 1970-1980	6.2	8.0	6.9
Exports 1980-89	1.7	4.7	2.8
Exports 1970-1980	3.3	4.5	3.8
Imports 1980-89	-0.9	0.2	-0.4
Imports 1970-1980	4.2	6.0	4.9
Private Consumption 1980-89	2.0	2.7	2.3
Private Consumption 1970-1980	4.1	4.9	4.5
Composition of Expenditures			
Av Public Share of GNP 72-79	23.3	26.3	24.5
Av Public Share of GNP 80-89	26.5	26.7	26.6
Govt Consumption / GDP 1989	13.6	12.0	13.0
Investment / GDP 1989	18.2	23.5	20.3
Savings / GDP 1989	14.4	20.7	16.8
Exports / GDP 1989	27.1	27.3	27.2
Resource Balance / GDP 1989	-3.9	-2.9	-3.5
External Debt			
Total Debt / Exports 1980	147.7	158.6	151.9
Total Debt / Exports 1989	303.4	335.3	315.7
Total Debt / GNP 1980	41.8	47.8	44.1
Total Debt / GNP 1989	81.4	81.9	81.6
Debt Service / Exports 1980	18.6	20.3	19.3
Debt Service / Exports 1989	24.9	22.8	24.1
Interest / Exports 1980	9.6	10.0	9.7
Interest / Exports 1989	10.9	10.6	10.8

High/Low groups based on the discriminant score in Table 7.4.

Source: Economic variables are from The World Bank, *World Development Report*, various issues; military variables are from USACDA, *World Military Expenditures and Arms Transfers* (Washington D.C.: United States Arms Control and Disarmament Agency), various issues.

rates of growth, although the low group had a higher rate of growth in investment during the 1970s. In part the high group grew faster because of its superior export growth and resulting ability to sustain higher rates of import growth. Government consumption for each group was about the same in the 1980s, with the high group having a somewhat higher, 8.0 versus 6.2, rate of government consumption in the 1970s. Third, again the high group had a greater share of resources devoted to savings and investment, with the low group a higher proportion of resources claimed by government consumption. Exports accounted for about the same share of GDP in both groups. Finally, the high group had somewhat higher debt to export ratios, although their debt to GNP was similar to that of the low group by 1989. Interestingly, the low group of countries had higher debt servicing to exports and interest payments to exports in 1989.

The picture that emerges from these comparisons is one whereby the high defense group appears more dynamic economically: they have greater rates of growth, higher investment and savings rates, together with similar debt servicing burdens. This is not to say that the high defense countries spend more on defense simply because they can afford this type of allocation. It simply suggests that these countries have been able to sustain their high rates of economic expansion despite their relatively high defense burdens.

Budgetary Trade-offs: Cross Section Analysis

To gauge the differential impact defense expenditures may have had on growth in the high and low groups, a model of the general form:

$$GY = f[GI, GYL, MEY, MEGE, MEGEL]$$
$$\quad\quad + \quad + \quad ? \quad\quad ? \quad\quad ?$$

Where:

GY = the rate of GDP growth, 1980-1989

GI = the rate of growth in investment, 1980-89

GYL = the rate of growth in GDP 1970-1979

MEGE = the average share of defense expenditures in the central government budget 1980-1989

MEGEL = the average share of defense expenditures in the central government budget 1972-1979.

This formulation is based on the normal developing country assumption that investment is the key element in growth.[42] It also draws on an empirical pattern first noted by Nugent "...for the aggregate growth rates of individual countries to be rather similar from one decade to the next."[43]

---

42. Obviously this is a simplification, but investment has traditionally been introduced as the starting point in models of this sort. See for example, Riccardo Faini, Patricia Annez, and Lance Taylor, "Defense Spending, Economic Structure, and Growth: Evidence Among Countries and Over Time," *Economic Development and Cultural Change* 32, 3 (April 1984), pp. 487-498.

This pattern was observed above where the high military expenditure countries achieved higher rates of growth in both the 1970s and 1980s.

In explaining the role of momentum in the growth process, Nugent drew on the theory of disequilibrium and suggested that many of the stabilizing and growth equalizing mechanisms assumed for the less developed countries were often inappropriate in developing countries. Specifically, he suggested (a) the nature of technological selection and change, (b) the process of capital formation, and (c) the way in which human capital and income distribution tends to vary with growth as the primary reasons why disequilibrium tends to be more prevalent in developing countries.[44] Past growth was therefore included in the regression equation to control for the apparent existence of this phenomenon in our two groups of sample countries.

The third term, the military burden (MEG), has been used in a number of studies of this type to examine the overall impact defense expenditures have on relative growth rates in developing countries.[45] While the usual presumption is that this impact is negative, several studies, and the analyses presented earlier in Chapters 4 and 5, found sub-groupings of countries where the military burden is positively associated with growth.[46]

Finally, the last term reflects the budgetary effects of defense expenditures. After controlling for investment, momentum, and the military burden, do excessively high shares of defense in central government budgets preempt funds that might have had a higher growth impact, that is, do economic or human capital building programs suffer proportionately?

A series of regressions were performed to examine the effects of increased levels of defense burden and budgetary share on growth. In the first set the total sample of countries was examined, with variables added in a stepwise manner (Table 7.6). This procedure enables us to determine the robustness of the model, that is, the sensitivity of coefficient size to model specification.

The results are consistent with the general pattern that emerged out of the discriminant analysis. As Table 7.6 indicates, investment was the most important factor affecting growth and its standardized coefficient was quite stable. Momentum was also present with countries tending to main-

43. Jeffrey Nugent, "Momentum for Development and Development Disequilibria," *Journal of Economic Development* (July 1977), p. 35.

44. Robert E. Looney and P.C. Frederiksen, "The Iranian Economy in the 1970s: Examination of the Nugent Thesis," *Middle Eastern Studies* 24, 4 (October 1988), p. 492.

45. The classic study is Emile Benoit, "Growth and Defense in Developing Countries," *Economic Development and Cultural Change* 26, 2 (January 1978), pp. 271-280.

46. See also, Peter Frederiksen and Robert Looney, "Defense Expenditures and Economic Growth in Developing Countries," *Armed Forces and Society* 9, 4 (Summer 1983), pp. 633-645; and Robert E. Looney, *Third World Military Expenditure and Arms Production* (London: Macmillan, 1988).

TABLE 7.6 Military Expenditures, Budgetary Shares and Economic Growth:
Total Sample (standardized coefficients)

Average annual rate of economic growth 1980-1989 (GY), Total Sample

Average annual rate of growth in investment 1980-89 (GY)
(1) GY = 0.67 IG
        (6.42)
r²(adj) = 0.432; F = 41.33; df = 52

Average annual rate of economic growth 1970-79 (GYL)
(2) GY = 0.67 IG + 0.35 GYL
        (7.24)   (3.83)
r²(adj) = 0.551; F = 33.46; df = 51

Average share of defense expenditures in GNP 1980-89 (MEY)
(3) GY = 0.63 IG + 0.32 GYL + 0.33 MEY
        (7.66)   (3.93)   (3.97)
r²(adj) = 0.651; F = 33.98; df = 50

Average share of defense in government budget 1980-89 (MEGE)
(4) GY = 0.65 IG + 0.32 GYL + 0.42 MEY - 0.16 MEGE
        (7.93)   (4.08)   (4.21)   (-1.59)
r²(adj) = 0.662; F = 26.90; df = 49

Average share of defense in government budget 1972-79 (MEGEL)
(5) GY = 0.64 IG + 0.32 GYL + 0.38 MEY - 0.18 MEGE + 0.07 MEGEL
        (7.48)   (3.70)   (2.93)   (-1.63)   (0.46)
r²(adj) = 0.656; F = 21.21; df = 48

Ordinary least squares estimates. r²(adj) = the adjusted coefficient of determination; F = the F statistic; df = the number of degrees of freedom; ( ) = the t statistic. For a description of the estimation program and interpretation of the results see *SPSS/PC+* (Chicago: SPSS Inc., 1990).

tain their growth patterns from one decade to another. This variable was also quite stable with a standardized value about half that of investment. Next, the overall military burden was positive, that is, countries with relatively high military burdens also experienced the most rapid rates of economic expansion. The standardized coefficient for this variable was less stable than the other two and slightly larger than the momentum term. Finally, the budgetary variables do not appear to be statistically significant for developing countries as a whole after accounting for investment, momentum, and the defense burden.

The next set of regressions attempted to identify any gradual trends as countries become more and more militarized. Do the general patterns noted for the total sample of countries hold for individual sub-groupings, or do these relationships change as countries with higher than average defense burdens and military budget shares are examined separately?

As noted above, the discriminant score was originally used to classify countries as having a high or low defense expenditure pattern (Table 7.4). This score assumed values between -5.34 (for Lesotho, the least militarized) to 17.78 (for Syria, the most militarized). Beginning with most of the

TABLE 7.7   Country Groupings, Ascending Militarization: Military Burden,
            Budgetary Shares, and Economic Growth (standardized coefficients)

Discriminant Score > -2.5
(1) GY = 0.64 IG + 0.32 GYL + 0.37 MEY - 0.18 MEGE + 0.07 MEGEL
         (7.13)   (3.52)   (2.77)   (-1.62)   (0.49)
r^2(adj) = 0.639; F = 18.91; df = 45

Discriminant Score > -2.0
(2) GY = 0.64 IG + 0.30 GYL + 0.32 MEY - 0.17 MEGE + 0.15 MEGEL
         (7.06)   (3.20)   (2.35)   (-1.51)   (1.00)
r^2(adj) = 0.652; F = 17.91; df = 40

Discriminant Score > -1.5
(3) GY = 0.68 IG + 0.25 GYL + 0.25 MEY - 0.20 MEGE + 0.17 MEGEL
         (7.32)   (2.69)   (1.94)   (-1.85)   (1.17)
r^2(adj) = 0.705; F = 19.64; df = 34

Discriminant Score > -1.0
(4) GY = 0.67 IG + 0.24 GYL + 0.26 MEY - 0.20 MEGE + 0.17 MEGEL
         (6.81)   (2.39)   (1.89)   (-1.84)   (1.16)
r^2(adj) = 0.703; F = 17.11; df = 29

Discriminant Score > -0.5
(5) GY = 0.70 IG + 0.22 GYL + 0.18 MEY - 0.21 MEGE + 0.19 MEGEL
         (6.70)   (1.98)   (1.24)   (-1.90)   (1.25)
r^2(adj) = 0.722; F = 16.10; df = 24

Discriminant Score > 0
(6) GY = 0.72 IG + 0.08 GYL - 0.03 MEY - 0.31 MEGE + 0.34 MEGEL
         (5.30)   (0.58)   (-0.20)   (-2.47)   (1.87)
r^2(adj) = 0.728; F = 11.70; df = 15

Discriminant Score > 0.5
(7) GY = 0.74 IG + 0.03 GYL - 0.22 MEY - 0.44 MEGE + 0.53 MEGEL
         (5.76)   (0.26)   (-1.26)   (-3.33)   (2.67)
r^2(adj) = 0.781; F = 13.86; df = 13

For definition of terms and statistics see Table 7.6.

sample (countries with a discriminant score greater than -2.5), countries
were systematically excluded from the analysis if their discriminant score
fell below a certain value—increments of 0.5 in the discriminant score
were used for this purpose. The results produced several interesting patterns (Table 7.7).

As Table 7.7 indicates, since only three countries had a discriminant
score lower than -2.5, countries with a discriminant score of greater than
this figure experienced a pattern quite similar to that of the total sample.
However, as more and more of the low defense countries were dropped
from the analysis the military burden gradually lost its statistical significance. This was also true for the momentum variable. For the high group
of countries as a whole, those with a discriminant score greater than zero,
the military burden (MEY) was not correlated with growth. At the same
time the military burden term was weakening, the defense share of the
central government budget was becoming more and more statistically sig-

TABLE 7.8   Country Groupings, Descending Militarization: Military Burden,
Budgetary Shares, and Economic Growth (standardized coefficients)

Average annual rate of economic growth 1980-1989 (GY)

Discriminant Score < 2.5
(1) GY = 0.64 IG + 0.29 GYL + 0.45 MEY - 0.27 MEGE + 0.17 MEGEL
          (6.74)   (3.19)   (3.36)   (-1.84)   (1.31)
r^2(adj) = 0.630; F = 17.67; df = 44

Discriminant Score < 2.0
(2) GY = 0.61 IG + 0.23 GYL + 0.62 MEY - 0.32 MEGE + 0.10 MEGEL
          (6.53)   (2.61)   (4.49)   (-2.31)   (0.75)
r^2(adj) = 0.685; F = 20.10; df = 39

Discriminant Score < 1.5
(3) GY = 0.69 IG + 0.28 GYL + 0.55 MEY - 0.33 MEGE + 0.01 MEGEL
          (5.98)   (2.48)   (3.83)   (-2.18)   (0.04)
r^2(adj) = 0.518; F = 9.81; df = 36

Discriminant Score < 1.0
(4) GY = 0.75 IG + 0.33 GYL + 0.56 MEY - 0.14 MEGE - 0.17 MEGEL
          (6.79)   (3.05)   (4.47)   (-1.04)   (-1.23)
r^2(adj) = 0.602; F = 12.20; df = 32

Discriminant Score < 0.5
(5) GY = 0.78 IG + 0.41 GYL + 0.41 MEY - 0.03 MEGE - 0.24 MEGEL
          (6.64   (3.62)   (3.19)   (-0.17)   (-1.69)
r^2(adj) = 0.619; F = 12.06; df = 29

Discriminant Score < 0
(6) GY = 0.80 IG + 0.42 GYL + 0.34 MEY + 0.13 MEGE - 0.37 MEGEL
          (6.38)   (3.43)   (2.45)   (0.66)   (-2.20)
r^2(adj) = 0.604; F = 10.77; df = 27

Discriminant Score < -0.5
(7) GY = 0.93 IG + 0.38 GYL + 0.41 MEY + 0.50 MEGE - 0.82 MEGEL
          (4.40)   (2.29)   (1.98)   (1.32)   (-2.18)
r^2(adj) = 0.472; F = 5.12; df = 18

Discriminant Score < -1.0
(8) GY = 1.00 IG + 0.63 GYL + 0.07 MEY + 1.42 MEGE - 1.56 MEGEL
          (4.99)   (3.69)   (0.33)   (3.24)   (-3.73)
r^2(adj) = 0.635; F = 7.27; df = 13

For definition of terms and statistics see Table 7.6.

nificant. For the high defense spenders this term was negative. On the other hand, as the sample contained a greater proportion of the high defense group, the lagged budgetary term (MEGE—the average share of defense in the central government budget) became increasingly significant, but with a positive term.

Looking at the countries in terms of descending militarization also produced several interesting patterns (Table 7.8). Table 7.8 indicates that as countries with high levels of military expenditures were systematically excluded from the analysis there was a gradual weakening of the negative budgetary term (MEGE). Certainly those countries in the low group (discriminant scores less than 0) did not experience a depressing effect on growth associated with this variable. For countries with very low levels of military expenditure (discriminant scores less than 1) this term was actually positive and statistically significant. On the other hand the lagged budgetary term became negative as the sample was concentrated with countries with a low level of military expenditures.

In sum, developing countries are far from homogeneous with regard to the manner in which defense expenditures impact on their economies. Countries with high defense burdens (discriminant scores less greater than zero) appear to have an environment that generates higher rates of overall growth in a manner independent of the defense burden. On the other hand there is some evidence these countries experience negative effects stemming from high budgetary shares allocated to the military. In contrast, countries with a low defense burden tend to experience relatively depressed rates of growth. Within this group however countries with higher defense burdens experience more rapid rates of growth. For extreme cases (countries with very low defense burdens) increased shares of the budget allocated to the military are also associated with higher rates of growth in Gross Domestic Product.

Budgetary Trade-offs: Time Series Analysis

While these patterns are clear, their explanation is not. It would be easy to argue that military expenditures do have a net positive impact on these economies (the result from the total sample) and that the countries with high defense burdens are simply experiencing diminishing returns from this source. Similarly, countries with a low defense burden have not reached this point of diminishing returns. Regarding budgetary shares, these arguments could be extended: countries with high proportions of their budget allocated to defense may derive some stimulative effects in the short run but over time the deterioration in economic services and human capital offsets any positive stimulus derived from expenditures of this type.

The defense burden patterns have been analyzed earlier in this book and need not be addressed here.[47] However it is pertinent to attempt to

---

47. See Chapters 4 and 5. The analysis in those chapters suggests that countries that are relatively unconstrained in terms of foreign exchange and/or savings/investment tend to have a net positive impact from defense expenditures. Often, however, in resource scarce countries this impact becomes negative. The speed of defense mobilization may also be very important in this regard with a gradual expansion in the defense burden neutral or simulative but a serge in defense expenditures producing negative impacts on the economy. On this latter point, see Robert E. Looney, "The Role of Military Expenditures in Pre-Revolutionary Iran's Economic Decline," *Iranian Studies* XXI, 3-4 (1988), pp. 52-81.

shed some light on the budgetary effects on growth. Returning to our sample of Middle Eastern, North African, and South Asian countries, a model similar to that of Saudi Arabia noted above was estimated:

SHARE = f[GDEFEX, GDEFUX, MILXU, MILXE]

Where:[48]
    GDEFEX = the expected government budgetary position (- = deficit, +
          = surplus)
    GDEFUX = the unexpected government budgetary position
    MILXU = unexpected defense expenditures
    MILXE = expected defense expenditures.

All the variables are defined in terms of their share of government expenditures.

In this formulation, we assume the expected deficit reflects a structural imbalance between revenue and expenditure. Similarly, transitory government deficits are assumed to be depicted by that component of the public deficit that was unanticipated. Admittedly, this may occur because of a revenue shortfall. In those circumstances, however, the expected deficit could be attained simply by cutting expenditures accordingly. Therefore if an unanticipated deficit occurs, it is assumed that it reflects the decision to fund priority sectors. Similarly, if a sector's budgetary share falls with an increase in the unanticipated deficit, it is assumed that sector's funding was reduced to support other programs of a higher priority.

This form of prioritizing is consistent with (although not proof of) some form of lexicographic ordering of budgetary priorities.[49] That is, the government tries to maintain certain budgetary categories at pre-defined levels. When these levels are met, the authorities are then willing to provide additional funding for categories and programs of lower priority. The expected and unexpected military expenditure terms can be interpreted in a similar manner.

Two sets of regressions were estimated. The first, of the form noted above, reflects short run budgetary adjustment to changes in the deficit and defense expenditures. The second set examines longer term budget-

---

48. Expected values were estimated by regressing each year's actual figure on that of the previous year. The predicted value for each year was assumed to be that expected. Unexpected values were calculated as the difference between what actually occurred in a given year and that which was expected. See Robert Looney, "Budgetary Priorities in Saudi Arabia: The Impact of Relative Austerity Measures on Human Capital Formation," *OPEC Review* XV, 2 (Summer 1991), pp. 133-152 for a more detailed explanation of this method.

49. See J. Encarnacion, "Some Implications of Lexicographic Utility in Development Planning," *The Philippine Economic Journal* IX, 2 (Second Semester, 1970), pp. 231-240.

TABLE 7.9   Patterns of Short-Run Budget Impact and Trade-off (nature of impact)

Country	Budgetary Position		Defense Expenditures	
	Expected	Unexpected	Expected	Unexpected
Public Services				
Egypt	+	+	ins	+
Syria	+	ins	-	ins
Jordan	+	+	ins	+
Israel	ins	ins	+	+
Pakistan	+	ins	ins	ins
Morocco	+	+	-	ins
Iran	ins	ins	-	ins
Oman	ins	ins	ins	ins
Malta	ins	-	-	ins
Tunisia	ins	ins	ins	ins
Cyprus	ins	ins	ins	ins
Bahrain	ins	ins	ins	ins
Education				
Egypt	+	ins	+	-
Syria	-	ins	+	+
Jordan	+	+	+	+
Morocco	ins	-	+	-
Israel	ins	ins	ins	ins
Pakistan	ins	-	+	-
Iran	+	+	ins	ins
Oman	ins	ins	ins	ins
Malta	ins	ins	ins	-
Tunisia	+	+	ins	-
Cyprus	-	-	ins	ins
Bahrain	ins	ins	ins	-
Health				
Egypt	-	+	ins	ins
Syria	-	-	ins	+
Jordan	-	ins	+	ins
Morocco	ins	ins	ins	ins
Israel	ins	ins	ins	+
Pakistan	-	ins	+	-
Iran	ins	ins	-	ins
Oman	ins	ins	-	-
Malta	ins	ins	-	-
Tunisia	ins	ins	ins	-
Cyprus	ins	ins	ins	ins
Bahrain	ins	ins	ins	ins
Social Security, Welfare				
Egypt	-	-	ins	ins
Syria	+	ins	ins	-
Jordan	+	-	ins	-
Israel	ins	-	-	-
Pakistan	-	ins	+	+
Morocco	ins	-	ins	-
Iran	+	ins	ins	ins
Malta	ins	ins	ins	ins
Oman	ins	ins	ins	ins
Tunisia	ins	-	-	-

TABLE 7.9   (continued)

Country	Budgetary Position		Defense Expenditures	
	Expected	Unexpected	Expected	Unexpected
Cyprus	ins	ins	ins	ins
Bahrain	ins	ins	ins	ins
Housing, Community Activities				
Egypt	ins	-	+	-
Syria	+	ins	-	-
Morocco	+	+	-	ins
Jordan	+	+	ins	-
Israel	-	ins	ins	ins
Pakistan	-	ins	+	+
Iran	-	-	ins	ins
Oman	ins	+	-	-
Malta	+	+	ins	ins
Tunisia	ins	+	ins	+
Cyprus	ins	+	ins	+
Bahrain	-	ins	-	-
Economic Services				
Egypt	-	-	+	-
Syria	-	-	-	-
Morocco	-	-	+	ins
Jordan	+	ins	ins	-
Israel	+	-	-	-
Pakistan	+	ins	-	-
Iran	ins	ins	ins	+
Malta	+	ins	-	-
Oman	+	+	+	+
Tunisia	ins	ins	+	ins
Cyprus	+	+	ins	-
Bahrain	ins	ins	ins	+

ary adjustment to year-to-year changes in the deficit position and military shares. These longer term adjustments are assumed to follow a distributed lag and thus were estimated by including the lagged value of the dependent variable as one of the regressors.[50] The results for total sample of countries are summarized in Tables 7.9 and 7.10.[51]

In summarizing the results for the entire sample of Middle Eastern, North African and South Asian countries, several patterns stand out better if countries are grouped according to their classification by the discriminant analysis performed above. In particular that analysis classified Morocco and Pakistan as high defense countries. Unfortunately, Iran and Oman could not be included in the discriminant analysis because of miss-

---

50. First formulated in L.M. Koyc, *Distributed Lags and Investment Analysis* (Amsterdam: North Holland, 1954). For the economic interpretation of this phenomenon see M. Nerlove, "Lags in Economic Behavior" *Econometrica* 40, 2 (March, 1972) pp. 221-251.

51. A full set of results is available from the authors upon request.

TABLE 7.10 Patterns of Long-Run Budgetary Impact and Trade-off
(nature of impact)

Country	Budgetary Position	Defense Expenditures	
		Expected	Unexpected
Public Services			
Egypt	+	ins	+
Syria	+	ins	ins
Jordan	ins	ins	ins
Morocco	+	-	ins
Pakistan	ins	ins	ins
Israel	ins	ins	ins
Iran	ins	ins	ins
Malta	ins	ins	ins
Oman	ins	ins	ins
Tunisia	+	ins	ins
Cyprus	ins	ins	ins
Bahrain	+	+	-
Education			
Egypt	+	+	-
Syria	+	+	+
Jordan	ins	ins	-
Pakistan	ins	+	ins
Israel	-	ins	+
Morocco	-	+	ins
Iran	+	ins	ins
Malta	+	ins	-
Oman	ins	ins	ins
Tunisia	ins	ins	-
Cyprus	ins	ins	ins
Bahrain	+	ins	+
Health			
Egypt	ins	ins	ins
Syria	ins	+	ins
Jordan	ins	ins	ins
Morocco	-	ins	+
Israel	ins	ins	ins
Pakistan	+	+	-
Iran	ins	ins	ins
Malta	+	-	-
Oman	+	ins	ins
Tunisia	ins	ins	-
Cyprus	ins	ins	ins
Bahrain	ins	ins	ins
Social Security, Welfare			
Egypt	-	ins	ins
Syria	+	ins	-
Jordan	ins	ins	-
Israel	-	ins	-
Pakistan	-	ins	+
Morocco	-	ins	-
Iran	+	-	ins
Malta	-	ins	ins
Oman	ins	ins	ins
Tunisia	ins	-	ins
Cyprus	ins	-	-
Bahrain	ins	ins	ins

TABLE 7.10 (continued)

Country	Budgetary Position	Defense Expenditures	
		Expected	Unexpected
Housing, Community Activities			
Egypt	ins	ins	ins
Syria	+	ins	-
Jordan	ins	ins	ins
Israel	+	+	+
Morocco	ins	ins	ins
Pakistan	ins	ins	ins
Iran	ins	ins	ins
Malta	+	ins	+
Oman	-	-	-
Tunisia	ins	ins	ins
Cyprus	-	-	-
Bahrain	ins	ins	-
Economic Services			
Egypt	+	+	ins
Syria	-	-	-
Jordan	-	+	-
Morocco	ins	+	ins
Israel	-	-	-
Pakistan	ins	ins	-
Iran	ins	ins	-
Malta	ins	ins	ins
Oman	ins	+	ins
Tunisia	ins	ins	ins
Cyprus	ins	ins	ins
Bahrain	ins	+	ins

ing observations. However, from the initial grouping of these countries (Table 7.1) a good case could can be made that they are better placed in the relatively low defense group as their level of defense expenditures is not in a class with that of Israel, Egypt, Syria or Jordan.

Using this new grouping, several patterns are apparent (Table 7.9 and 7.10).

First, public services appear to have fairly high priority in the high defense group, but not in the low defense group. For all of the high defense countries, other than Israel, increases in the expected deficit were used to fund expanded levels of public services.

Second, expanded defense shares (particularly unexpected increases) also appear to support public services in the high defense group.

Third, in contrast, with the exception of Malta, public services in the low defense group are not affected one way or another with changing deficit and defense shares.

Fourth, education presents an interesting contrast with the high defense countries usually increasing its share along with expansion in the expected defense share. On the other hand, several countries reduce its share along with unexpected increases in defense. This pattern was also found in the low defense countries.

Fifth, health expenditures appear to be a major casualty of expected deficits in the high defense group, although in several cases this is offset by increased defense expenditures (either expected or unexpected, but usually not both). While this category does not get hurt by budgetary strategies in the low defense group, it is an area likely to be cut by any increase in defense expenditures.

Sixth, as with health, social security and welfare in the high defense group does receive some budgetary support from increases in the intended deficit. However, this sector suffers cuts with increases in the unintended deficit. With the exception of Pakistan, it is also susceptible to lost shares when defense increases.

Seventh, housing and community activities receive considerable budgetary support in both the high and low defense countries. This is particularly true of unexpected deficits in the low defense group. This sector's budgetary shares are affected in most countries by developments in defense, but there are no appreciable differences in patterns between the high and low defense groups.

Eighth, economic services provide some interesting contrasts. In the high defense countries, shares to this activity are almost certain to be cut with expanded defense expenditures, particularly if these expenditures are unanticipated. This group of countries also reduces allocations to this budgetary category when unanticipated deficits appear.

Ninth, still, several of the high defense countries, notably Jordan, Israel and Pakistan, increase the share of the budget for these activities with increases in the budget deficit. However, this effect may be offset by developments in defense and the existence of unexpected deficits.

Finally, in contrast, economic services fair considerably better in the low defense countries with many of these countries supporting expanded economic activities with budgetary deficits. In addition, a number of countries expanded economic services along with military expenditures.

Roughly the same pattern emerges over time with several notable exceptions (Table 7.10). First, public services benefit over time from expanded deficits in several of the high and low defense countries. However their expansion with military expenditures observed in the short term in high defense countries does not appear to carry over into the longer term. Second, the negative impacts on health in the low defense group produced by defense expenditures largely disappear in the longer term. They do however still occur with increases in defense expenditures in Pakistan and several of the low defense countries. Third, reductions in allocations to social security and welfare programs seem to be more vulnerable to budgetary cuts in the high defense countries. For these countries, increases in the unintended share of defense expenditures, as in the short run, also reduce the relative allocations to these programs. These programs are also more vulnerable over time to increases in expected defense expenditures in the low defense group. Lastly, economic services are still quite vulnerable to unexpected increases in military expenditures in the high defense group. However several of the low defense countries no longer expand these allocations with increases in the deficit.

Conclusions

There are several main findings from the analysis presented in this chapter. Perhaps the most important is simply that defense budgetary trade-offs in the Third World are complex. In part, this is a natural reflection of differences in budgetary priorities across countries. However, this complexity also stems from the fact that increased levels of government deficits can offset or reinforce the impacts that expanded defense expenditures have on other budgetary shares.

Our analysis indicated that defense socio-economic trade-offs also vary considerably depending on whether the country has an environment characterized by a high or low level of military expenditures. This usually occurs in both the central government budget and in relation to the overall size of the economy. During the 1980s, defense expenditures in these two environments also had a differential impact on economic growth. In the high defense expenditure countries, increases in the share of resources allocated to defense did not provide any appreciable positive stimulus to the economy. For these countries, increases in defense in the central government budget actually tended to reduce the overall rate of growth. In the low defense countries, however, increases in the defense burden did provide a positive stimulus to economic growth. Furthermore increases in the share of defense in the central government budget did not retard that growth.

At least in the Middle East, there is a partial explanation for these patterns. In this region, the high defense countries (with several exceptions) appear to cut economic expenditures to free up resources for further expansions in the military. This may occur because of the political costs in cutting non-defense expenditure, particularly over long periods of time. Again, with several exceptions, the low defense countries seem to have more flexibility in accommodating increased levels of military expenditure. Perhaps as a result, economic programs are not as susceptible to cuts in these economies.

Most likely there are long run costs associated with the manner in which Middle Eastern countries alter budgetary shares to accommodate increased military expenditures. For high defense countries as a whole, increased budgetary shares allocated to defense in the 1970s had a positive impact on growth in the 1980s. However, increased budgetary shares to defense in the 1980s impacted negatively. Given the observed lagged nature of many of the negative impacts in these countries on economic services, this may indicate the neglect of economic services, infrastructure, and similar sectors. If that is the case, this group's high defense burdens are starting to take a heavy toll on economic growth. If these lagged impacts are stable, we can expect growth in these economies to expand at rates somewhat below their long run growth paths at least until the mid-1990s. For these countries, a reorientation of budgetary priorities may not provide an immediate stimulus to their economies.

Thus far in this book we have investigated the effects of defense spending in developing countries in general, and the Middle East and South Asia in particular, in a sequence of thematically-oriented quantitative assessments. We began with a factor analytic assessment of the patterns of defense expenditures and economic development. This was followed by an analysis of the causality of arms races. Next we examined the impact of defense expenditures on economic growth generally in the Third Word followed by a specific assessment of the Middle East and South Asia. Then we undertook an in-depth assessment of the impact of defense expenditures on human capital development. In the final chapter in Part One, we examined the budgetary impact of defense expenditures, seeking to gauge the differential impact that defense expenditures may have on budgetary allocations in different sub-groupings of countries. In each of these chapters, we have sought to contribute to the theoretical and empirical understanding of the economic causes and consequences of defense expenditures by developing a series of models, by a rigorous quantitative assessment of the data, and by using an "atheoretical" methodology to identify patterns.

Now we turn to four country-specific chapters. In undertaking a more in-depth quantitative examination of Iran, Iraq, Saudi Arabia, and Pakistan, we seek to develop further insights into these particular cases and into the more general processes at work in the Middle East and South Asia. Our analysis in Part Two draws upon the theoretical perspectives we have advanced, and methodological procedures we have utilized, in Part One.

Case Studies

8

Iran: Budgetary Priorities in a Revolutionary State

Now in its second decade, the Iranian Revolution would appear to be at an important and uncertain point, not because it is necessarily in imminent danger of collapse or overthrow, but because many issues it confronts remain unresolved and the cost of failing to resolve them is rising. The long war with Iraq in the 1980s,[1] followed by regional uncertainties generated by the end of the cold war and the aftermath of the 1990-91 Gulf War,[2] only exacerbated these problems.[3]

As Clawson observed, in the 1980s the country faced a set of circumstances remarkably unfavorable to its economic growth—the oil price decline (and later collapse), the Iraqi invasion, and the departure of many professionals and entrepreneurs in the early 1980s.[4] Simultaneously, grave complications have been created by the government's basic political decisions including continuing the war with Iraq for so long before it concluded essentially in a stalemate, granting few concessions to those traditionally tied to the West,[5] maintaining a policy of thorough-going Islamisization, coupled with the deterioration of the country's oil produc-

---

1. Fred Halliday, "The Revolution's First Decade," *Middle East Report* 19, 1 (January-February 1989), p. 19.

2. See David Winterford and Robert E. Looney, "Gulf Oil: Geo-Economic and Geo-Strategic Realities in the Post-Cold War and Post-Gulf War Era," in M.E. Ahrari and James H. Noyes, eds., *The Persian Gulf After the Cold War* (Westport: Praeger, 1993), pp. 149-171.

3. For a politico-military evaluation of the impact on Iran's defense policy of its eight-year war with Iraq, that war's relationship to the Revolution, and Iran's reaction to the 1990-91 Gulf War, see Shahram Chubin, "Iran and the Lessons of the War with Iraq: Implications for Future Defense Policies," in Shelley A. Stahl and Geoffrey Kemp, eds., *Arms Control and Weapons Proliferation in the Middle East and South Asia* (New York: St. Martin's Press, 1992) pp. 95-119.

4. Patrick Clawson, "Islamic Iran's Economic Politics and Prospects," *Middle East Journal* 42, 3 (Summer 1988), p. 371.

ing capabilities,[6] and the adverse consequences of the 1990-91 Gulf War for world oil prices.[7]

Most evident for Iran are the economic problems.[8] Iran endures high inflation; continued mass migration to the cities despite early attempts to reverse this trend; and, the underproduction and inefficient utilization of industrial capacity. During the war with Iraq, the government converted many of the country's most modern and best equipped industrial plants to munitions production. This was especially true of the factories for assembling motor vehicles in the Teheran region. The process of reconversion will be complex and is likely to be long.[9]

Much as the regime has been able to stave off its problems, it will be increasingly difficult to ignore them, not least because of the demographic explosion. Iran's population has increased from a population 28 million in 1966, to 47 million in 1986 and over 57 million in 1991.[10] By the year 2000, the country's population will likely reach 70 million.[11] In this regard perhaps the key problem for the future is tackling unemployment. By the early 1990s, estimates placed the country's unemployed at nearly 4 million.[12] The war mobilization in the 1980s resulted in millions of men serving in the regular armed forces, thus forgoing further training during this period.

In the long term, the ability of the country to deal with these problems will be largely dependent on the ability of Iran to upgrade its stock of human capital through the provision of increased amounts of education and training. The government has made a major commitment toward addressing these problems through the drawing up of an ambitious five year plan that envisages a growth of 8% per annum in Gross Domestic Product (GDP) and that lays out targets for sectoral regeneration particularly in agriculture. Measures to lower the fertility rate, create two million jobs, and

---

5. This policy has changed somewhat in the early 1990s, with more Iranian exiles returning to the country. See Scheherazade Daneshku, "Iranian Exiles Returning to the Economic Fold," *Financial Times* (May 3, 1990), p. 5.

6. Scheherazade Daneshku, "Iran in No Position to Fill Oil Supply Gap," *Financial Times* (August 30, 1990), p. 23.

7. Winterford and Looney, "Gulf Oil: Geo-Economic and Geo-Strategic Realities in the Post-Cold War and Post-Gulf War Era."

8. For an assessment of the political and foreign policy circumstances confronting Iran in the 1990s, see M.E. Ahrari, "Iran in the Post-Cold War Persian Gulf Order," in Ahrari and Noyes, eds., *The Persian Gulf After the Cold War*, pp. 81-98.

9. Anthony Hyman, "Iran," in *The Middle East Review, 1990* (Saffron Walden: World of Information, 1990), p. 69.

10. The World Bank, *World Development Report, 1993* (New York: Oxford University Press, 1993), p. 239.

11. The World Bank, *World Development Report, 1990* (New York: Oxford University Press, 1990), p. 228.

12. Hyman, "Iran," p. 71.

increase the government's tax income as a proportion of its expenditures, are all included in the plan period ending in 1993.[13]

Of particular importance is the anticipated expansion of public expenditures. In recent years, because of growing budget deficits and the consequent effect on inflation, real public expenditures have followed a downward trend. Given the plan's policies aimed at reducing the budget deficit, and as a corollary, the inflation rate, over the next five years, real public expenditure is to increase by an average of 3.8 percent a year. Included in the plan are provisions for a major expansion of the country's school system. Specifically, the plan hopes to increase the number of university students by 7.8 percent, while the number of school students will reach 16 million, requiring construction of 46,000 extra classrooms.[14]

The plan originated initially in 1983, but the government was then unable to push it through a hostile parliament. Starting in early 1990 the Rafsanjani government began to work in earnest on a change in economic philosophy. After years of an isolationist and war mentality, the government had a mandate to borrow from abroad, to liberalize, and to reconstruct the economy.

Several interesting issues arise for the future. First, how sound is the educational/human capital base upon which the plan must build? In this regard, how have educational expenditures fared following the Revolution and the Iran-Iraq War? What priorities for the 1990s does the government appear to have set concerning education? Have the government's allocations to the educational system been biased? And if so, in any particular way? How do the Islamic Republic's budgetary priorities toward education differ from those of the Shah?

The analysis in this chapter examines these questions. Based on the results of this analysis, several conclusions are drawn concerning the Iran's stock of human capital and the impact on its economic direction for the rest of the 1990s.

Education

The first serious attempts at eradicating illiteracy in Iran occurred in the 1930s under Reza Shah. Yet a coordinated push to improve the fundamental skills of the population was not undertaken until the 1960s when a mass campaign occurred under a Literacy Corps program as part of the Shah's "White Revolution." A great deal was accomplished in a short time, and by 1979, the literacy rate had improved substantially to 55 percent of

13. Scheherazade Daneshku, "Frail Economic Underpinning," *The Middle East* 194 (December 1990), p. 8.
14. "Iran Budgets for High Spending," *Middle East Economic Digest* (December 21, 1990), p. 11.

males and 30 percent of females. By the early 1990s, adult illiteracy stood at 46 percent.[15]

Enrollment rates have shown steady increases over time, especially in the primary levels. Still, male enrollment rates appear to have leveled off at the secondary level in the mid-1980s (Tables 8.1 and 8.2). As a basis of comparison, Iran's enrollment rates are favorable relative to its regional neighbors and countries with a similar level of income. On the other hand, the country's illiteracy rate is considerably above other countries in its income range.

Following the Revolution, the educational system evolved so that all teaching conformed to Islamic principles as required by the regime. The government placed great emphasis on ensuring that the young would be brought up as totally committed Muslims. Also, in some ways, the quality of education also improved. Still, higher education presented the government with continuing problems since the universities, especially the two main foundations in Teheran, were, by traditional standards, politically liberal and secular. They were closed for a long period, reopening in 1983 with modified Islamic syllabi and a controlled intake of "acceptable" students.[16]

Iran has been in almost total intellectual and literary isolation since the Revolution. Ideas, literature, and new scientific advances from outside penetrate only slowly into the Iranian system because of attitudes, policies, and recently, a severe shortage of financial resources.[17] The fact that over 50 percent of the population is under 15 years of age means that the imprint of Islamic education is very powerful. This is especially evident since a growing number of the population have experienced no real schooling other than of the Islamic Revolutionary type. Simultaneously, there has been a contraction in higher education.[18]

In the wake of the Revolution, there was a significant outflow of people and capital from Iran, the former even more damaging to the country's future prospects than the latter. Most of those who fled the country in the early years of the Revolution were professional people, industrial capitalists, landowners, and experienced administrators or technocrats. These groups represented many years and even generations of expensive and time consuming training and education. By the early 1990s approximately two million Iranians were living outside the country.[19] For all its faults, this stratum of society possessed the skills necessary for running what was be-

15. The World Bank, *World Development Report, 1993* p. 239.

16. EIU, *Iran: Country Profile 1990-1991* (London: Economist Intelligence Unit, 1990), p. 13.

17. Daneshku, "Iran in No Position to Fill Oil Supply Gap," p. 23.

18. EIU, *Iran: Country Profile, 1988-89*, p. 13.

19. Daneshkhu, "Iranian Exiles Returning to the Economic Fold," p. 4.

TABLE 8.1   Iran: Progress Towards Educational Attainment, 1970-1986

	Year					
	1970	1975	1977	1982	1985	1986
Education Exp (% GDP)		3			3	
					11	11
Enrollment Ratio (Primary/Total)	72	93	101	97	2	7
					10	10
Enrollment Ratio (Primary/Female)	52	71	80	82	1	7
Enrollment Ratio (School Age)	27	45	42	39	46	47
Enrollment Ratio (Secondary/Female)	18	33	32	32	37	38
Science/Engineering Students	32	38	35	35	29	28
Pupil/Teacher Ratio: Primary	32	29	32	20	22	28
Pupil/Teacher Ratio: Secondary	36	27	24	15	16	21
Pupil/Teacher Ratio:		79				
Repeater Rate (Primary)	9				10	12
Illiteracy Rate (Overall)					49	
Illiteracy Rate (Female)					61	

Enrollment Ratios = % of school age group. Science/engineering students = % of tertiary students. Pupil/Teacher ratio = pupils per teacher. Pupils reaching grade 4 = % of cohort. Repeater rate = percentage of total enrollment. Illiteracy rate = % 15 years old and over.

Source: The World Bank, *Social Indicators of Development, 1989* (Baltimore: Johns Hopkins University Press, 1989), p. 147.

TABLE 8.2   Iran: Relative Progress in Education

	25 to 30 Years Ago	15 to 20 Years Ago	Most Recent Group	Same Income	Same Region
Enrollment Ratio (Primary/Total)	63	93	117	103	87
Enrollment Ratio (Primary/Female)	40	71	107	99	78
Enrollment Ratio (School Age)	18	45	47	57	47
Enrollment Ratio (Secondary/Female)	11	33	38	56	38
Science/Engineering Students	17	37	27		
Pupil/Teacher Ratio: Primary	32	29	29	27	31
Pupil/Teacher Ratio: Secondary	30	27	22		18
Pupil/Teacher Ratio:		79		77	78
Repeater Rate (Primary)	9		11	18	7
Illiteracy Rate (Overall)			49	22	50
Illiteracy Rate (Female)			61	26	57

See Table 8.1 for definition of terms.

Source: The World Bank, *Social Indicators of Development, 1989* (Baltimore: Johns Hopkins University Press, 1989), p. 147.

coming an economically sophisticated state. The mark of this loss is still instantly apparent in present day Iran.

Employment

As noted above, the employment situation in Iran has deteriorated in recent years. This is in sharp contrast to the boom period of the seventies. During that earlier period a serious shortage of labor existed in certain key sectors.[20] As a result, during the 1970s up to one million Afghan immigrants moved into agriculture and general labor in Iran, while many Iranian migrants in the Gulf states were induced by the prosperous conditions in Iran to return to their homes.

The collapse of the economy after 1976 brought on growing but generally modest levels of unemployment as the level of activity fell off, especially in construction and services. Young males who had often been employed in multiple shift work occupations found work less easy to come by, and new immigrants were not absorbed into the labor force on the previous scale. Much distress arose from the fall in disposable income among the manual laboring groups as they faced rapidly increasing prices for their essential needs.

A downward trend in per capita income started with the revolutionary movement in 1978. According to official sources, based on the fixed prices of 1974, per capita income fell from 114,000 rials in 1978 to 5,500 rials by 1988. This reflected further deterioration on the employment front. In the period before and after the Revolution, what appeared to be a gradual decline on the employment front became a severe deterioration.[21] The causes of the problem varied. Flight by factory owners, continuing migration of rural people to the towns, shutdown of major construction projects, and displacement of people in the war zone all added to the government's difficulties. By 1986, there were some 3.8 million unemployed of the adult work force of 13.3 million, up from 3 million in 1984. By the late 1980s only 20 percent or so of the population was fully employed.

Even these figures mislead in the sense that large areas of disguised unemployment exist in all sectors. Most farming activity takes place during the warm months of the year. Industry retains many workers in employment for welfare purposes. Services are an all embracing term covering people in low productivity occupations such as cigarette selling and other similar activities. Given continuing poor economic conditions and a high

---

20. Robert Looney, *Economic Origins of the Iranian Revolution* (New York: Pergamon Press, 1982), chapter 7.

21. James Scoville, "The Labor Market in Prerevolutionary Iran," *Economic Development and Cultural Change* 24, 1 (October 1985), pp. 143-155.

rate of entry into the labor market, unemployment can only get worse in the 1990s despite the dedication of the government to full employment.

In terms of the country's school system, an average of only 4,000 of the total 23,000 graduates have been able to find jobs in recent years. By the late 1980s only one-fifth of the graduates meeting entry requirements were employed by the civil service. Some 70,000 of the country's doctors have found jobs abroad.

While massive brain drain is a major problem, this issue is not straight-forward. Ironically, while many qualified doctors must seek work abroad, Iran's industrial sector, at present operating at only about one-third of its capacity, is crying out for highly qualified recruits and potential managers to head the development plan for the next five years. The brain drain reflects not only the baby boom, but also the lack of co-ordination between industrialists and the country's higher education planners. The massive youth market remains largely untrained to do the jobs likely to unfold in the 1990s.[22]

Trends in the Government's Budget

Initially after the Revolution the new government favored a budget less dependent on oil and more on taxes. The public incomes were to be spent largely on such activities as agriculture, rural development, producer goods industries, electricity, and transportation. The least developed provinces, the working people, and small-scale productive operations were to receive more assistance from the state. These and similar policies were to be implemented to help realize the goals of economic self reliance, restructuring of the consumption patterns, and social justice.[23]

As Amirahmadi notes, unfortunately before much could be achieved in these areas, struggles over political and social questions of the Revolution began, the war with Iraq erupted, and oil revenues declined. In response to falling oil revenues, the government generally adopted a fairly orthodox policy. By continuing and drastic fiscal measures, the government deficit has been limited to between 7 and 8 percent of GDP. This was about the same level as the year before the Revolution. Exceptions were when oil income fell steeply in 1981-82 and 1986-87. During those two periods, the deficit reached 10-11 percent of GDP.

Clawson argues that the method by which the government curtailed its deficit constitutes the most stringent development in its domestic economic policy.[24] There has been an extraordinary shrinking of government

---

22. Alison Semple, "When the Baby Boom Explodes," *The Middle East* 168 (June 1990), p. 27.

23. Hooshang Amirahmadi, *Revolution and Economic Transition: The Iranian Experience* (Albany, New York: The State University of New York Press, 1990), p. 163.

TABLE 8.3   Iran: Central Government Budgetary Expenditures, 1970-1988
(billion Rials, 1985 prices)

Category	1970	1977	1980	1988	1970-1988	1970-1977	1980-1988
					Average Annual Growth		
General Public Services	157.7	316.1	500.4	69.8	-4.4	10.4	-21.8
Defense	391.9	1734.6	782.6	275.3	-1.9	23.6	-12.2
Education	162.4	677.8	1047.5	453.5	5.9	22.6	-9.9
Primary/Secondary	104.3	355.6	791.7	356.7	7.1	19.2	-9.5
University	30.9	179.0	85.1	69.6	4.6	28.5	-2.5
Other	27.5	143.2	172.8	27.3	0.0	26.6	-20.5
Health	60.4	223.8	313.7	166.2	5.8	20.6	-7.6
Social Security/Welfare	9.1	71.5	149.5	622.4	26.5	34.2	19.6
Housing/Commun Amenities	20.1	266.4	111.6	82.8	8.2	44.6	-3.7
Recreation	39.6	138.9	55.8	34.2	-0.8	19.6	-5.9
Economic Services	618.8	2606.5	1178.2	325.2	-3.5	22.8	-14.8

Source: Based on data from International Monetary Fund, *Government Finance Statistics Yearbook, 1982, 1990* (Washington, D. C.: International Monetary Fund).

expenditures in real terms (Tables 8.3 and 8.4). Specifically, total public expenditures fell from 4912 billion rials (1985 prices) in 1980 to 2353.8 billion in 1988, or a decline of 8.8 percent per annum in real terms. Interestingly, this was during a period when the GDP averaged a 4.1 percent increase in real terms. In terms of its share of GDP, the reduction in government expenditures over the period from 1977 to 1988 (Table 8.4) was 25.5 percent (declining from 41.2 percent to 15.7 percent).

This reduction in government expenditures would seem to be among the most rapid and far-reaching experienced by any government since such data began to be collected systematically after World War II. No industrialized nation has ever been able to reduce expenditures in any five year period by as much as 5 percent of its GDP. The much applauded efforts of Latin American governments to cut spending in response to the debt crisis were much more modest than Iran's response to its own crisis. Indeed elsewhere the International Monetary Fund (IMF) has been criticized for demand expenditure reductions that were as high as 10 percent of GDP.[25]

While the magnitude of the Iranian budgetary cutbacks was somewhat unprecedented, it is of some interest to determine whether the composition of the government's budget changed in a manner similar to that of other countries going through a major austerity program.

---

24. Amirahmadi, *Revolution and Economic Transition, p.* 163.
25. Clawson, "Islamic Iran's Economic Politics and Prospects," p. 378.

TABLE 8.4   Iran: Macroeconomic Trends, 1970-1987 (billion Rials, 1985 prices)

Category	1970	1977	1980	1987	1970-1987	1970-1977	1980-1987
					Average Annual Growth		
Public Consumption	3310.1	8322.5	7326.6	8027.2	3.8	20.6	-6.6
Public Investment	561.7	4079.0	2049.4	826.1	2.3	32.7	-12.2
Total Investment	1237.6	5525.9	2919.1	1745.3	2.0	23.8	-7.1
Private Investment	675.9	1446.9	869.7	919.2	1.8	11.5	0.8
Private Consumption	3310.1	8322.5	7326.6	8027.8	5.3	14.1	1.3
GDP	9075.3	18356.5	11299.8	14989.7	3.0	10.6	4.1
Total Pub Expenditure	1504.7	7578.1	4912.0	2353.8	2.5	26.0	-8.8
Public Revenues	1265.1	6768.2	2966.0	1276.7	0.1	27.1	-10.0
Deficit(-) Surplus(+)	-239.6	-809.9	-1945.2	-1077.1	8.7	19.0	-7.1
Deficit (% GDP)	-4.6	-4.4	-14.2	-6.8	-	-	-
Public Expenditures (% GDP)	16.6	41.2	43.0	15.7	-	-	-

Public Revenues, Public Expenditures and the Public Deficit are all for 1988 (rather than 1987).

Source: Based on data from International Monetary Fund, *International Finance Statistics Yearbook*, 1990, (Washington, D. C.: International Monetary Fund, 1990).

The manner in which governments in the developing world have dealt with austerity does not seem to have held up very well for the Iranian case.[26] In recent years, social security and welfare expenditures have increased substantially (19.6% average annual increase, 1980-1988) in absolute terms, while defense in the 1980s suffered a major reduction relative to other budgetary categories (Table 8.5).[27] On the other hand, the country has followed a typical path of diverting resources largely in the direction of more unproductive expenditures and provision of basic needs items.[28] This is also evidenced by the fact that public investment decreased at an average annual rate of 12.2 percent per annum (as compared with a 6.6 percent decrease in public consumption) during the 1980s (Table 8.4).

In short, the decline in oil revenues in the 1980s led to fiscal and monetary constraints, increased bottlenecks, and forced the state to change its priorities and policies in favor of more allocation for the war with Iraq and basic needs, largely at the expense of development funds.[29] The net result

26. For a description of the general pattern, see above, Chapter 7.

27. Our data do not permit us to examine Iranian defense expenditures in the 1990s. Anecdotal evidence suggests that Iran's expenditures on defense have accelerated in the 1990s as the country's leaders pursue a long-term Iranian ambition to be the leading regional power. The economic demands and consequences of these expenditures for Iran's growth, and in terms of its relative budgetary allocations, may be quite mixed. Although Iran has been acquiring an impressive array of advanced (and expensive) weapons, it has obtained favorable prices from cash-strapped suppliers such as Russia.

28. Amirahmadi, *Revolution and Economic Transition*, p. 163.

TABLE 8.5   Iran: Budgetary Shares, 1979-1988 (percentage of government
             budget)

Budgetary Category	Year									
	1970	1972	1974	1976	1978	1980	1982	1984	1986	1988
Public Services	10.5	8.8	5.0	5.3	6.1	10.2	9.7	9.9	3.0	3.0
Defense	26.0	24.1	29.1	29.4	25.9	15.9	10.2	10.2	14.2	11.7
Education	10.8	10.4	7.0	8.6	12.2	21.3	13.6	16.2	19.6	19.3
Primary/Sec	6.9	6.1	3.6	4.4	7.2	16.1	10.5	12.3	15.5	15.2
University	2.1	2.3	1.6	2.2	2.8	1.7	1.6	1.6	3.0	3.0
Other	1.8	2.0	1.8	2.1	2.2	3.5	1.6	2.3	1.1	1.2
Health	4.0	3.6	3.1	2.9	3.5	6.4	5.5	7.4	6.0	7.1
Soc Sec/Welfare	4.2	3.7	2.6	3.1	7.1	6.4	9.2	11.1	14.3	13.7
Recreation	2.6	1.8	2.1	1.8	1.8	1.1	1.4	1.4	1.5	1.5
Housing/Comm Amenities	1.3	2.4	3.2	3.9	2.2	2.3	3.1	2.2	3.1	3.5
Economic Services	41.1	30.6	23.6	28.9	29.4	24.0	24.3	25.0	15.7	13.8

Source: Based on data from International Monetary Fund, *Government Finance
Statistics Yearbook*, (Washington, D. C.: International Monetary Fund), various
issues.

was that during the 1980s, between 80 and 90 percent of the government's
current expenditure consisted of salary payments to civil servants and
procurement of consumer goods. This meant that only the remaining 10 to
20 percent was available to implement various economic policies. Obviously, the rise in current expenditure in recent years has automatically
reduced development expenditures and, as a result, investments for employment and the possibility of increasing the economic productivity
potential.

War expenditures in the 1980s in turn fell into two categories: current
and development. Development expenditure consisted of such things as
the construction of air raid shelters and other non-active defenses. In recent years, total war expenditure to total government expenditure went up
from 32 percent in 1986-87 to more than 34 percent by 1987-88. As noted
above, the rise in current expenditures is most dramatically evidenced by
the increase in social security and welfare expenditure from 6.4 percent of
the budget in 1980 to nearly fourteen percent by 1988 (Table 8.5).

With regard to specific categories, educational expenditures, while declining in absolute terms, were able to stay around fifteen to twenty
percent of total government expenditures over the 1980-88 period. This
was up from an average of eight to ten percent during the 1970s (Table 8.5).
Economic expenditures fell from 24.0 percent of the budget in 1980 to 13.8
percent in 1988.

---

29. Amirahmadi, *Revolution and Economic Transition*, pp. 163-164.

In terms of defense, in the 1980s, Iran seems to have suffered a more dramatic reduction in expenditures than might have been suggested by the comparative analysis noted above. Defense expenditures fell from 25.9 percent of the budget in 1978 to 11.7 percent by 1988. This decline in defense expenditures occurred while Iran was engaged in a major conflict with Iraq and reflects the fact that in financing the war Iran was constrained by lack of foreign exchange, especially after the 1986 oil price collapse. The result was to limit its expenditure on arms during the last several years of the war to $2-3 billion annually. In addition, the low levels of defense expenditures during the war were due to the government's inability to obtain sophisticated and expensive equipment, its greater reliance on voluntary forces, and a reluctance to impose austerity on the public.[30]

In general, therefore, Islamic Iran's expenditure reduction was only somewhat atypical and should be seen against the background of the oil boom. To a large extent, the Islamic Republic simply returned to the level of government that had prevailed until 1973. Also, much of the reduction was in development spending, which fell in inflation-adjusted terms by 80 percent from the pre-revolutionary past. Reducing expenditures on such development projects as roads, power plants or factories was relatively simple; as on-going projects were completed, work on new projects was postponed.

The 1990/91 budget covered the first financial year under the new economic planning forecasts.[31] It anticipated that IR 3,964.5 billion would be allocated for recurrent costs, up by almost 16 percent over the 1989/90 budget with nearly forty-six percent of the budget allocated to welfare sectors. The development budget, designed to initiate a process of planned growth in the economy, was up by sixty percent over the financial year 1989/90. Iranian authorities anticipated a total deficit of IR1,586 billion.

The corresponding budget took up the theme of the plan, setting physical targets for the year of which the principal ones were: oil output rising to a sustained 3.57 million barrels per day; construction of 5, 424 housing units for civil servants and workers; the laying of 1,800 km of highway; and, substantial expansion of school and hospital facilities.

Presumably, the heavy emphasis in the budget on the physical plan was to demonstrate that the government is serious about improving conditions and to muster popular support for the economic development program during its initial phases. Unfortunately when measured against the real post-war needs of the country, the budget was very modest. It had limited

30. "Iranian Economy: Picking Up the Pieces," *Middle East Economic Digest* (August 12, 1988), p. 8.

31. EIU, *Iran: Quarterly Review 1990, No. 2* (London: Economist Intelligence Unit, 1990), pp. 13-14.

objectives, and these were defined in material terms alone. There is no indication of the fiscal and other reforms to the state system that are needed to achieve a thorough going change in the country's economic fortunes. There are few signs that the government will be able to tackle the endemic problems such as high inflation, the instability of the rial and food subsidies.[32]

Budgetary Trade-offs Involving Education

Before any assessment can be made of the country's ability (and willingness) to maintain or even improve its stock of human capital, some idea must be gained about the factors affecting the government's expenditure decisions. To what extent did the war with Iraq affect educational expenditures? Has education been a priority of the Revolutionary government? Which budgetary categories compete with education for funding?

When public policy demands exceed the available public resources, budgetary trade-offs often occur between and among different policy areas with one program area gaining at the expense of others in the allocation of scarce resources.[33] Budgetary trade-off patterns range on a continuum between two extremes. For example, in the case of defense expenditures and allocations to education, it may be that allocations to defense come at the expense of educational spending, that is, as defense spending increases, spending on education may actually decrease, producing a negative trade-off. This pattern reflects a substitution effect.[34] A positive trade-off occurs if defense spending increases stimulate real increases in education spending. Of course, it is always possible that defense spending bears no relationship negative or positive to education spending, producing a either pattern in the middle of the trade-off continuum or no trade-off.

As Chapter 6 suggests, the defense/education trade-off is complex, and may be affected by several factors including changes in regime (military/ civilian; authoritarian/democratic), wars/regional conflicts, austerity measures/budget deficits, and foreign exchange shortages.[35] Some or all these factors must be included in the regression equation to obtain less biased estimates of any trade-offs between education and other categories of government expenditures.

---

32. EIU, *Iran: Quarterly Review,* p. 14.

33. For an earlier analysis of the Iranian situation, see Robert E. Looney, "The Role of Military Expenditures in Pre-Revolutionary Iran's Economic Decline," *Iranian Studies* XXI, 3-4 (1988), pp. 52-74.

34. See above, Chapter 6. Also see Joel Verner, "Budgetary Trade-offs Between Education and Defense in Latin America: A Research Note," *Journal of Developing Areas* 18, 1 (October 1983), p. 78.

Based on the general discussion in Chapter 6, and the specific situation in Iran indicated above, it is clear several factors have had a potential influence on the share of educational expenditures in the government budget.

The Revolution. The change in regime type from monarchy to Islamic republic is likely to have shifted priorities toward education, although this factor may be somewhat different depending on whether the level of education is primary, secondary or university. The impact of the Revolution was measured in two ways: (1) a pure structural change (depicted in a statistically significant change in the intercept of the regression equation). For this purpose a dummy variable (REV) with values of 0 for 1970-77 and one for 1978-88 was added to the regression equation; and (2) a change in propensity as measured by a shift in the slope of the regression equation. For this purpose all non-dummy independent variables were multiplied by REV. The new variables were then regressed on the budgetary share allocated to education. An improvement in the (t) value of that variable was considered indicative of the importance of the Revolution in shifting budgetary priorities.

The Iran-Iraq War. This seems to be a pure guns versus butter situation, with the government reducing its commitment to education to divert resources to the war effort. This is a dummy variable, depicted with zeros for the prewar years and ones for the years of the war.

Government Fiscal Deficit. This factor could work in either direction, depending in part on the priorities of the government toward the educational sector. Larger deficits may have occurred to maintain educational programs or larger deficits to finance other expenditures may have forced the government to reduce allocations to education as part of an austerity program.

Sectoral Priorities. This factor includes the guns versus butter analogy discussed above. Still, educational expenditures could be affected (positively or negatively) by movements in any of the other major budgetary categories. Besides education, the budgetary data presented by the International Monetary Fund for Iran include: (a) general public services, (b) defense, (c) health, (d) social security and welfare, (e) housing/community amenities, (f) recreation/religious services and (g) various economic services.[36]

---

35. See above Chapter 6. Also see Robert E. Looney and P.C. Frederiksen, "Consequences of Military and Civilian Rule in Argentina: An Analysis of Central Government Budgetary Trade-offs, 1961-1982"; and Robert E. Looney, "The Impact of Political Change, Debt Servicing and Fiscal Deficits on Argentinian Budgetary Priorities," *Journal of Economic Studies* 14, 3 (1987), pp. 25-39.

36. International Monetary Fund, *Government Finance Statistics Yearbook*, (Washington D.C.: IMF) various issues.

Operational Definitions

While the government's fiscal position provides some insights into the public sector's budgetary priorities, a more sensitive indicative indicator is the manner in which unforeseen shortfalls (and windfalls) in the public sector's budgetary position (deficit/surplus) are allocated. Here, unexpected (windfall) deficits are defined as the difference between the actual deficit in any year and the one that was expected to occur.

Operationally expected deficits were assumed to be depicted by the trend in the government's budgetary position. This trend was estimated using a linear regression with time. The expected deficit (as a percentage of the overall size of the budget) was calculated as:

(1) $DEFE(t) = a + b[DEF(t-1)]$

with the parameters (a) and (b) estimated over the period 1970-89.[37]

We assume that the expected deficit reflects a structural imbalance between revenues and expenditures. Similarly, transitory government deficits are assumed to be depicted by that component of the public deficit that was unexpected. Operationally, the unexpected public sector budgetary position DEFU (GIU) was defined as the difference between the actual (realized) deficit (DEF) and that which was expected (DEFE). Clearly, the basic assumption underlying these proxies is that the expected deficit represents an on going budgetary process that moves slowly over time and cannot be changed very rapidly.

The relationship between a sector's budgetary share and the government's fiscal position (revenues minus expenditures) in any year should also be indicative of the priority accorded that sector.[38] Sectors with a relative high priority would be protected during periods of budgetary deficit—their budgetary shares should increase during periods of growing budgetary deficits. Similarly, their budgetary shares should decrease during periods of growing budgetary surplus, that is, during times when the government has ample funds to allocate to lower priority activities.

Incorporating these elements, the general form of the equation used for examining the patterns of Iranian educational spending over the 1970-86 period (with expected signs) was:

---

37. For an application of this procedure, see Mario Blejer and Moshin Khan, "Public Investment and Crowding Out in the Caribbean Basin Countries," in Michael Connolly and John McDermott, eds., *The Economics of the Caribbean Basin* (New York: Praeger Publishers, 1985), pp. 219-236.

38. This situation may have changed somewhat in the last several years as the individual ministries are becoming more responsible for raising their own revenues through fees and other service charges. We are indebted to Asghar Rastegar for pointing out this development.

(2) EDU = [DEFE, DEFU, WAR, REVOLUTION, OTHER BUDGETARY]
          (+)   (-)   (+)   (+)   (-)

In other words, we might expect the share of the government budget al-located to education (EDU) to be greater: (a) the greater the deficits (DEFE—the expected deficit and DEFU—unanticipated changes in the deficit), (b) during peace time, (c) after the Revolution and (d) in the ab-sence of other strong budgetary priorities. Because it appears that the Revolutionary government treats allocations to primary and secondary education (SCH) in a somewhat different manner than its funding of uni-versities (UNIV), regressions were also performed on the funds allocated to each type of school. Similar tests were performed on the share of the budget allocated to total educational expenditures and those educational expenditures (other education) not directly associated with primary/sec-ondary and university education.

Main Findings

Analysis consisted of a multiple regression technique for the period 1970-88.[39] The results (Tables 8.6-8.9) are presented using standardized re-gression coefficients, thus enabling a tentative assessment concerning the relative strength of the various independent variables.

Education

In the case of the share of total educational expenditures in the govern-ment's budget, the overall coefficient of determination (r^2 adj) was high (usually around 90 percent). In addition several interesting patterns were found.

First, as anticipated, the Revolution introduced a new set of budgetary priorities, with education's share of the budget increasing in relative sig-nificance (but not necessarily in absolute terms) after the overthrow of the Shah.

Second, fiscal deficits were also very important in affecting educational expenditures. These variables (together with the Revolution shift variable, REV) accounted for nearly ninety percent of the fluctuations in the share of the budget allocated to education. The positive sign on the deficits (the deficits are defined as expenditures minus revenues) suggests that in-creased deficits were used to expand the educational share of the budget,

---

39. Regression analysis was performed using *Soritec Version 6.4* (Springfield, Virginia, The Sorites Group, 1990). Although the degree of serial correlation was considered based on the Durbin Watson (DW) statistic, regressions were performed using a Cochrane-Orcutt tech-nique that corrected for first-order autocorrelation in the disturbances.

TABLE 8.6 Iran's Budgetary Trade-offs: Total Education, 1970-1987 (beta coefficients)

Total Education (EDB)

Impact of Revolution (REV), War (WAR) and Deficits (DEFU, DEFE)
(1) EDB = 0.56 REV - 0.26 WAR + 0.58 DEFU + 0.48 DEFE
$\quad\quad\quad$ (3.09) $\quad\quad$ (-1.63) $\quad\quad\quad$ (4.96) $\quad\quad\quad$ (3.03)
r^2(adj) = 0.890; F = 29.59; DW = 1.61; (t)rho = 1.37

Impact of Revolution on slopes of deficits (DEFU, DEFE)
(1a) EDB = 0.69 REV - 0.18 WAR + 0.41 DEFU + 0.36 DEFE
$\quad\quad\quad$ (3.51) $\quad\quad$ (-1.18) $\quad\quad\quad$ (4.95) $\quad\quad\quad$ (1.89)
r^2(adj) = 0.896; F = 31.21; DW = 1.92; (t)rho = 0.88

Impact of General Public Services (GPS)
(2) EDB = 0.36 REV - 0.45 WAR + 0.53 DEFU + 0.46 DEFE + 0.19 GPS
$\quad\quad\quad$ (1.78) $\quad\quad$ (-2.11) $\quad\quad\quad$ (4.92) $\quad\quad\quad$ (3.45) $\quad\quad$ (1.67)
r^2(adj) = 0.897; F = 25.54; DW = 1.21; (t)rho = 7.40

Impact of Defense Expenditures (MILX)
(3) EDB = 0.94 REV - 0.96 WAR + 0.58 DEFU + 0.51 DEFE + 0.53 MILX
$\quad\quad\quad$ (3.17) $\quad\quad$ (-0.56) $\quad\quad\quad$ (5.19) $\quad\quad\quad$ (3.46) $\quad\quad$ (1.55)
r^2(adj) = 0.904; F = 27.25; DW = 1.72; (t)rho = 0.90

Impact of Health Expenditures (HEALTH)
(4) EDB = 0.18 REV - 0.36 WAR + 0.53 DEFU + 0.52 DEFE + 0.55 HE
$\quad\quad\quad$ (1.61) $\quad\quad$ (-4.45) $\quad\quad\quad$ (8.57) $\quad\quad\quad$ (6.65) $\quad\quad$ (5.35)
r^2(adj) = 0.981; F = 92.52; DW = 1.48; (t)rho = 0.59

Impact of Revolution on Slopes
(4a) EDB = 0.47 REV - 0.25 WAR + 0.34 DEFU + 0.26 DEFE + 0.40 HEALTH
$\quad\quad\quad$ (2.27) $\quad\quad$ (-1.71) $\quad\quad\quad$ (4.07) $\quad\quad\quad$ (1.45) $\quad\quad$ (1.82)
$r^{2(}$adj) = 0.915; F = 31.27; DW = 1.96; (t)rho = 1.11

Impact of Social Security and Welfare (SOSCW)
(5) EDB = 0.54 REV - 0.39 WAR + 0.50 DEFU + 0.43 DEFE + 0.24 SOSCW
$\quad\quad\quad$ (2.94) $\quad\quad$ (-1.61) $\quad\quad\quad$ (3.58) $\quad\quad\quad$ (2.72) $\quad\quad$ (0.90)
r^2(adj) = 0.887; F = 22.90; DW = 1.66; (t)rho = 0.68

Impact of Recreation and Religious Affairs (RECR)
(6) EDB = 0.96 REV - 0.19 WAR + 0.65 DEFU + 0.34 DEFE + 0.43 RECR
$\quad\quad\quad$ (3.21) $\quad\quad$ (-1.42) $\quad\quad\quad$ (4.72) $\quad\quad\quad$ (2.19 $\quad\quad$ (1.62)
r^2(adj) = 0.896; F = 31.21; DW = 1.92; (t)rho = 0.88

Impact of Economic Services (ECON)
(7) EDB = 0.54 REV - 0.31 WAR + 0.51 DEFU + 0.41 DEFE - 0.22 ECON
$\quad\quad\quad$ (3.27) $\quad\quad$ (-2.14) $\quad\quad\quad$ (4.50) $\quad\quad\quad$ (2.93) $\quad\quad$ (1.73)
r^2(adj) = 0.906; F = 27.95; DW = 1.80; (t)rho = 0.47

Impact of Mining, Manufacturing and Construct (MMC)
(8) EDB = 0.54 REV - 0.31 WAR + 0.48 DEFU + 0.39 DEFE - 0.26 MMC
$\quad\quad\quad$ (3.64) $\quad\quad$ (-2.45) $\quad\quad\quad$ (4.64) $\quad\quad\quad$ (3.08) $\quad\quad$ (-2.54)
r^2(adj) = 0.927; F = 36.70; DW = 1.56; (t)rho = 0.73

Impact of Revolution on Slopes (MMC)
(8a) EDB = 0.70 REV - 0.21 WAR + 0.46 DEFU + 0.52 DEFE - 0.18 MMC
$\quad\quad\quad$ (3.55) $\quad\quad$ (-1.36) $\quad\quad\quad$ (4.80) $\quad\quad\quad$ (2.00) $\quad\quad$ (-0.93)
r^2(adj) = 0.895; F = 24.79; DW = 1.94; (t)rho = 0.84

TABLE 8.6   (continued)

Total Education (EDB)

Impact of Other Economic (OE)
(9) EDB = 0.72 REV - 0.12 WAR + 0.47 DEFU + 0.51 DEFE - 0.32 OE
            (3.92)   (-0.70)   (4.18)   (3.62)   (-2.03)
   r^2(adj) = 0.915; F = 31.27; DW = 1.46; (t)rho = 2.30

Impact of Revolution on Slopes
(9a) EDB = 0.90 REV + 0.02 WAR + 0.39 DEFU + 0.57 DEFE - 0.60 OE
            (4.67)   (0.10)   (5.48)   (3.04)   (-2.17)
   r^2(adj) = 0.923; F = 34.67; DW = 1.86; (t)rho = 1.41

REV = Dummy Variable depicting the Iranian Revolution; WAR = Dummy variable depicting the Iran/Iraq War; EDB = the share of in the government budget; DEFU = the budgetary share of the unexpected government deficit; DEFE the budgetary share the expected government deficit; GPS = the budgetary share of general public services; MILX = the budgetary share of defense expenditures; HE = the budgetary share of health expenditures; r^2(adj) = the adjusted coefficient of determination; F = the F statistic; DW = the Durbin Watson Statistic; (t) rho = the t statistic on (rho) the serial correlation coefficient; SOSCW = the budgetary share of social security and welfare; RECR = the budgetary share of recreation and religious affairs; MMC = the budgetary share of economic services for mining manufacturing and constructions economic services.

that is, the government appears to have been willing to increase its deficit to maintain a certain level of instruction.

Third, the share of education in the government's budget does not appear to be greatly affected by military expenditures (Table 8.6, equation 3). In fact, the major budgetary trade-off was a positive one associated with expanded health expenditures (Table 8.6, equation 4). On the other hand, while the revolution resulted in increased emphasis on education, it did not result in a further expansion to education's share with the expansion in health expenditures, that is, the propensity to increase educational expenditures with expanded budgetary shares allocated to health (Table 8.6, equation 4b).

Fourth, the major negative trade-offs with education came from several economic services: (a) mining, manufacturing and construction (Table 8.6, equation 8), and (b) other economic services (Table 8.6, equation 9). However, the coefficients on the economic variable were small. Also they were only marginally significant.

Fifth, somewhat surprisingly, the war with Iraq did not, in and of itself, reduce the share of the budget allocated to education (in several instances the war was marginally significant, albeit with a fairly small standardized coefficient).

TABLE 8.7   Iran's Budgetary Trade-offs: Primary and Secondary Education, 1970-1987 (beta coefficients)

Primary and Secondary Education (SCH)

Impact of Revolution (REV), War (WAR) and Deficits (DEFU, DEFE)

(1) SCH =   0.50 REV - 0.07 WAR + 0.51 DEFU + 0.44 DEFE
                   (2.62)   (-0.38)   (4.06)   (2.59)
r^2(adj) = 0.876; F = 25.77; DW = 1.83; (t)rho = 0.78

Impact of General Public Services (GPS)

(2) SCH =   0.42 REV - 0.12 WAR + 0.53 DEFU + 0.43 DEFE + 0.15 GPS
                   (1.95)   (-0.56)   (4.39)   (2.48)   (1.16)
r^2(adj) = 0.867; F = 19.27; DW = 1.52; (t)rho = 2.84

Impact of Defense Expenditures (MILX)

(3) SCH =   1.01 REV + 0.17 WAR + 0.53 DEFU + 0.48 DEFE + 0.73 MILX
                   (3.75)   (1.17)   (4.53)   (3.82)   (2.33)
r^2(adj) = 0.906; F = 28.04; DW = 2.04; (t)rho = - 0.54

Impact of Revolution on Slopes (MILX)

(3a) SCH =   0.61 REV - 0.01 WAR + 0.39 DEFU + 0.31 DEFE + 0.02 MILX
                    (2.74)   (- 0.03)   (2.23)   (1.05)   (0.11)
r^2(adj) = 0.883; F = 22.20; DW = 2.03; (t)rho = 0.33

Impact of Health Expenditures (HEALTH)
(4) SCH =   0.14 REV - 0.20 WAR + 0.49 DEFU + 0.48 DEFE + 0.52 HEALTH
                   (0.95)   (-1.84)   (6.04)   (4.58)   (3.97)
r^2(adj) = 0.950; F = 54.27; DW = 1.78; (t)rho = 0.77

Impact of Revolution on Slopes
(4a) SCH =   0.40 REV - 0.08 WAR + 0.33 DEFU + 0.26 DEFE + 0.35 HEALTH
                    (1.77)   (-0.52)   (3.65)   (1.38)   (1.49)
r^2(adj) = 0.905; F = 27.68; DW = 1.99; (t)rho = 0.81

Impact of Social Security and Welfare (SOSCW)
(5) SCH =   0.49 REV - 0.16 WAR + 0.47 DEFU + 0.40 DEFE + 0.16 SOSCW
                   (2.46)   (-0.61)   (3.07)   (2.34)   (0.55)
r^2(adj) = 0.866; F = 19.14; DW = 1.84; (t)rho = 0.48

Impact of Recreation and Religious Affairs (RECR)
(6) SCH =   0.88 REV - 0.27 WAR + 0.61 DEFU + 0.30 DEFE + 0.54 RECR
                   (3.13)   (-0.21)   (4.21)   (1.82)   (1.82)
r^2(adj) = 0.883; F = 21.18; DW = 1.07; (t)rho = -0.97

Impact of Economic Services (ECON)
(7) SCH =   0.49 REV - 0.16 WAR + 0.44 DEFU + 0.35 DEFE - 0.27 ECON
                   (3.06)   ·   (-1.19)   (3.90)   (2.75)   (-2.27)
r^2(adj) = 0.905; F = 27.66; DW = 2.08; (t)rho = - 0.49

Impact of Mining, Manufacturing and Construct (MMC)
(8) SCH =   0.48 REV - 0.13 WAR + 0.41 DEFU + 0.35 DEFE - 0.26 MMC
                   (2.92)   (-0.98)   (3.51)   (2.59)   (-2.17)
r^2(adj) = 0.908; F = 28.63; DW = 1.85; (t)rho = 0.19

Impact of Energy (ENERGY)
(9) SCH =   0.47 REV - 0.07 WAR + 0.56 DEFU + 0.40 DEFE - 0.20 MMC
                   (2.89)   (-0.57)   (4.79)   (3.19)   (-2.19)
r^2(adj) = 0.905; F = 27.75; DW = 1.99; (t)rho = -0.24

TABLE 8.7   (continued)

Primary and Secondary Education (SCH)

Impact of Other Economic (OE)
(10) SCH =   0.76 REV + 0.11 WAR + 0.37 DEFU + 0.45 DEFE - 0.48 OE
                     (4.52)   (0.64)   (4.07)   (3.93)   (-3.76)
r^2(adj) = 0.938; F = 43.12; DW = 1.36; (t)rho = 3.71

Impact of Revolution on Slopes
(10a) SCH =   0.92 REV + 0.26 WAR + 0.34 DEFU + 0.64 DEFE - 0.85 OE
                     (6.48)   (2.03)   (6.81)   (4.71)   (-4.33)
r^2(adj) = 0.959; F = 65.75; DW = 1.85; (t)rho = 1.70

See Tables 8.1 and 8.6 for complete definition of statistics and variables; SCH =
the share of primary and secondary education in the budget.

Roughly similar patterns were found when the share of the budget allocated to primary and secondary education was used as the dependent variable (Table 8.7). Keeping in mind the absolute decline in educational expenditures during the 1980s, these results are consistent with assessments of the Revolution that stress its orientation toward trying to improve the general quality of life of the lower segments of the population.[40]

It is worth noting that the rural population has benefited most, although the mass exodus to urban centers that started in the 1960s continues. To stop or reverse the flow, the government has limited development spending in the cities leading to a deterioration in urban life and greater public dissatisfaction. The situation is exacerbated by the boom in the population, which is growing by about 2 million a year. Demand for education, particularly by politicized village families, is very high, but there is a severe shortage of teachers and schools. Health standards have improved, particularly in terms of child mortality rates. Yet medical facilities are strained because of lack of equipment and the departure of many doctors with the Revolution.

In general, therefore, while total educational expenditures and the proportion allocated to primary and secondary schools have declined in absolute terms they have not suffered serious reductions stemming from expansions in the other major budgetary areas. It should be noted, however, that a (albeit fairly weak) negative trade-off occurred with several categories of economic services.

For university education, a much different pattern emerged (Table 8.8). First, the overall coefficient of determination (r^2 adj) was much lower for university education. In addition the number of statistically significant

---

40. Vahe Petrossian, "Iran's Changing State," *Middle East Economic Journal* (February 10, 1989), p. 2.

TABLE 8.8   Iran's Budgetary Trade-offs: University Education, 1970-1987 (beta coefficients)

University Education (UNV)

Impact of Revolution (REV), War (WAR) and Deficits (DEFU, DEFE)
(1) UNV =   -0.34 REV - 0.52 WAR + 0.39 DEFU + 0.83 DEFE
                   (-0.67)   (-1.14)   (1.23)   (1.92)
r^2(adj) = 0.189; F = 1.81; DW = 1.83; (t)rho = 1.78

Impact of General Public Services (GPS)
(2) UNV =   0.07 REV - 0.63 WAR + 0.33 DEFU + 0.73 DEFE - 0.70 GPS
                   (0.18)   (-2.04)   (1.32)   (2.38)   (-3.15)
r^2(adj) = 0.537; F = 4.26; DW = 1.79 (t)rho = 0.46

Impact of Health Expenditures (HEALTH)
(3) UNV =   0.10 REV - 0.93 WAR + 0.29 DEFU + 0.73 DEFE - 1.07 HEALTH
                   (0.18)   (-1.76)   (1.09)   (2.23)   (-2.60)
r^2(adj) = 0.359; F = 2.57; DW = 1.72; (t)rho = 6.74

Impact of Social Security and Welfare (SSW)
(4) UNV =   -0.84 REV - 1.71 WAR + 0.32 DEFU + 0.61 DEFE + 1.94 SSW
                   (-3.84)   (-6.08)   (1.69)   (3.91)   (6.53)
r^2(adj) = 0.701; F = 7.85; DW = 2.79; (t)rho = - 3.92

Impact of Community Amenities (CA)
(5) UNV =   -0.11 REV - 0.72 WAR + 0.11 DEFU + 0.43 DEFE + 0.74 CA
                   (-0.28)   (-2.13)   (0.43)   (1.22)   (2.86)
r^2(adj) = 0.515; F = 3.97; DW = 1.75; (t)rho = 1.01

Impact of Revolution on Slopes
(5a) UNV =   0.03 REV - 0.80 WAR - 0.21 DEFU - 0.16 DEFE + 1.13 CA
                   (0.07)   (-2.57)   (-0.99)   (-0.36)   (3.88)
r^2(adj) = 0.569; F = 4.70; DW = 1.79; (t)rho = 0.44

Impact of Economic Services
(6) UNV =   -0.37 REV - 0.56 WAR + 0.37 DEFU + 0.81 DEFE - 0.13 ECON
                   (-0.70)   (-1.11)   (1.08)   (1.76)   (1.67)
r^2(adj) = 0.107; F = 1.33; DW = 1.89; (t)rho = 1.67

See Tables 8.1 and 8.6 for complete definition of statistics and variables; UNIV= the share of primary and secondary education in the budget.

variables was considerably lower. Apparently the government was unwilling to incur larger budgetary deficits simply to fund this type of activity. The fiscal deficits were insignificant in most cases when regressed on the share of university education in the budget.

Second, also in contrast to primary and secondary education, the war with Iraq tended to take a toll on university education. It is also interesting that the change in budgetary priorities associated with the overthrow of the Shah may have actually resulted in a reduction in the relative importance of secondary education. This relationship is fairly weak, however, and probably does not reflect a major bias of the current regime against secondary education *per se*.

Third, also in contrast to primary and secondary education, the share of university education in the government budget was influenced by several other budgetary categories. A strong positive association exists between social security and welfare and university education. The same also applies to community amenities. On the other hand, university education appears to be forced to compete with general public services and health for funding.

Finally, the percentage of variance on the share of university education explained by the model is considerably lower than was the case with either total or primary education. In part, this most likely reflects a weak commitment by the government to instruction at this level.

Next, other types of education (non-primary/secondary or university) followed another distinct pattern (Table 8.9). First, as with university education, the overall coefficient of determination was low relative to that obtained for total and primary/secondary education. Despite this, other education appears to have been favored by the Revolution (the positive sign for REV). Second, offsetting this was its susceptibility to cuts during the war years. In addition this type of education does not appear to have received a very high priority (the sign of the deficit term was negative).

Third, also in contrast to the other educational categories, other education appears to be complementary with certain types of educational services. It did however suffer reduced shares stemming from allocations to defense and community activities.

Other Budgetary Categories

One of the more interesting (and surprising) findings from this analysis was the role of the budget deficit in funding education, particularly the primary/secondary school component. Again, increases in the share of the budget associated with increased budget deficits (both expected and unexpected) appear to reflect this expenditure category's relatively high priority.

It is of some interest therefore to assess if other areas in the budget were afforded similar status. To this end a set of similar regressions were undertaken for each major non-educational budgetary categories.[41] The main findings of this analysis suggests several patterns (Tables 8.10 and 8.11).

First, the only non-educational categories that received a stimulus from the budgetary deficits were housing and community amenities, and other transport. In absolute levels of expenditure, however, both categories were rather minor budgetary items.

---

41. Due to space limitations, only a summary of the main findings is presented here. A complete set of results is available from the authors upon request.

TABLE 8.9   Iran's Budgetary Trade-offs: Other Types of Education, 1970-1987
(beta coefficients)

Other Types of Education (OTE)

Impact of Revolution (REV), War (WAR) and Deficits (DEFU, DEFE)
(1) OTE =   1.05 REV -0.89 WAR - 0.19 DEFU - 0.37 DEFE
              (2.18)   (-2.38)   (-0.36)   (-0.94)
r^2(adj) = 0.166; F = 1.70; DW = 1.92; (t)rho = - 0.91

Impact of Revolution on Slopes
(1a) OTE =   1.66 REV - 1.02 WAR - 0.44 DEFU - 0.78 DEFE
               (3.08)   (-3.55)   (-1.64)   (-1.67)
r^2(adj) = 0.232; F = 2.06; DW = 2.03; (t)rho = - 2.18

Impact of General Public Services (GPS)
(2) OTE =   0.52 REV - 0.64 WAR - 0.01 DEFU - 0.35 DEFE + 0.72 GPS
              (2.11)   (-4.20)   (-0.01)   (-2.52)   (5.81)
r^2(adj) = 0.775; F = 10.65; DW = 2.46; (t)rho = -3.49

Impact of Revolution on Slopes
(2a) OTE =   0.68 REV - 0.66 WAR - 0.01 DEFU - 1.16 DEFE + 1.15 GPS
               (2.28)   (-4.67)   (-0.06)   (-5.22)   (5.80)
r^2(adj) = 0.807; F = 12.70; DW = 2.58; (t)rho = -5.16

Impact of Defense Expenditures (MILX)
(3) OTE =   0.31 REV -1.41 WAR - 0.61 DEFU - 0.65 DEFE - 1.60 MILX
              (0.58)   (-4.82)   (-2.45)   (-2.61)   (-2.47)
r^2(adj) = 0.377; F = 2.69; DW = 2.46; (t)rho = - 3.18

Impact of Community Activities (CA)
(4) OTE =   0.66 REV - 0.53 WAR + 0.11 DEFU + 0.01 DEFE - 0.73 CA
              (2.55)   (-2.86)   (0.52)   (0.03)   (-5.11)
r^2(adj) = 0.750; F = 9.38; DW = 2.45; (t)rho = -2.12

Impact of Recreation and Religious Affairs (RECR)
(5) OTE=   0.27 REV - 0.93 WAR - 0.83 DEFU - 0.19 DEFE - 1.22 RECR
             (0.39)   (-3.44)   (-2.55)   (-0.63)   (-1.83)
r^2(adj) = 0.260; F = 1.99; DW = 2.10; (t)rho = 0.17

Impact of Economic Services (ECON)
(7) OTE =   1.45 REV - 0.65 WAR - 0.50 DEFU - 0.36 DEFE + 0.61 ECON
              (4.58)   (-2.53)   (-2.14)   (-1.60)   (2.74)
r^2(adj) = 0.415; F = 2.99; DW = 2.75; (t)rho = - 3.57

Impact of Revolution on Slopes
(7a) OTE =   1.26 REV - 0.67 WAR - 0.23 DEFU - 1.49 DEFE + 0.88 ECON
               (2.68)   (-2.34)   (-1.07)   (-2.92)   (2.43)
r^2(adj) = 0.479; F = 3.58; DW = 2.08; (t)rho = - 1.04

Impact of Mining, Manufacturing and Construct (MMC)
(8) OTE =   1.08 REV - 0.89 WAR - 0.21 DEFU - 0.37 DEFE + 0.02 MMC
              (2.14)   (-2.14)   (-0.55)   (-0.91)   (0.05)
r^2(adj) = 0.074; F = 1.22; DW = 1.91 (t)rho = - 0.23

Impact of Revolution on Slopes (MMC)
(8) OTE =   1.41 REV - 0.77 WAR - 0.33 DEFU - 1.58 DEFE + 0.87 MMC
              (2.83)   (-2.61)   (-1.41)   (-2.61)   (1.94)
r^2(adj) = 0.394; F = 2.81; DW = 2.21; (t)rho = -1.31

Impact of Transportation and Communications (TC)
(9) OTE =   1.63 REV - 0.66 WAR - 0.68 DEFU - 0.79 DEFE + 0.64 TC
              (4.87)   (-2.63)   (-2.81)   (-3.07)   (3.03)
r^2(adj) = 0.521; F = 4.04; DW = 2.36; (t)rho = - 1.94

TABLE 8.9   (continued)

Other Types of Education (OTE)

Impact of Roads (ROADS)
(10) OTE =   1.17 REV - 0.64 WAR - 0.50 DEFU - 0.60 DEFE + 0.48 ROADS
                 (3.07)   (-2.04)   (-1.79)   (-2.01)   (2.20)
r^2(adj) = 0.392; F = 2.80; DW = 2.24; (t)rho = - 1.12

Impact of Revolution on Slopes
(10a) OTE =   1.61 REV - 0.63 WAR - 0.31 DEFU - 1.60 DEFE + 0.77 ROADS
                  (3.94)   (-2.46)   (-1.57)   (-3.52)   (3.13)
r^2(adj) = 0.586; F = 4.97; DW = 2.11; (t)rho = - 1.04

See Tables 8.1 and 8.6 for complete definition of statistics and variables; OTE= the share of other education in the budget.

Second, several other non-educational categories saw their budgetary shares decreased with expanded deficits. These included public services, health, and recreation.

Third, several sectoral allocations again appear complementary with total educational expenditures. These include health and recreation. However, trade-offs tended to occur between total education and economic services.

Fourth, in terms of shifts in the budget slope of the educational term, the Revolution tended to produce a complementary relationship between education and public services. However, the Revolution appears to have created several trade-offs between education and housing/community activities, and between education and other transport services and other economic services. With regard to the slope of the education term, the Revolution seems to have had its major impact with total education and primary and secondary education, with little effect on university or other types of education.

The data reveal several findings after regressing the war and revolution dummies together with the budgetary shares on the actual (realized) deficit. Thus, education (either total or primary) was the only budgetary category associated with increases in the deficit. In fact, increases in the share of funds allocated to education accounted during the period under consideration for over seventy percent of the increase in the fiscal deficit. Also, the revolutionary regime appears slightly more disposed than its predecessor to run deficits, but this effect is not particularly strong. Moreover, contrary to the situation in most countries, the war in general (and military expenditure in particular) does not appear to have had much, if any, effect in increasing the size of the deficit. Finally, substituting the share of the budget allocated to defense for the war term also does not enable one to account for the increase in the deficit in recent years. In fact, the

TABLE 8.10 Summary: Trade-offs Between Educational and Non-Educational Budgetary Shares, Total Educational Expenditures, and Primary and Secondary Expenditures, 1970-1988

	Independent Variables					
	Revolution	*War*	*Unexpected Deficit*	*Expected Deficit*	*Education Budgetary Share*	*Primary Secondary School Share*
Public Services	ins	ins	-	-	ins (+/r)	ins (+/r)
Defense	-	ins	ins	ins	ins	+ (ins/r)
Health	ins	+	-	-	+ (+r)	+
Social/ Security Welfare	ins	ins	ins	ins	ins	ins
Housing/ Community Amenities	+	-	+	+	ins (-r)	ins (-/r)
Recreation	-	ins	-	ins	+ (ins/r)	+ (ins/r)
Economic Services	ins	-	ins	ins	ins	- (ins/r)
Manufact/ Mining	+	-	ins	ins	- (ins/r)	- (ins/r)
Roads	-	ins	ins	ins	ins (+ r)	ins
Other Transport	ins	+	+	+	- (-/r)	- (ins/r)
Other Economic	+	+	ins	ins	ins (-/r)	-

ins = statistically insignificant at the 95% level; + = significant at the 95% level with a positive sign; - = significant at the 95% level with a negative sign. Two forms of the educational share of the budget were specified. The first specification involved the budgetary share of the educational variable. The second term (indicated by a parenthesis) represents the educational share weighted by the revolution dummy variable. Here: (+/r) = slope of education term was positive and statistically significant at the 95% level when weighted with Revolution dummy variable. (-/r) = slope of education term negative and statistically significant at the 95% level when weighted with the Revolution dummy variable. When no result is given for the dummy specification, the result using the dummy weighting was the same as that obtained with the simple budgetary share.

defense term has a positive sign, suggesting that higher levels of defense expenditure are actually associated with lower deficits.

It appears, therefore, that both the Shah and the Islamic leaders gave a high enough priority to (primary) education so as to be willing to risk the inflationary impact usually associated with increased budgetary deficits. No other sector appears to have been elevated to this status by either regime.

TABLE 8.11 Summary: Trade-offs Between Educational and Non-Educational Budgetary Shares, University Educational Expenditures, and Other Educational Expenditures, 1970-1988

	Independent Variables					
	Revolution	*War*	*Unexpected Deficit*	*Expected Deficit*	*University Budgetary Share*	*Other Education Budgetary Share*
Public Services	ins	ins	-	-	- (ins/r)	+
Defense	-	ins	ins	ins	ins	+ (ins/r)
Health	ins	+	-	-	- (ins/r)	ins
Social/ Security Welfare	ins	ins	ins	ins	+	ins
Housing/ Community Amenities	+	-	+	+	ins	-
Recreation	-	ins	-	ins	+ (ins/r)	ins
Economic Services	ins	-	ins	ins	ins	ins
	+	-	ins	ins	ins	ins
Manufact/ Mining	-	ins	+	+	ins	+
Roads	-	ins	ins	ins	ins	+
Other Transport	-	-	ins	ins	ins (-/r)	ins
Other Economic	ins	+	+	+	- (-/r)	ins

See Table 8.10 for complete definitions of statistics and variables.

Conclusions

Since assuming power, the Islamic regime has been able to maintain, if not increase, the country's stock of human capital. Most likely, this has come at some cost in terms of inflation, and perhaps resources that could have been allocated more effectively to the higher levels of training. Following the end of the war with Iraq, and given Iran's by-stander role in the 1990-91 Gulf War, the country's focus for the rest of the 1990s most likely will turn to increasing its investment in its younger citizens. It is unlikely that education, at least at the primary level, will face major problems in maintaining its budgetary share, despite the increasing economic costs associated with on-going reconstruction. Increases in the absolute amounts of resources allocated to both activities should help revive the economy. However, it is hard to see major increases in growth occurring in the longer term unless the government is willing to alter its priorities toward increased funding of university level education.

9

Iraq: War, Military Expenditures, and Human Capital Development

A common thesis is that even in the more affluent oil exporting countries military expenditures have preempted funds that might otherwise have been allocated to education and the improvement of human capital.[1] If this view is correct then Iraq, particularly following its defeat in the 1990-91 Gulf War, should suffer a major decline in its human capital development in the 1990s. Even in Iraq's case, however, there may be mitigating factors undermining the widely-held belief that a decline in human capital is all but inevitable. In fact our analysis in Chapter 6 suggested that, at least in the Middle East, there tends to be a fairly close association between increases in military participation (number of soldiers per capita) and improvements in the literacy rate. Obviously, whether or not Iraqi educational and military expenditures complement each other or compete for scarce funds will ultimately depend on the government's budgetary priorities.

This chapter explores several aspects of the education versus military expenditures issue as it relates to Iraq. Sufficient usable data for the period after the 1990-91 Gulf War is not yet available.[2] Therefore in our analysis we will examine the effects of the eight-year long Iran-Iraq war in the 1980s for insights into the relationship in Iraq between the military and

---

1. See Chapter 6 above for an analysis and assessment of this view. For a well articulated statement of this thesis, see John Cummings, Hossein Askari, and Michael Skinner, "Military Expenditures and Manpower Requirements in the Arabian Peninsula," *Arab Studies Quarterly,* 2, 1 (Winter 1980), pp. 38-49.

2. For a political analysis of Iraq's role in the strategic affairs of the post-cold war and post-Gulf War era, see Ahmad Hashim, "Iraq and the Post-Cold War Order," in M.E. Ahrari and James H. Noyes, eds., *The Persian Gulf After the Cold War* (Westport: Praeger, 1993), pp. 99-124. Hashim argues that Iraq has a deep-rooted ambition to be the paramount political, economic, technological, and military power in the Arab world. He also believes that Iraq's weakened state in the 1990s poses a serious threat to the survival of Iraq as a state and consequently believes it does not bode well for the continued stability of the Gulf region.

non-military sectors. Did Iraq's human capital development suffer during the Iran-Iraq war, and if it did, in what manner? Does Iraq follow a pattern of military/human capital development typical of the Arab world? How does the country's human resource development during the 1980s compare to that of Iran? What are the implications of Iraq's human development patterns for the country's reconstruction in the 1990s?

Economic Conditions Before the Iran-Iraq War

In the years following the nationalization of the Iraq Petroleum Company in 1972 and the 1973 oil price increases, Iraq made major efforts to develop its infrastructure, its oil sector, and its goods producing sectors. Simultaneously, the government also worked to modernize the military. The 1975 Algiers Accords with Iran allowed Iraq to pursue its economic development plans unhindered by the cost of quelling a Kurdish rebellion. By 1979, Iraq had displaced Iran as the second largest OPEC oil producer/exporter after Saudi Arabia.[3]

While the Baath tradition of controlling expenditure to avoid debt and economic overheating was maintained until the end of the 1970s, it was evident by 1979 that Iraq had not escaped the classic structure of an oil rich rentier state. In addition, the government was coming under increased pressure to expand expenditures following the second round of oil price increases in the late 1970s.[4]

The government's stepped up expenditures, particularly after Saddam Hussein's accession to the presidency in 1979, placed severe strains on the economy, and many of the problems which the Iraqi economy faced in the late 1980s began to develop at this time. In particular, shortages of skilled manpower began to appear and bureaucratic inefficiency started to have a serious effect on the development process.

Ironically, the over abundance of non-productive labor in the government service sector was matched by a serious labor shortage in productive sectors. By the early 1980s industrial projects in the development plan called for nearly half a million additional semi-skilled workers, 375,000 craftspersons, and 1,500,000 degree holders. However, the total annual output of graduates was less than 20,000, and the situation in vocational fields was even more inadequate. It is impossible to say how much the labor bottleneck as opposed to other factors contributed to the shortcomings of the Plan, but abundant anecdotal evidence indicates it was a major factor:

---

3. Abbas Alnasrawi, "Economic Consequences of the Iraq-Iran War," *Third World Quarterly*, 8, 3 (July 1986), p. 872.

4. George Joffe and Keith McLachlan, *Iran and Iraq: the Next Five Years*. (London: Economist Intelligence Unit, 1987), p. 19.

Japanese firms working on Iraqi projects have had to import thousands of Chinese workers from the People's Republic and Yugoslav construction firms have an edge in bidding on Iraqi projects owing to their ability to supply the necessary labor. A recent World Bank study estimates that by 1985 Iraq will depend on non-Iraqis for between 4.3 and 10 percent of its entire labor force. The outlook may be even further complicated if the armed forces draw more heavily on the limited pool of skilled labor.[5]

This last concern was realized with the mobilization of major segments of the labor force as the Iran-Iraq war escalated and size of the armed forces increased. During the early years of the war, the armed forces expanded from 140,000 persons in 1978 to 450,000 in 1982, and further to 642,000 in 1984.[6]

The mobilization of the military has several important implications. In 1978, the size of the labor force in Iraq was 2.97 million or 24 percent of the total population of 12.41 million. Applying the same percentage to the 1982 population of 14.11 million yields a labor force of 3.39 million.[7] This means that the proportion of the labor force enlisted in the army increased from 4.7 percent in 1978 to 13.3 percent in 1982. By the mid 1980s, however, with a population of 15.25 million (and an implied labor force of 3.66 million), it is likely that around 17.5 percent of the labor force was in the military.

It should be noted that the loss of a major segment of the domestic labor force to the military economy was more than offset by the rise in the number of women in the labor force and, more importantly, by imported workers, mainly Egyptians. Thus between 1978 and 1982, the size of the labor force increased by 2.7 million (from 2.97 million to 5.67 million), while the population of Iraq increased by only 1.7 million during the same period.

Partially as a result of labor and infrastructural bottlenecks, inflation rose, imports piled up as ports in the Gulf began to clog and recourse had to be made to expensive overland routes from Turkey and Jordan. Despite these adverse signs, the political imperative combined with the doubling of oil revenues meant that the overall national growth rate in 1979 was set at 16.8 percent, compared with average annual real growth of 10.5 percent in 1973. In fact, nominal growth in 1979 was 27 percent and real growth about half that rate. When the war with Iran broke out in September 1980, the Iraqi economy was already seriously off balance, with accelerating inflation and virtually complete dependence on oil for export revenues.[8]

---

5. Joe Stork, "Iraq: The War in the Gulf," *MERIP Reports*, 9, 7 (June 1981), pp. 16-17.

6. Ruth Leger Sivard, *World Military and Social Expenditures*. (Washington: World Priorities), various issues.

7. Alnasrawi, "The Economic Consequences of the Iraq-Iran War," pp. 875-76.

There is no doubt that the war profoundly distorted Iraq's economy, quite apart from its incalculable human cost which included more than a million dead and injured and between 1 and 2 million displaced persons. The fact that Iraq has not published detailed national statistics since 1977 means that any attempt to estimate the cost of the war is extremely difficult. The difficulty is compounded because various estimates select different components of cost and thus are not comparable with the others. Furthermore, the estimates refer to different time periods.[9] As Joffe and McLachlan note, annual costings of the war show similar variations.[10] Most observers assumed that in the years during the mid-to-late 1980s Iraq spent $4-5 billion on arms purchases, with some estimates ranging as high as $6.25 billion. Iraq's economic losses have been estimated at around $16 billion a year.[11]

Patterns of Human Resource Development and Military Expenditures

The consequences for human capital development of increased military expenditures in Iraq can be best assessed within the context of comparative developments taking place simultaneously in neighboring Arab countries. In fact, government initiative in this area has expanded in recent years, with Arab countries as a whole increasing their educational expenditures as a percent of GNP from 3.87 in 1974 to 5.08 by 1984. The corresponding figures for non-Arab countries were 3.33 percent and 4.01 percent. Health expenditures have not shown such a dramatic increase, however, increasing from 1.39 percent of GNP in 1974 for the Arab countries to 1.59 in 1984.[12]

A similar pattern was observed in the non-Arab countries, where health expenditure increased from 1.32 to 1.62 percent of GNP over the 1974-84 decade. Whereas Arab countries had a higher average annual rate of education/GNP growth (2.8 percent versus 1.9 percent) for the decade 1974/84, non-Arab countries had higher rates of expansion of per capita education expenditures (12.1 percent versus 10.2 percent).

8. George Joffe and Keith McLachlan, *Iran and Iraq: the Next Five Years.* (London: Economist Intelligence Unit 1987), p. 19.

9. George Joffe and Keith McLachlan, *Iran and Iraq: Building on the Stalemate--Special Report No 1164.* (London: Economist Intelligence Unit, November 1988), p. 23.

10. Joffe and Keith McLachlan, *Iran and Iraq: the Next Five Years.*, pp. 23-24.

11. Hashim suggests that $200 billion was spent by Baghdad on the Iran-Iraq war. Although our data do not permit a quantitative assessment of the direct cost to Iraq of its invasion of Kuwait in 1990, he cites a figure of another $200 billion. See Hashim, "Iraq and the Post-Cold War Order," p. 112.

12. The data in the next several paragraphs is calculated from Ruth Leger Sivard, *World Military and Social Expenditures* (Washington D.C.: World Priorities), various issues.

In general, the Arab countries have experienced higher rates of growth of military expenditures per capita relative to education or health expenditures (14.5 percent versus 10.2 percent and 11.3 percent) over the 1974/84 period. Non-Arab countries, on the other hand, had higher rates of per-capita growth of education and health expenditures relative to military expenditures (12.1 percent and 11.5 percent versus 8.8 percent) over the same time period. In short, concurrent with rapid economic growth in the Arab world, there was an acceleration in military spending.[13]

For the region as a whole, military purchases have been partially financed by oil revenues and by military aid and grants from the major industrial country arms suppliers. According to Lebovic and Ishaq:[14]

Middle Eastern defense accounted for one third of the military spending of developing countries and almost one-half of world arms imports. During the 1973-1982 period, the average annual economic growth rate for individual Middle Eastern states was about 6.0%, while military expenditures grew by approximately 13.0 percent per year. Although military expenditure levels vary greatly across countries, in a great majority of the countries the growth rate of military spending outpaced economic growth. This indicates a striking trend in the region toward higher military burdens (military expenditures as a ratio of Gross Domestic Product).[15]

As might be expected, comparable figures during this period for Iraq show that the country had a considerably higher increase in military expenditures than that of Arab countries as a whole. While Iraq's per capita military expenditures were below Arab countries in 1974, $112.42 versus $139.82, Iraq's per capita military expenditures increased at an average annual rate of 23.37 percent over the 1974/84 period (versus 14.5 percent for Arab countries).

Interestingly, in contrast, Iran's military expenditures increased fairly modestly during the period under consideration. While increasing at an annual average rate of 14.6 during the 1979-84 period, they still averaged only 2.80 percent for the 1974/84 period as a whole. On the other hand, Iran's educational expenditures were considerably above those of Iraq; by 1984 Iran had a per-capita educational expenditure about twice that of Iraq.

Several other measures of socio-economic/military development indicate substantial differences between the Arab countries and other non-

---

13. The data is calculated from Sivard, *World Military and Social Expenditures*, various issues.

14. James Lebovic and Ashafaq Ishaq, "Military Burden, Security Needs, and Economic Growth in the Middle East," *Journal of Conflict Resolution*, 31, 1 (March 1987), p. 107.

15. Lebovic and Ishaq, "Military Burden, Security Needs, and Economic Growth in the Middle East," p. 107.

Arab developing countries.[16] First, for the Arab countries government expenditures (as a percentage of GNP) on education, health and defense were about twice those of non-Arab countries (19.1 per cent vs. 9.3 per cent in 1984). The rate of growth of the share of these expenditures in GNP was also about twice as fast as those of non-Arab countries (3.8 percent vs. 1.9 percent) over the 1974/84 period. Second, the Arab countries also have higher teacher per capita ratios than their non-Arab counterparts in the Third World together with higher rates of growth of this ratio (3.0 percent versus 1.9 percent) over the 1974/84 period. Third, despite having a higher ratio of teachers per capita, the Arab countries experienced, relative to non-Arab countries, slower rates of expansion in the proportion of the school age population attending school. As a result, the Arab countries, while having a higher proportion of their population in school in 1974 (42.5 percent versus 41.9 percent), ended the decade with a lower ratio of their school age population actually in school. Fourth, the relative expansion of teachers in the Arab world resulted in this group of countries experiencing a relatively rapid decline in the ratio of school age population per teacher. Fifth, despite the relatively slow increase in the percentage of school age population in school, the Arab countries were able to achieve considerably greater improvements in literacy than their non-Arab counterparts. Finally, consistent with their relatively high level of military expenditures, Arab countries had much higher military participation ratios (armed forces per 1,000 population) than their non-Arab counterparts. In 1974 Arab countries had 11.7 soldiers per 1,000 population, while at the same time non-Arab countries had 4.5. By 1984 the respective rates were 14.4 and 5.6.

Again, although Iraq began the period as a relatively typical Arab country, it tended to magnify several of the ten year patterns experienced by this group of states. Thus while Iraq's expenditures on education, health and defense were nearly the same as the mean for the Arab group in 1974, by 1984 the country was spending over half (54.2 percent) of its GNP on these items, compared to only 22.4 percent for Arab countries as a group. Similarly, Iraq began the period with a military participation rate slightly below that of Arab countries (10.5 vs. 11.7), and ended it with a rate considerably higher (42.1 vs. 14.4). As well, Iraq's literacy rate was slightly below that of Arab countries in 1975 (26.0 percent versus 27.5 percent). By 1984, however, Iraq's literacy rate had increased to 58 percent compared to 48.0 percent for the Arab group of countries. The relative improvement in Iraq's literacy rate occurred despite the fact that the country experienced the same increase in school age population in school (2.1 percent 1974/84)

---

16. The data is calculated from Sivard, *World Military and Social Expenditures*, various issues.

and school age population per teacher (-4.9 percent) as the other Arab countries. In part, the improvement in literacy must have stemmed from Iraq's rapid increase in teachers per capita (8.4 percent) compared to other Arab countries (3.0 percent) over the 1974/84 period. Clearly, the Arab world, given its relatively low levels of human capital formation, should be one of the areas most receptive to a link between military expenditure, military participation, human capital formation, and economic growth. Finally, during this period, (non-Arab) Iran tended to have more stable, albeit lower, expansions in most of the key ratios described above. The one exception was school age population in school, where Iran's increase was 3.4 percent per annum over the 1974/84 compared to 2.1 percent for Iraq.

Despite Iraq's heavy commitment to the military during this period, it is not obvious that the country suffered any particularly severe retardation in human capital development. As our analyses in Chapters 5, 6, and 7 point out, besides the simple guns-versus-butter trade-off, economic theory does not unambiguously indicate whether a higher military burden retards or promotes economic growth in general and human capital development in particular.[17] Empirical evidence on the subject is the focus of controversy.

The analysis below examines Iraq by placing it within the context of the arguments put forth in Chapters 5, 6, and 7. As we noted in Chapter 5, with several exceptions, previous studies have tended to concentrate on developing countries as a whole. However, in this chapter we are primarily interested in drawing comparisons between Iraq and the Middle East states, a set of countries characterized as having very high military burdens (military expenditures as a percentage of GNP) by Third World standards, together with lower than average levels of human capital. We are interested in determining whether and to what extent military expenditures act independently of total government expenditures in affecting human capital development either in the region or it Iraq. Finally, are the linkages between military expenditures and human capital development

---

17. See our analysis in Chapter 5 for an assessment of the economic consequences of defense expenditures, Chapter 6 for the impact of defense expenditures on human capital development, and Chapter 7 for the budgetary impact and trade-offs associated with defense expenditures. Our analysis suggests that the relationship between military expenditures and economic growth is not as straightforward as it may seem. This supports the work of others, for example, see Lebovic and Ishaq, "Military Burden, Security Needs, and Economic Growth in the Middle East," pp. 106-138; Cummings, Askari and Skinner, "Military Expenditures and Manpower Requirements in the Arabian Peninsula," pp. 38-49; Mohammed Raief Mousad, "Human Resources, Government Education Expenditure and the Military Burden in Less Developed Countries: With Special Reference to Arab Countries," *Bulletin of Arab Research and Studies* (Number 11, 1984), pp. 35-55; Saadat Deger, "Human Resources, Government Education Expenditure, and the Military Burden in Less Developed Countries," *Journal of Developing Areas* 20, 1 (October 1985), pp. 37-48.

in Iraq and elsewhere in the region fundamentally different from those experienced in other parts of the world, and if they are, why?

Framework for Analysis

The main quantifiable variables pertain to allocations to defense, government expenditures and the public education that may generate human capital. Following the reasoning we advanced in Chapter 6, the analysis below is based on several methodological premises.

First, human capital is proxied by the ratio of public education expenditure as a proportion of GDP. That is, we assume that public education spending as a proportion of the national product is a crucial determinant of human capital formation (HC). If this ratio falls, then the rate of growth of human capital may, in all probability, fall too.

Second, total government expenditures were included in the analysis in addition to military expenditures, with each defined in terms of a different ratio. Specifically, government expenditures (GEY) were treated in terms of their share of GNP. This avoids the problem of lack of clarity as to whether the military burden acted in some way as a statistical proxy for government expenditures.

Third, allocations to defense were defined in ways other than the traditional military burden (military expenditures share of GNP) to avoid spurious correlations with government expenditures. Since the literature is unclear as to the most appropriate definition of the defense burden, three alternative measures were used: (i) military expenditures per soldier (MEAF), (ii) the defense share of the central government budget (MEGE), and (iii) the military participation rate—the number of soldiers per 1000 population (AFP).

Fourth, the rate of human capital development (HCo) at the beginning of the period (that is, 74 for the 1974-84 interval) was introduced into the regression equation. This controls for effect of the initial level of human capital.

Finally, the increase in per-capita income (YP) with an expected negative sign was also introduced into the regression equations. This controls for rapid increases in per capita income reducing the ratio of educational expenditures to Gross Domestic Product.[18]

---

18. Rapid increases in per capita income may reduce the ratio of educational expenditures to Gross Domestic Product, particularly in the oil exporting countries where, due to absorptive capacity problems, oil revenues may outrun the government's capability to expand productive expenditures. For an excellent description and application of the concept of absorptive capacity to Iraq, see Ragaei El Mallakh and Jacob K. Atta, *The Absorptive Capacity of Iraq* (Lexington, Mass: Lexington Books, 1981).

In sum, the model with expected signs used for examining the impact of military expenditures on human resource development was of the form:[19]

(1)   HC = [GEY, MEAF, MEGE, AFP, YP, HCo]
            (+)   (?)   (?)   (?) (-) (-)

Where:

HC = educational expenditures/GNP

GEY = total government expenditures/GNP

MEAF = military expenditures per soldier

MEGE = the share of defense in the central government budget

AFP = the number of soldiers per 1000 population

YP = per capita income (GNP/population)

HCo = educational expenditures/GNP in the base year.

All variables except HCo were defined in terms of their rate of growth over the specified time interval. To get an idea of the robustness of the results, step-wise regressions were undertaken for the entire time interval 1974-84, together with its two five-year sub-periods, 1974-79 and 1979-84.

Results

The results for the period as a whole (1974-84) produced several interesting findings (Table 9.1). First, for developing countries in general, increases in the share of government expenditures in GNP explain approximately 60 percent of the changes in human capital formation. The coefficient for the government expenditure term (GEY) is very stable, not changing appreciably with varying model specification.

Second, while increased military expenditures per soldier (MEAF) did not detract from human capital development, increases in the defense share of the public sector budget as well as increases in military expenditures per soldier, tended to reduce the expansion of human capital development relative to GDP during this period. The same was also the case for increase in the military participation rate (AFP).

---

19. Data were taken from Sivard, *World Military and Social Expenditures*, various issues. The original sample of developing countries consisted of 109 nations. Because of missing observations on several countries the usual sample size was around 90 countries. The Arab countries consisted of the twenty members of the Arab Monetary Fund and consisted of: Jordan, UAE, Bahrain, Tunisia, Algeria, Saudi Arabia, Sudan, Syria, Somalia, Iraq, Oman, Qatar, Kuwait, Lebanon, Libya, Egypt, Morocco, Mauritania, Yemen Arab Republic and the Peoples Democratic Republic of Yemen. Because of missing observations, Lebanon, Qatar and Mauritania were absent from most of the regressions.

TABLE 9.1   Factors Affecting Human Capital Formation in the Third World, 1974-1984 (standardized regression coefficients)

(1) HC = 0.77 GEY	
(11.23)	
r^2 = 0.589; F = 126.01; df = 89	
Student Residual Iraq = - 4.60	Student Residual Iran = 1.56
(2) HC = 0.78 GEY - 0.03 MEAF	
(10.05) (-0.36)	
r^2 = 0.590; F = 61.17; df = 87	
Student Residual Iraq = - 4.74	Student Residual Iran = 1.52
(3) HC = 0.77 GEY + 0.06 MEAF -0.28 MEGE	
(10.86) (0.77) (-4.24)	
r^2 = 0.662; F = 54.92; df = 87	
Student Residual Iraq = - 5.05	Student Residual Iran = 1.38
(4) HC = 0.74 GEY + 0.05 MEAF - 0.26 MEGE - 0.09 HCo	
(10.00) (0.65) (-3.77) (-1.34)	
r^2 = 0.670; F = 42.04; df = 87	
Student Residual Iraq = - 4.96	Student Residual Iran = 1.37
(5) HC = 0.75 GEY + 0.01 MEAF - 0.25 MEGE - 0.09 HCo + 0.06 YP	
(9.84) (0.17) (-3.58) (-1.37) (0.77)	
r^2 = 0.671; F = 33.58; df = 87	
Student Residual Iraq = - 5.03	Student Residual Iran = 1.40
(6) HC = 0.84 GEY - 0.11 MEAF - 0.17 MEGE - 0.13 HCo + 0.10 YP - 0.20 AFP	
(9.84) (-1.16) (-2.31) (-1.89) (1.37) (-2.62)	
r^2 = 0.697; F = 31.12; df = 87	
Student Residual Iraq = - 5.06	Student Residual Iran = 1.56

HC= education expenditures/GNP; GEY = government expenditures/GNP; MEAF = military expenditures per soldier; MEGE = share of military expenditures in central government budget; YP = per capita income; AFP = the military participation rate (armed forces per capita). HCo = education expenditure/GNP for 1974. All variables except HCo are rates of growth.

Third, in terms of Iraq, it appears that the country spent considerably less than predicted by the model, with the student residual for Iraq varying (depending on model specification) between - 4.60 and - 5.06. In other words, even after controlling for military expenditures and military participation rates, Iraq was unable, relative to most other Third World countries, to increase its commitment to human capital formation during this period.

Fourth, in sharp contrast, Iran's commitment to human capital formation was considerably above that anticipated by the model.

However, looking at countries in terms of Arab/non-Arab groupings (Tables 9.2 and 9.3), produces a picture considerably different than that obtained above for the Third World countries as a whole over the 1974/84 period.

As Table 9.2 indicates, the growth in the share of government expenditures in GNP by itself accounts for well over 65 percent of the observed

TABLE 9.2 Factors Affecting Human Capital Formation in the Arab World, 1974-1984 (standardized regression coefficients)

(1) HC = 0.82 GEY
       (5.56)
$r^2 = 0.659$; F = 30.90; df = 17
Student Residual Iraq = - 3.01

(2) HC = 0.54 GEY + 0.40 MEAF
       (3.07)   (2.27)
$r^2 = 0.746$; F = 22.02; df = 17
Student Residual Iraq = - 2.52

(3) HC = 0.48 GEY + 0.44 MEAF -0.25 MEGE
       (2.96)   (2.75)   (-2.10)
$r^2 = 0.807$; F = 19.51; df = 17
Student Residual Iraq = - 2.50

(4) HC = 0.32 GEY + 0.47 MEAF - 0.21 MEGE - 0.25 HCo
       (1.99)   (3.20)   (-1.95)   (-2.01)
$r^2 = 0.852$; F = 30.90; df = 17
Student Residual Iraq = - 2.36

(5) HC = 0.01 GEY + 0.91 MEAF - 0.28 MEGE - 0.27 HCo - 0.41 YP
       (0.02)   (5.03)   (-3.19)   (-2.76)   (-3.13)
$r^2 = 0.919$; F = 27.16; df = 17
Student Residual Iraq = - 1.22

(6) HC = - 0.26 GEY + 1.74 MEAF - 0.49 MEGE - 0.26 HCo - 0.90 YP + 0.42 AFP
       (0.02)   (5.03)   (-3.19)   (-2.76)   (-3.13)   (2.15)
$r^2 = 0.942$; F = 30.21; df = 17
Student Residual Iraq = - 1.29

(7) HC = 0.91 MEAF - 0.28 MEGE - 0.27 HCo - 0.41 YP
       (8.84)   (-3.41)   (-3.13)   (-4.22)
$r^2 = 0.918$; F = 36.78; df = 17
Student Residual Iraq = - 0.65

For definitions of terms see Table 9.1.

fluctuations in the share of human capital formation in GDP for the Arab countries. However this relationship breaks down with more complete model specification (Table 9.2, equations 5, 6 and 7). Perhaps more importantly, several of the military expenditure terms are now statistically significant. Both expanded rates of military expenditures per soldier (MEAF), and the military participation rate (AFP), tended to increase human capital development during this time period. However, as with the total sample of Third World countries, increases in the defense share of the budget (MEGE) tended to reduce the growth in human capital formation.

Table 9.2 also reveals that Iraq's pattern of human capital is much better accounted for in the context of the larger group of Arab development patterns than it was when the total sample of countries was used. While Iraq's human capital expenditures still expanded somewhat below the rate anticipated by the total Arab group equations, this difference was much less than that predicted in the total sample case. In addition Iraq's pattern of

TABLE 9.3   Factors Affecting Human Capital Formation in the non-Arab World, 1974-1984 (standardized regression coefficients)

(1) HC =   0.67 GEY
            (7.56)
$r^2 = 0.449$; F = 57.12; df = 71

Student Residual Iran = 2.47
(2) HC =   0.68 GEY - 0.27 MEAF
            (43.76)   (-3.19)
$r^2 = 0.525$; F = 37.06; df = 69

Student Residual Iran = 2.40
(3) HC =   0.81 GEY - 0.18 MEAF - 0.33 MEGE
            (10.0)   (-2.19)   (-4.10)
$r^2 = 0.622$; F = 36.14; df = 69

Student Residual Iran = 2.40
(4) HC =   0.76 GEY - 0.20 MEAF - 0.29 MEGE - 0.14 HCo
            (8.80)   (-2.41)   (-3.42)   (-1.63)
$r^2 = 0.637$; F = 28.45; df = 69

Student Residual Iran = 2.43
(5) HC =   0.77 GEY - 0.21 MEAF - 0.29 MEGE - 0.13 HCo + 0.03 YP
            (8.25)   (-2.26)   (-3.37)   (-1.56)   (0.30)
$r^2 = 0.637$; F = 22.46; df = 69

Student Residual Iran = 2.42
(6) HC =   0.87 GEY - 0.34 MEAF - 0.21 MEGE - 0.17 HCo + 0.06 YP - 0.23 AFP
            (8.89)   (-3.27)   (-2.41)   (-2.01)   (0.69)   (-2.52)
$r^2 = 0.670$; F = 21.35; df = 69

Student Residual Iran = 2.42

For definitions of terms see Table 9.1

human capital development tended to converge toward the Arab world norm, once military expenditures were introduced explicitly into the model.

For the non-Arab countries, much the reverse was true (Table 9.3). In addition to increased levels of defense expenditures in the central government budget, these countries as a group experienced negative impacts on human capital formation stemming from expanded military expenditures per soldier and increased military participation rates.

In addition to the distinctive differences observed between Arab and non-Arab countries, several interesting contrasts were found between the two five year intervals (Table 9.3).[20] Other than the negative effect on human capital associated with increased shares of the government budget being allocated to defense, military expenditures in the developing world as a whole do not appear to have diverted resources away from education during the 1974/79 period.[21]

---

20. Because of their length these results are only summarized here. A complete set of tables with the detailed findings is available from the authors upon request.

During the 1974/79 period, Iraq closely followed the pattern predicted by the model. In this sense, its efforts at human capital formation were "typical" of those taking place in the developing world. Iran, on the other hand, experienced rates of capital formation considerably above that predicted by increases in government expenditures, the share of the budget allocated to defense, and the initial (1974) share of educational expenditures in Gross Domestic Product.

During the 1979/84 period, Iraq's human capital development was considerably below that anticipated by the model. In fact, the short-fall in capital formation from that predicted increased as the share of defense expenditures in the government's budget was added to the regression equation. On the other hand, over the 1974/79 sub-period, Iran was a "typical" Third World country, following very closely the increase in human capital development predicted by the model.

The patterns observed for developing countries during the 1974/79 were quite stable (in terms of the size of the regression coefficients). They did not carry over into the 1979-84 period. Specifically, the overall coefficient of determination (r^2) was much lower in the latter interval as was the strength of the expansion in government expenditures to increase the importance of education in economic activity. In addition, the military participation rate which was slightly significant (and negative) for the period as a whole was not statistically significant in either of the two five year sub-periods.

For Arab countries as a group the model with government expenditures (GEY) and the share of defense in the government budget (MEGE) accounted for around 65 percent of the fluctuations in human capital formation during the 1974/79 period. In contrast to the 1974/84 period, however, increased rates of military expenditures per soldier were no longer associated with expanded levels of human capital formation. In addition, increased levels of military participation were associated with reductions in human capital formation.

During the first five year interval, Iraq closely followed the pattern of human capital development predicted by the Arab world equations. In addition, the predicted value for Iraq's human capital development improved once we controlled for the increase in the military participation rate. A much different pattern emerged in the second (1979/84) time interval. As with the case for the 1974/84 interval, both military expenditures per soldier and the military participation rate were positively associated with increases in human capital development. In Iraq's case, introducing increased levels of military participation tended to increase considerably

---

21. For lack of space, statistically insignificant results are not reported here. They are obtainable from the authors upon request.

the level of human capital development predicted for that country by the model.

Finally, in terms of the patterns of human capital development in the non-Ārab world as a whole, military expenditures per soldier (MEAF) during the 1974-79 interval (in contrast to the period) were not statistically significant in retarding the expansion of human capital development. Again, at this time, expanding the share of defense in the government budget apparently came (at least partially) at the expense of educational expenditures. Once more Iran's performance with regard to human capital development was superior to most developing countries. Iran's positive student residual of 2.12 to 2.22 was one of the highest in the non-Arab world during this period.

These patterns changed in the latter five year interval. During this period, military expenditures per soldier were now associated with reduced rates of growth in human capital development (the military participation rate was statistically insignificant). For this period Iran's human capital formation was slightly below that for the non-Arab countries as a whole and its position vis-a-vis these countries did not change considerably upon controlling for military expenditures.

Conclusions

To sum up, the process of human capital development in the Third World appears to be affected to a certain extent by the pattern of military expenditures simultaneously undertaken by these states. The patterns vary considerably by sub-grouping—Arab versus non-Arab, and by time period—the late 1970s versus the early 1980s. In general, these patterns have become more extreme with time.

A major finding of the analysis in this chapter was that Arab countries have tended (particularly in more recent times) to experience positive associations between military expenditures per soldier (and to a certain extent increased military participation rates) and human capital development. On the other hand, increased military expenditures per soldier (and to a lesser extent the military participation rate) appear to have come at the expense of human capital development in the non-Arab world.

During the 1970s, Iraq appears to have followed pretty closely the patterns experienced by most Third World countries, and certainly those of the Arab world. This situation deteriorated somewhat in the 1980s, however, with Iraq missing many of the apparent linkages between expanded military expenditures per soldier and allocations to education which existed in many other Arab states. On the other hand, there is some evidence that increased military participation during the 1979/84 period stimulated increased rates of human capital development in Iraq. As a basis of comparison, Iran appears to have done relatively well with regard to its human capital development, particularly during the earlier period.

Based on the results presented in this chapter, again, we can only speculate as to the mechanisms linking military expenditures and human capital formation in the Iraq. Given shortages of skilled labor in Iraq in the 1980s,[22] the government may have assigned a very high priority to attracting available skilled labor to the military services.[23]

More likely, the Iraqi government opted to subsidize education for increased numbers of civilians during periods of stepped up military expenditures with the understanding that upon completion of training those individuals would serve some time in the military. This strategy would have allowed the military to absorb the large volume of sophisticated weapons flowing into the country without requiring drastic increases in the numbers of foreign military advisors.

---

22. Documented in Abbas Salih Mehdi and Olive Robinson, "Economic Development and the Labor Market in Iraq," *International Journal of Manpower* 4, (1983), pp. 3-39.

23. A possibility noted by Cummings, Askari and Skinner, "Military Expenditures and Manpower Requirements in the Arabian Peninsula," p. 42.

10

Saudi Arabia: Budgetary Priorities, Relative Austerity Measures, and Human Capital Formation

Throughout the 1980s, Saudi Arabia experienced a period of relative fiscal austerity. Falling oil revenues forced a number of significant budgetary cutbacks. However, by 1989, the situation had stabilized to the point that the Saudi Arabian government announced that its budget would be equal to that of two years earlier. To many observers, this signaled a welcome end to the deflationary effects of successive reductions in government budgetary expenditures over the last few years. In practice, it permitted ministries to prepare sufficient projects for implementation in the event that revenue constraints did not force cutbacks during the year.[1] Shortly thereafter, in August 1990, Iraq invaded Kuwait, putting significant new strains on Saudi revenue and expenditure patterns which have continued into the mid-1990s.[2]

This chapter examines how the Saudi government set priorities between major expenditure categories given its fluctuating revenues. In particular, we are interested in determining the manner in which the Saudi government revised, in light of revenue developments during the fiscal year, its allocation to the major budgetary categories. Did expenditures on certain categories vary systematically with unanticipated changes in revenues? If they did, which sectors gained or lost? Do these patterns provide insights in to the manner in which the Saudi government established budgetary priorities during this period?

---

1. Economist Intelligence Unit, *Saudi Arabia: Country Report No. 1 1989* (London: Economist Intelligence Unit, 1989), p. 3.

2. For a political assessment of the impact on Saudi Arabia of Iraq's invasion of Kuwait, the breakup of the Soviet Union, and the continuing concern with revolutionary Iran, see Joseph Twinam, "The Saudi Role in the New Middle East Order," in M.E. Ahrari and James H. Noyes, eds., *The Persian Gulf After the Cold War* (Westport: Praeger, 1993), pp. 125-146.

Fiscal Patterns

Budgetary revenue and expenditure increased steadily to 1974, except for 1967/68 when dislocation following the Israeli-Arab war affected all economies in the region.[3] However, the 1973/74 and 1979 oil price jumps, world recession, fluctuations in the world demand for oil, and political instability and warfare in the Gulf have led to sizable year to year fluctuations in budgetary receipts compared to expectations.

Although the general trend remained buoyant until 1981/82, in 1977/78 and 1978/79 slight budget deficits followed unexpectedly low oil revenues, whereas expenditure and revenue both rose over projected amounts during the next two years. The 1982/83 budget was the first in which an absolute decline in revenue was projected, the objective being to arrive at a balance, while in 1983/84 a planned deficit of SR35 billion was budgeted for the first time in many years.

Since then, budgetary positions have shown increased volatility. In 1984/85, the planned deficit was increased to SR46 billion with budget revenue and expenditure figures of SR214 billion and SR260 billion respectively. The 1985/86 budget was supposed to balance at SR200 billion, but ended with a SR50 billion deficit. The 1986/87 budget was not published in March 1986 as due, because of uncertain revenue forecasts. Monthly disbursements continued on the basis of average spending in 1984/85. A new budget was finally released at the end of December 1986 to cover the 1987 calendar year. The projected revenue at that time was SR117 billion. As a basis of reference the budget for 1981/82 was for SR340 billion.

Over the same period, the government had reduced government spending from SR298 billion to SR160 billion, a significant achievement, but not enough to close the deficit gap. In 1988, another large budget deficit was projected but the government acknowledged the dwindling size of its budget reserves by launching a local borrowing scheme to cover a substantial portion of the revenue shortfall. Import duties were also raised in an attempt to generate more non-oil revenue, but other measures such as tax increases were rescinded following public protest.

In addition to declining oil revenues, the government has had to contend with a drop in overseas investment income which resulted from a fall in international interest rates and a reduction in the size of the government's overseas assets (from around $150 billion in the early 1980s to less than an estimated $60 billion by the late 1980s). This figure is not official, as the Saudi leadership has not released figures concerning the size and composition of its portfolio.[4]

---

3. The following is based largely on Economist Intelligence Unit, *Saudi Arabia: Country Report* (London: Economist Intelligence Unit), various issues.

One of the main problems for the government is that current expenditure has proven very difficult to pare back; there are huge costs involved in running and maintaining the activities established by development project capital inputs in social services as well as physical infrastructure. Defense expenditure remains a major budget item. The growing government preoccupation with cutting its budget deficit is being translated into a number of schemes devised to tap the savings of state organizations (the Pension Fund has around SR60 billion) and the private sector. Expenditure rationalization and efficiency increases have also been initiated.

Government bond issues are the most obvious example of attempts to tap sources of savings other than the government's own dwindling reserves, the more so since various amendments to the offering terms have been introduced. These changes have gradually widened the groups of potential end-investors. Before the bonds were even offered to banks, it was estimated that some SR14 billion may have been placed with the government Pension Fund. The bonds were then offered to banks. In turn, a number of these institutions gained permission to include the bonds in a package of national assets offered to private investors in the form of a unit trust.

Finally, in the late 1980s the Saudi Arabian Monetary Agency (SAMA) permitted banks to sell the bonds directly to the Saudi public in minimum tranches of SR1 million. Purchasers got a certificate of purchase rather than the bonds themselves as the banks still collected interest from them, and were forbidden to sell them to non-Saudis. Firm details on the number and success of the bond offerings are sparse, which seems to confirm both that the banks' take was lower than hoped for, and that the scheme itself was still seen at the time as rather controversial.

The success of the government borrowing program will be judged not just by the levels of commercial bank and private sector subscriptions to each issue, but also by the extent to which these investors are prepared to repatriate their foreign asset holdings to purchase the bonds. As yet there is no firm evidence to show whether the purchases are being financed from domestic or foreign savings.

If the government could cover its direct foreign exchange spending with foreign currency repatriated via the bond issues, it would mean that government oil revenue and overseas investment income could all be put

---

4. The figure is however widely viewed as reflecting the approximate size of the government's foreign assets. For example Sharif Ghaleb, Middle East analyst for the Institute of International Finance in Washington, estimated in September 1985 that the Kingdom's total foreign assets were worth $92 billion. However, after adjusting for irretrievable loans to Iraq and developments in the currency and bond markets, the real value of the Saudi asset portfolio was probably no more than $75 billion at that time. See Michael Richie, "Saudi Arabia," in *The Middle East Review, 1987* (London: World of Information, 1987), pp. 167-83.

at the disposal of SAMA to meet private sector foreign exchange demand. On the other hand, if government borrowings are to be covered by riyal savings, and could therefore be classified in the same vein as domestic revenue, it becomes clear that this method of borrowing will decrease the net domestic cash flow, along with the stimulus that the government budget has traditionally given to the economy. This might be expected eventually to lead to less demand for foreign exchange throughout the economy, rather than to bring about an increase in foreign exchange availability. Funding the bond issues from domestic resources thus has a much clearer deflationary impact which might be expected to hurt the independent growth of the private sector.

The Gulf War of 1990-91 placed an additional strain on the government's finances. During the War the government paid out more for the war than it received in extra oil revenues. As a result, its budgetary situation deteriorated. A $13.5 billion cash pledge, made to the USA soon after the war started, represented the type of drain on reserves that the Kingdom could have afforded over a year, but not all at once. To alleviate the problem the Kingdom successfully raised its first commercial sovereign loan in February 1991. The overseas loan was for $3.5 billion and was clearly the best option for the government in meeting its twin objectives of securing extra hard currency at short notice and minimizing disruption to the local economy.[5]

With the momentum of war gaining pace at the beginning of 1991 it was no surprise that the Saudi authorities decided to postpone publication of the annual budget, and to use the powers available to them to sanction expenditure on the basis of levels established in 1990. However delaying the budget also meant that the government was deprived of an opportunity to adjust taxes, subsidies, or the government bond program. The latter continued to run via fortnightly auctions of SR1.5 billion ($400 million), but budget breakdowns by the Ministry of Finance indicated that interest and repayment charges were running at around SR15 billion year,[6] reducing the net contribution that this borrowing made to fund the government's expenditure program.

At the end of that conflict, and despite higher oil production and for a short time higher oil prices, the Saudi government's liquid foreign exchange reserves had been stretched because of the need to make large payments to certain coalition partners and allies in that war and by the ongoing acquisition of additional military equipment. After the war, oil prices continued to decline. Even with higher production oil revenues did not

---

5. EIU, *Saudi Arabia: Country Report, No. 1, 1991* (London: The Economist Intelligence Unit, 1991), p. 11.

6. EIU, *Saudi Arabia: Country Report, No. 1, 1991*, p. 12.

hold and the government has confronted great difficulties in raising sufficient funds to continue expenditures at recent levels,[7] including an accelerated program of defense acquisitions.[8]

Composition of the Budget

Relatively little is known about how OPEC governments make expenditure decisions concerning which programs to cut back during periods of austerity. As Chapter 7 indicated, when determining budgetary allocations many other governments typically have a bias toward maintaining expenditures in the social services and defense. This may reflect a government's preference for present consumption over investment and future consumption, since social sectors and defense typically have a heavy bias toward recurrent expenditures and within these there is a sizable employment component. Since the social sectors and defense/administration are relatively labor intensive with high recurrent costs, reducing expenditures on them not only cuts back services highly valued by the public, but also causes relatively high unemployment per unit reduction.[9]

The general characterization of the manner in which a government deals with austerity seems to hold up fairly well for the Saudi Arabian case. In recent years, most of the major categories of the budget have been cut (Table 10.1). Infrastructure spending in particular has been cut drastically, with few new projects commissioned. The budget for education and health has also been cut, reflecting in part a decline in capital expenditure on new schools and hospitals. However, the wage bill for teachers, nurses and doctors continues to rise. Similar conditions arise with defense expenditures; even though expenditure on basic defense infrastructure is past its peak, post 1990-91 Gulf War conditions suggest that the need to purchase new equipment and to maintain existing systems is still great.

Several points are worth noting in terms of specific allocations (Table 10.1). First, government lending institutions have experienced the greatest reduction in their allocations, declining by 51.9 percent over the 1983/88

---

7. For an analysis of prospects for a prolonged glut in global oil markets with resulting downward pressure on oil prices, see David Winterford and Robert E. Looney, "Gulf Oil: Geo-Economic and Geo-Strategic Realities in the Post-Cold War and Post-Gulf War Era," in Ahrari and Noyes, eds., *The Persian Gulf After the Cold War*, pp. 149-171.

8. By some estimates during the early 1990s Saudi authorities can expect an annual oil income of about $36 billion, once Kuwaiti and Iraqi exports return to pre-Gulf War levels. However, Riyadh seeks to buy $14 billion in weapons from the United States (and more from other sources). The authorities disbursed more than $2 billion in economic aid to Syria, and perhaps more to Egypt. They have committed $3 billion to the new republics of the former Soviet Union. Indeed the list of foreign aid claimants is long suggesting difficult choices for the Saudi government. See Twinam, "The Saudi Role in the New Middle East Order," p. 142.

9. See our extended analysis in Chapter 7.

TABLE 10.1 Saudi Arabia: Central Government Budgetary Expenditures, 1980-88
(billions of Saudi Riyals)

					Average Annual Rate of Growth		
Category	1980	1983	1985	1988	1980/ 1983	1983/ 1988	1985/ 1988
Human Resource Development	18.2	31.9	30.4	23.7	20.6	-5.8	-8.0
Transportation and Communications	24.4	32.5	22.2	10.9	10.0	-6.1	-21.1
Economic Resource Development	14.9	22.0	12.5	5.9	13.9	-23.1	-22.1
Health	9.8	17.0	16.1	10.8	20.2	-8.7	-28.5
Infrastructure	6.9	11.7	9.8	3.6	19.3	-21.0	-28.4
Municipal Services	12.7	26.2	17.1	7.0	27.3	-23.3	-25.7
Defense	56.5	92.9	79.9	50.1	18.0	-11.6	-14.4
Public Administration	48.0	44.6	43.9	25.1	-2.4	-10.9	-17.0
Government Lending Institutions	24.8	23.4	17.5	0.6	-1.9	-51.9	-67.5
Local Subsidies	0.0	11.2	10.5	5.3	—	-13.9	-20.4

Source: Based on data from Saudi Arabian Monetary Agency, *Annual Report*, various issues.

period, and with cutbacks accelerating to 67.5 percent for the more recent 1985/88 period. Second, after expanding at an average rate of 20.6 percent over the period following the second oil price increase (1980-82), human resource development averaged reductions of 5.8 and 8.0 percent per annum over the 1983-88 and 1985-88 period respectively. It appears, however, that of the major budgetary categories, human resource development experienced the smallest cutbacks during the 1983/88 period, and over the 1985/88 period. Third, despite the common perception of their high priority, defense expenditures contracted at a fairly rapid rate of 11.6 and 14.4 percent per annum over the 1983/88 and 1985/88 periods. Fourth, the same also applies to local subsidies which have declined at 13.9 and 20.4 percent per annum during the 1983/88 and 1985/88 periods respectively.

As a result of these differential rates of contraction, the relative shares of the major expenditure items have undergone a fairly large realignment. As Table 10.2 indicates, there has been a major increase in human resource development, from 8.5 percent of government expenditures in 1980 to 16.6 percent in 1988. Again, this increase reflects more the contraction of human resource expenditures at a rate considerably less than that experienced by other major categories. On the other hand, defense expenditures have maintained their dominant position increasing from around twenty-six percent of the budget in 1980 to over thirty-five percent by 1988. Third, government lending institutions have experienced a dramatic decline in importance, experiencing a decline in their share of government

TABLE 10.2 Saudi Arabia: Composition of Central Government Budget 1980-88
(Percent of Central Government Expenditures)

Category	1980	1982	1984	1985	1986	1987	1988
Human Resource Development	8.5	8.8	10.7	11.7	12.3	14.8	16.6
Transportation and Communications	11.3	11.9	9.6	8.5	7.2	6.8	6.7
Economic Resource Development	6.9	7.6	5.1	4.8	4.5	4.1	4.2
Health	4.6	4.6	5.2	6.2	6.4	7.0	7.7
Infrastructure	3.1	4.7	3.7	3.8	3.5	2.7	2.5
Municipal Services	5.9	8.8	7.3	6.6	5.9	5.1	5.0
Defense	26.1	27.7	29.0	30.7	32.0	34.0	35.5
Public Administration	22.2	14.4	18.2	16.9	19.8	19.4	17.8
Government Lending Institutions	11.5	8.3	7.7	6.7	4.7	2.2	0.4
Local Subsidies	0.0	3.1	3.5	4.1	4.2	3.9	3.8

Source: Based on data from Saudi Arabian Monetary Agency, *Annual Report*, various issues.

expenditure. This fell from over 11 percent (1980) to less than half a percent (1988). Fourth, infrastructure expenditures in 1988 were about one half their 1983 share. Finally, a similar percentage decline was experienced by transportation and communications.

Human resource expenditures have enabled the country to achieve significant increases in both enrollment rates and teacher student ratios. Although the country lags somewhat behind comparable countries in terms of enrollment rates, it appears to be closing the gap fairly quickly. In addition, the pupil teacher ratio is one of the lower ones in the region.[10] On the other hand, the relatively low number of pupils reaching the sixth grade indicates that perhaps a number of difficulties exist in terms of the quality of education received.[11] It is clear that the country has made some great strides in its efforts to increase the Kingdom's stock of human capital. However, it is just as apparent that a great deal more needs to be accomplished.

Operational Definitions

The evolving budgetary patterns examined above are suggestive of the manner in which the Saudi Government sets priorities for its expenditures. However, while certainly suggestive, simple comparisons in the

10. The World Bank, *Social Indicators of Development, 1988* (Washington D.C.: The World Bank, 1988), p. 209.
11. The World Bank, *Social Indicators of Development, 1989* (Baltimore: The Johns Hopkins University Press, 1989), p. 264.

TABLE 10.3 Saudi Arabia: Budgetary, 1979-1988 (in percentages)

	1979	1980	1981	1982	1983	1984	1985	1986	1987	1988
(Percent of Gross Domestic Product)										
Expected Deficit	0.0	4.4	21.3	10.1	0.0	10.0	14.7	0.0	19.1	12.7
Actual Deficit	6.6	-4.9	-21.3	-20.7	-0.3	6.8	14.3	18.6	32.1	24.7
Unanticipated Deficit	6.6	-8.8	-42.5	-30.2	-0.3	-3.2	-0.4	18.6	13.0	12.0

Government expenditures for 1987 are given as 137,422 million riyals for the first ten months of the year. This figure was proportioned up to 164,906 million Riyals for a twelve month period. The same was done for revenues. The deficit is computed as expenditures minus revenues. Therefore a positive figure indicates a deficit has occurred.

We assume that the expected deficit reflects a structural imbalance between revenues and expenditures. Similarly, transitory government deficits are assumed to be depicted by that component of the public deficit that was unexpected. The basic assumption underlying these proxies is that the expected deficit represents an on-going budgetary process that moves slowly over time and cannot be changed very rapidly.

Source: Computed from Saudi Arabian Monetary Agency, *Annual Report*, various issues.

relative growth of budgetary allocations to individual sectors (or their share of the total) are not sufficient in and of themselves to infer the existence of any particular pattern of budgetary priorities. These measures fail to capture the dynamics of the budgetary process.

While the government's fiscal position provides an insight into the public sector's budgetary priorities, a more sensitive (and indicative) indicator is the manner in which the government uses the deficits to fund or reduce allocation to certain budgetary categories (Table 10.3).

Three types of deficits are relevant: (a) Actual Deficits—those that actually occur during the budgetary period. Deficits are defined as the difference between government expenditure and government revenues.[12] (b) Expected Deficits—those anticipated at the beginning of the fiscal year, that is, the difference between anticipated expenditures and forecast revenues. And, (c) Unexpected Deficits—changes in the public sector's budgetary position, defined as the difference between the actual deficit in any year and the one that was expected to occur at the beginning of the fiscal year.

---

12. This definition of the deficit makes it easier to interpret the empirical results presented in Tables 10.5 through 10.9. That is, since an increase in the deficit has a positive sign, we can easily determine which budgetary categories owe their increased budgetary share to the government's willingness to run a higher deficit. Likewise, we can determine which budgetary categories are vulnerable to cutbacks associated with a growing fiscal deficit.

TABLE 10.4 Saudi Arabia: Fiscal Budgetary Impact Summary of Main Findings by Budgetary Category, 1979-1988 (standardized regression coefficients)

Budgetary Category	Unexpected Deficit	Expected Deficit	Actual Deficit	Expected Revenues
Human Resource Development	+	ins	+	ins
Health and Social Development	+	ins	+	ins
Transportation and Communications	-	ins	-	+
Economic Services	-	ins	-	+
Infrastructure	-	ins	-	+
Municipal Services	ins	ins	ins	+
Defense	ins	ins	ins	+
Government Lending	ins	-	-	+
Administration	ins	ins	ins	ins
Subsidies	ins	ins	ins	ins

+ = positive and consistently statistically significant at the 95 percent level;
- = negative and consistently statistically significant at the 95 percent level;
ins = insignificant at the 95 percent level.

Based on Tables 10.5 through 10.9.

Given the Saudi government's aversion in the 1980s to run deficits,[13] the relationship between a sector's budgetary share and the government's fiscal position (revenues minus expenditures) in any year should be indicative of the priority accorded that sector. More specifically, the government is willing to run deficits only for the purpose of funding high priority expenditures. The shares of these budgetary categories would therefore be expected to increase during periods of growing budgetary deficits. Similarly, their budgetary shares should decrease during periods of growing budgetary surplus, that is, during times when the government has ample funds to allocate to lower priority activities.

Incorporating these elements into a model of budgetary priorities (with expected signs for high priority categories in parenthesis) yields:

(A)   BUDGETARY SHARE = [DEFU, DEFA, DEFB, GOVEE]
                                      (+)   (+)   (-)   (+)

Where:

DEFU = the unexpected budgetary deficit
DEFA = the actual budgetary deficit
DEFB = the expected budgetary deficit
GOVEE = expected government expenditures.

_____

13. Robert E. Looney, *Economic Development in Saudi Arabia: Consequences of the Oil Price Decline* (Greenwich, Connecticut: JAI Press, 1990), chapter 11.

TABLE 10.5 Saudi Arabia: Fiscal Budgetary Impact of Human Resource
Development, Health and Social Development, 1979-1988
(standardized regression coefficients)

Category	Fiscal Measure				Statistics	
	Unexpected Deficit	Expected Deficit	Actual Deficit	Expected Revenues	r^2 (adj)	F
Human Resource Development						
(1)	0.74 (3.81)				0.732	22.9
(2)	0.99 (4.88)	0.36 (1.92)			0.805	17.5
(3)		-0.02 (-0.12)	0.85 (4.8)		0.805	17.5
(4)			1.00 (6.02)	0.27 (1.66)	0.866	26.9
(5)	0.72 (3.40)			-0.08 (-0.40)	0.697	10.2
Health and Social Development						
(6)	0.67 (2.55)				0.495	8.8
(7)	0.74 (2.15)	0.11 (0.35)			0.501	3.9
(8)		-0.17 (-0.63)	0.63 (2.17)		0.433	3.9
(9)			1.03 (4.28)	0.60 (2.58)	0.707	10.6
(10)	0.72 (2.63)			0.24 (0.90)	0.480	4.7

Equations estimated with a Cochraine-Orcutt iterative procedure to correct for serial correlation; r^2 (adj) is the adjusted (for degrees of freedom) coefficient of determination; F is the F-statistic; ( ) is the t-statistic of significance. All variables are defined in terms of their percentage of total (actual) government expenditures. The unexpected deficit is the difference between the actual deficit and that projected at the beginning of the fiscal year. Expected expenditures are those projected at the beginning of the fiscal year. The deficit is defined as expenditures minus revenues. Positive numbers therefore signify that a larger deficit increases budgetary shares.

Following our reasoning in Chapter 7, in terms of indices of budgetary priorities, we hypothesize that the unanticipated deficit should be the most indicative measure of the priority afforded a budgetary category. During the fiscal year additional (emergency) borrowing would likely only be used to assure adequate funding of the government's most important programs. The actual deficit is less volatile, and therefore would be next in importance as an indicator of priority. The expected deficit provides an initial bench mark measure of budgetary priorities.[14]

The expected level of government expenditures was entered as a control variable. That is, as the share of government expenditures in GDP increase, certain budgetary categories tend to have their budgetary shares

TABLE 10.6 Saudi Arabia: Fiscal Budgetary Impact of Transportation and
           Communications, Economic Services, 1979-1988 (standardized
           regression coefficients)

| | Fiscal Measure | | | | Statistics | |
Category	Unexpected Deficit	Expected Deficit	Actual Deficit	Expected Revenues	r^2 (adj)	F
Transportation and Communications						
(1)	-0.76				0.512	9.4
	(-3.29)					
(2)	-1.08	-0.63			0.793	16.3
	(-6.01)	(-3.24)				
(3)		-0.20	-0.92		0.795	16.4
		(-1.25)	(-6.01)			
(4)			-0.63	0.41	0.894	34.7
			(-4.95)	(3.03)		
(5)	-0.57			0.61	0.919	46.2
	(-5.94)			(6.14)		
Economic Services						
(6)	-0.80				0.554	10.9
	(-3.64)					
(7)	-1.09	-0.60			0.811	18.1
	(-6.36)	(-3.24)				
(8)		-0.17	-0.92		0.813	18.2
		(-1.12)	(-6.36)			
(9)			-0.69	0.35	0.887	32.4
			(-5.09)	(2.48)		
(10)	-0.61			0.56	0.901	37.5
	(-5.67)			(5.08)		

See Table 10.5 for definitions of terms and statistics.

systematically increase. This is the so-called Wagner's Law effect whereby
countries allocate a higher proportion of their resources to certain public
goods (usually defense) with the general expansion of the government in
the economy.[15]

---

14. As indicated in Chapter 7, this form of prioritizing is consistent with (although not
proof of) some form of lexicographic ordering of budgetary priorities. That is, the government tries to maintain certain budgetary categories at pre-defined levels. When these levels
are met, the authorities are then willing to provide additional funding for categories and programs of lower priority.

TABLE 10.7 Saudi Arabia: Fiscal Budgetary Impact of Infrastructure and
                    Municipal Services, 1979-1988 (standardized regression coefficients)

| | Fiscal Measure | | | | Statistics | |
Category	Unexpected Deficit	Expected Deficit	Actual Deficit	Expected Revenues	r^2 (adj)	F
Infrastructure						
(1)	-0.66				0.484	8.5
	(-2.33)					
(2)	-1.11	-0.57			0.699	10.3
	(-3.92)	(-2.45)				
(3)		-0.14	-0.94		0.700	16.5
		(-0.77)	(-3.92)			
(4)			-0.60	0.47	0.848	23.3
			(-3.19)	(2.75)		
(5)	-0.53			0.66	0.896	35.4
	(-4.20)			(5.46)		
Municipal Services						
(6)	-0.42				0.295	4.3
	(-1.27)					
(7)	-0.95	-0.70			0.616	7.4
	(-3.05)	(-2.63)				
(8)		-0.32	-0.81		0.615	7.4
		(-1.56)	(-3.06)			
(9)			-0.33	0.66	0.822	19.5
			(-1.64)	(3.56)		
(10)	-0.29			0.76	0.833	20.9
	(-1.80)			(4.93)		

See Table 10.5 for definitions of terms and statistics.

Results

Because of the limited number of observations, the available degrees of
freedom did not permit the estimation of the full model described in Equation A above. Instead, a series of regressions were estimated utilizing sets
of two of the independent variables. This method had the advantage of
testing for the consistency and robustness of results. That is, were the in-

15. For a description of this effect together with empirical evidence see Robert E. Looney,
Third World Military Expenditure and Arms Production (London: Macmillan, 1988), chapter 5.

TABLE 10.8 Saudi Arabia: Fiscal Budgetary Impact of Defense, Government Lending, 1979-1988 (standardized regression coefficients)

	Fiscal Measure				Statistics	
Category	Unexpected Deficit	Expected Deficit	Actual Deficit	Expected Revenues	r^2 (adj)	F
Defense						
(1)	0.45				0.166	2.6
	(1.35)					
(2)	0.24	-0.33			0.171	1.6
	(0.59)	(-0.83)				
(3)		-0.42	0.20		0.127	1.7
		(-1.28)	(0.59)			
(4)			0.90	1.00	0.761	13.7
			(4.23)	(4.72)		
(5)	0.64			0.67	0.569	6.3
	(2.58)			(2.75)		
Government Lending						
(6)	-0.59				0.221	3.3
	(-2.18)					
(7)	-0.92	-0.77			0.679	9.5
	(-4.88)	(-3.34)				
(8)		-0.41	-0.78		0.681	9.6
		(-2.03)	(-4.88)			
(9)			-0.40	0.55	0.789	16.0
			(-2.76)	(3.22)		
(10)	-0.36			0.67	0.782	15.3
	(-2.75)			(4.68)		

See Table 10.5 for definitions of terms and statistics.

dependent variables statistically significant across a number of alternative specifications?

The main results are presented in Tables 10.5 through 10.9 and summarized in Table 10.4. They provide a number of important insights concerning Saudi Arabian budgetary priorities, and in particular, the importance afforded human capital formation.

First, human resource development and health and social development were the only budgetary categories to have their budgetary shares increase with expanded unanticipated deficits. They were also the only sectors to have their budgetary shares increase during periods of increased

TABLE 10.9 Saudi Arabia: Fiscal Budgetary Impact of Administration, Subsidies, 1979-1988 (standardized regression coefficients)

Category	Unexpected Deficit	Expected Deficit	Actual Deficit	Expected Revenues	r^2 (adj)	F
Administration						
(1)	0.37				0.530	10.0
	(1.82)					
(2)	0.26	-0.24			0.506	5.1
	(1.08)	(-0.86)				
(3)		-0.34	0.22		0.507	5.2
		(-1.36)	(1.08)			
(4)			0.59	0.55	0.688	9.8
			(3.07)	(2.51)		
(5)	0.49			0.34	0.624	7.7
	(2.54)			(1.66)		
Subsidies						
(6)	0.05				0.634	15.4
	(0.22)					
(7)	-0.06	-0.09			0.591	6.8
	(-0.15)	(-0.32)				
(8)		-0.06	-0.05		0.597	6.8
		(-0.04)	(-0.02)			
(9)			0.10	0.33	0.693	10.0
			(0.32)	(1.48)		
(10)	-0.06			0.32	0.692	10.0
	(-0.28)			(1.57)		

See Table 10.5 for definitions of terms and statistics.

actual (realized) budgetary deficits.

Second, human resource development and health did not have their budgetary shares expanded with increases in expected revenues. This finding is consistent with the notion that because of their high priority their funding levels were assured. Therefore marginal increases in revenues could be safely used by the authorities to fund lower priority projects.

Third, the deficit-related expansion in human capital seems to have come in part at the expense of longer term investments in economic capacity. Specifically transportation and communications, economic services, and infrastructure all had their budgetary shares contract during periods of increased unexpected and actual deficits. This finding is consistent with the findings of Hicks and Kubisch.[16]

In general the main findings confirm the high priority granted human resource development by the Saudi authorities. Resources to this sector have been preserved relative to other sectors during the current period of austerity. Budgetary cuts have occurred in Saudi Arabia but education has been relatively spared. The long term nature of the commitment by the government to this sector is also evidenced by the fact that it appears relatively safe from budgetary cuts during periods of budgetary deficit. In fact deficits may owe their size to the government's commitment to provide adequate funding for these programs. The same could be said for health and social expenditure.

Conclusions

As a result of the Gulf War in 1990-91, and given increasing worries over both relations with its neighbors and internal security, defense spending may well have a higher priority than ever in Saudi Arabia. While defense retained its leading share of the budget during the recent period of relative fiscal austerity, the country does not appear to have fallen into the guns-versus-education syndrome. In fact the two types of expenditure appear to complement each other in the minds of the Saudi budgetary authorities.

The country appears firmly committed to its responsibility of providing educational opportunities for the majority of its citizens. There is little reason to believe this commitment will be sacrificed for the sake of maintaining foreign reserves. Apparently the government takes a longer term view in which the rate of return on its citizens is higher than the financial return on its foreign savings.

Saudi leaders seem well aware of the demographic constraints confronting their defense forces. Riyadh knows that the Kingdom remains dependent on foreign workers for technical skills, services, and labor. While tightly bound to the United States for defense, Saudi authorities must confront the prospect of Iraq continuing to rebuild its military after the Gulf War and of on-going trouble with an apparently belligerent Iran.

---

16. Norman Hicks and Anne Kubisch, "Cutting Government Expenditure in LDCs," *Finance and Development* 21, 3 (September 1984), pp. 37-40.

11

Pakistan: Budgetary Conflicts, Military Expenditures, and Infrastructural Development

Toward the end of the 1980s, a deteriorating resource situation caused a financial crisis in Pakistan. The government's budget deficit reached over 8% of Gross Domestic Product (GDP), inflation accelerated, the current account deficit doubled to over 4% of Gross National Product (GNP), the external debt service ratio reached 28% of export earnings, and foreign exchanges reserves fell in half to $438 million, equal to less than three weeks of imports.[1]

With this backdrop, not surprisingly, resources for investment are scarce in the 1990s. However, part of the problem also lies in the fact that current expenditures account for the major part of government budgetary allocations, averaging 65-75 percent in recent years. In fact, by the early 1990s defense expenditure and debt servicing together accounted for over 80 percent of current expenditure.[2]

While not necessarily arguing that reduced defense expenditures would free up sufficient funds to restore the country's deteriorating capital stock,[3] the purpose of this chapter is to examine in more depth the extent to which defense expenditures in this South Asian country have reduced allocations to other budgetary categories, especially physical infrastructure.

Specifically, this chapter addresses the following questions:

1. Have increases in defense expenditures in Pakistan come at the expense of both economic and social programs or, instead, have

---

1. The World Bank, *Pakistan: Current Economic Situation and Prospects*, Report No. 9283-PAK (Washington: The World Bank, March 22, 1991), p. ii.

2. EIU, *Pakistan, Afghanistan Country Profile 1990-91*. (London: Economist Intelligence Unit, 1990), pp. 39-40.

3. See above, Chapters 4 and 5.

the reductions been confided to one area?

2. If allocations to defense have reduced the share of resources flowing into longer term infrastructure investment, have these reductions been across the board or confined to certain categories such
   as transport, communications, or energy?

Recent Developments

By the late 1980s, the deteriorating economic situation forced the Pakistan Government to enter agreements with the International Monetary
Fund (IMF), The World Bank, the Asian Development Bank and several bi-
lateral donors to implement a medium-term adjustment and structural
reform program aimed at restoring resource balances to sustainable levels
while at the same time improving the efficiency of the economy.

To date, progress has been slow with the government unable to implement successfully a major tax reform. Complicating the problem is the fact
that the country's chronically low level of domestic savings has resulted in
an on-going deterioration of the nation's physical and human capital
stock. The uncertain outlook for aid flows is exacerbating these problems.

The suspension of both U.S. and IMF aid funds is a major limitation on
public spending. Even if inflows from these sources resume, the overall
thrust of government policy will be austere for some time, both because
commitments from the Arab Emirates States and other donors will be lower than in previous years and because a resumption of IMF funds will
require stricter adherence to the Fund's structural Adjustment Program.
The result is a deceleration in growth and associated tax revenues.

Pakistan's fiscal problems stem from two basic constraints. First, the
country has a narrow tax base and a heavy commitment of expenditure to
two current items, namely, defense, which consumes about a third of the
budget and debt servicing (Table 11.1). Both of these have proven to be ir-
reducible and in fact continued to increase even after the initiation in the
late 1980s of the government's austerity programs (Table 11.2). By the early
1990s, debt service burden continued to increase reaching 42 percent of
current expenditure. The annual development plan (ADP) has regularly
had to be revised downwards in the light both of reduced flows of foreign
aid, on which it depends heavily, and of local resources.[4]

While there is no doubt that a large proportion of private household
savings are being channeled to the public sector, there is some evidence
that the public sector is "crowding out" investment in small enterprise
manufacturing, that is, that government spending is displacing private
sector investment in these activities. In recent years the government has

---

4. EIU, *Pakistan, Afghanistan Country Profile 1990-91*, p. 40.

TABLE 11.1 Pakistan: Expenditure Patterns, 1973-1986 (budgetary shares)

Year	Economic	Military	Energy	Infrastructure	Social
1973	21.4	39.9	0.5	5.9	5.5
1974	20.9	34.1	1.2	5.6	5.4
1975	22.9	35.4	2.4	8.2	7.6
1976	27.8	36.2	2.9	9.6	9.3
1977	30.5	33.1	2.7	10.6	10.5
1978	30.0	31.4	2.2	9.4	9.3
1979	35.0	28.8	2.4	12.2	8.7
1980	37.2	30.6	2.5	11.6	8.3
1981	32.4	28.5	2.5	9.5	11.8
1982	31.0	33.5	2.6	9.8	10.1
1983	28.0	34.8	2.5	8.2	13.4
1984	27.8	32.3	2.2	8.8	14.2
1985	25.8	33.9	2.6	9.0	14.7
1986	34.5	29.5	2.5	13.2	12.2

Source: Compiled from the International Monetary Fund, *Government Financial Statistics Yearbook, 1990* and various years.

TABLE 11.2 Pakistan: Budgetary Components, 1988-89 to 1990-91 (millions of rupees)

Category	1988-89 Initial	1988-89 Revised	1989-90 Budget	1989-90 Revised	1990-91 Budget	% Change
Total Expenditure	193,553	190,239	208,316	214,809	230,185	7.2
Current	124,879	129,616	142,400	152,883	161,779	5.8
Defense	47,268	51,103	52,220	61,926	63,273	2.2
Debt Service	48,854	52,447	59,479	60,351	68,419	13.4
Subsidies	6,920	8,313	7,585	8,559	6,622	-22.6
Public Admin	8,547	5,561	6,073	5,863	7,017	19.7
Social Services	5,643	5,582	4,940	4,896	5,097	4.1
Annual Development Plan	50,538	48,000	56,000	55,000	63,000	14.5
Non-ADP Grant	18,136	12,713	9,915	6,926	5,406	-21.9
Total Resources	189,806	192,848	203,828	209,800	214,475	2.2
Internal	160,872	151,026	161,345	171,382	173,385	11.7
Direct Taxes	13,924	13,974	16,486	16,486	18,135	10.0
Indirect Taxes	77,901	77,275	89,323	90,229	97,343	7.9
Surcharges	17,285	15,009	10,939	11,051	12,238	10.7
Non-Tax	37,032	37,251	42,687	43,336	47,691	10.0
Less Transfers to provinces	-18,134	-23,931	-26,405	-30,879	-34,218	10.8
Net Capital Rec	27,325	27,081	24,776	35,610	25,649	-28.0
Self-Financing	5,540	4,367	3,539	5,549	6,547	18.0
External	28,934	41,822	42,483	38,419	41,090	7.0
Resources Gap	3,746	-2,520	4,488	5,009	15,710	213.6

Sources: Compiled from the International Monetary Fund, *Government Financial Statistics Yearbook*, various years and EIU, *Pakistan, Afghanistan: Country Profile, 1990-91* (London: Economist Intelligence Unit, 1990), pp. 41-42.

been able to attract large amounts of private savings through the National Savings Schemes. These schemes offer high rates of return compared to more conventional savings instruments offered by the commercial banks.[5] It would seem natural to assume that these schemes are a drain on the deposits of the commercial banks in Pakistan, thus constraining their ability to extend credit to small scale firms. Presumably large scale manufacturing firms have alternative sources of funding and are not affected.

The Federal budget has two main parts, the ordinary budget covering current expenditures, and the development budget (ADP) which covers capital investment and development programs. A portion of federal income is passed on as statutory and discretionary grants to the provinces, which have their own budgets and also raise some of their own resources.[6]

The country's constitution specifies areas of exclusive federal responsibility and areas of concurrent federal responsibility with residual powers left to the provinces.[7] Areas of exclusive federal responsibility include defense, external affairs, foreign aid, banking and currency, air, sea and land transport, national highways and strategic roads, communications, and fuels (oil and gas). The concurrent list includes functions such as maintenance of law and order, labor legislation and population planning. Residual areas of responsibility which devolve to the provinces include education, heath, agricultural support services, maintenance of the irrigation system, provincial and rural roads and internal law and order.

Under a constitutional provision the Federal Government and the provinces may entrust responsibilities to each other with mutual consent. Several functions of the provincial government in various sectors have been federalized under this constitutional provision. These include university education, medical colleges, agricultural universities, urban transport, preventive health programs, flood control, and canal rehabilitation.

Tax collections have historically represented a low proportion of GDP and continue to do so. In the early 1980s total tax revenues were 13.3 per-

---

5. Javed Hamid, et al., *Financing Public Sector Development Expenditure in Selected Countries: Pakistan* (Manila: Asian Development Bank, June 1988), p. 4.

6. In 1991 the central government and provinces agreed to a new plan that raises revenue to the four provinces by an estimated 58 percent by transferring an additional $930 million a year to them from the federal share. At the same time, however, the central government will no longer make up provincial budgetary deficits, nor pick up their surpluses. For an in-depth analysis of financial constraints confronting provincial governments and the relationship between investments in "hard" infrastructural development and inter-provincial and intra-provincial disparities in Pakistan, see Robert E. Looney and David Winterford, "Infrastructure and Regional Development in Pakistan," *Review of Urban and Regional Development Studies*, Vol. 5 (1993) pp. 95-114.

7. Hamid et al., *Financing Public Sector Development Expenditure*, pp. 21-22.

cent of GDP and had increased only to 14.2 percent by the late 1980s. The overall level of government revenue in Pakistan is lower than that in other comparable Asian countries by 2 to 3 percentage points. This reflects the weakness in the tax structure as well as the lower tax effort by the provisional governments.[8]

In terms of its composition, however, there are several important differences with the country's neighbors.[9] The level of Federal tax collected is the highest among comparable Asian countries, but this reflects more the commandeering of most sources of tax revenue by the Federal Government than the efficiency of the Federal tax system. Collections on income tax and corporate tax are low, both because of the loopholes in the existing tax structure and because of the exclusion of agricultural income. Also, domestic taxation on goods and services is low. On the other hand, taxes on international trade are among the highest in the world.

Overall, Pakistan's taxation system is geared towards raising Federal taxes in an administratively convenient manner (and transferring some of it under a revenue sharing formula to the provinces). However the structure of taxation exhibits serious flaws and is not optimal either in raising revenue or increasing economic efficiency.

By the late 1980s, attempts were being made at tax reform. For example, the 1987/88 budget initially provided for substantial increases in taxes and administrated prices in order to reduce the size of the resources gap. Widespread protests forced the government to withdraw most of the increases, and a revised budget was issued in which cuts were made in both current and development expenditure. The 1988/89 budget, produced by a caretaker government, made only limited changes to tax and expenditure levels, and therefore included a substantial fiscal deficit put initially at 69.5 billion rupees. The budget tried to introduce significant measures to reduce tax evasion by the business and trading classes, but these were later modified in the light of stiff opposition.

By the early 1990s, budgets introduced by the Government were cautious on both the fiscal and expenditure sides.[10] For example, the federal budget for 1991/92 continued the patterns of the past. It proposed a 10.1 percent increase in expenditure over the 1990/91 revised estimates, with defense and debt servicing again dominating expenditure. The debt interest payment of 80.8 billion rupees was 27 percent higher than the 1990/91 budget, and defense increased by 11.5 percent. These two items alone ab-

8. Hamid et al., *Financing Public Sector Development Expenditure*, p. 20.

9. Hamid et al., *Financing Public Sector Development Expenditure*, p. 20. Also see the comparative data on revenues and expenditures in The World Bank, *World Development Report, 1993* (New York: Oxford University Press, 1993).

10. EIU, *Pakistan, Afghanistan Country Profile 1990-91*, p. 40.

sorbed 99 percent of the projected 153.4 billion of federal revenue and accounted for 82 percent of current spending and 59 percent of total outlay.[11]

The Economics of Austerity: Budgetary Trade-offs

How typical are Pakistan's budgetary patterns? As we pointed out earlier, anecdotal evidence from other developing countries going through austerity programs suggests that officials follow ad hoc rules for making large contractions in a short period—cutting new rather than on-going projects, new rather than present employment, materials and travel expenses rather than personnel, and favoring ministries that are politically powerful or reducing those that have expanded most rapidly in the past. Some sectors are often thought to be more vulnerable than others to reductions; social sectors in particular are usually considered more and defense sectors less prone to budgetary cuts.[12]

On the other hand, as our analysis in Chapters 7 indicates, contrary to these expectations, we found several different patterns at work. Without repeating our earlier analysis, it is worthwhile highlighting some of the key findings before proceeding with our analysis of Pakistan. In brief, we found in the analysis of our sample countries that both social sectors and defense were relatively protected suggesting that there were high political costs associated with reducing them. Countries appeared to have been more willing to cut spending on infrastructure and production. The net result may have adverse implications for longer-term growth prospects but fewer early, direct, and immediate political costs.

These conditions were not very different for countries belonging to different income groups. The low income countries appear to have afforded slightly more protection to the social sectors and production and slightly less to administration ad defense, but the difference was marginal. The middle income countries, by contrast, gave more protection to administration and defense and less to productive and infrastructural sectors.

The apparent bias toward maintaining expenditures in social services and defense may reflect a government's preference for present consumption over investment and future consumption, since social sectors and defense typically have a heavy bias toward recurrent expenditures and within these there is a sizable employment component. Since social sectors and defense/administration are relatively labor intensive with high recur-

---

11. EIU, *Pakistan, Afghanistan: Country Report, No. 2* (London: Economist Intelligence Unit, June 25, 1991), p. 18-19.

12. See Chapter 7 for a review of the literature on budgetary trade-offs and our empirical assessment of trade-offs in the Middle East and South Asia.

rent costs, reducing expenditures on them not only cuts back services highly valued by the public, but also causes relatively high unemployment per unit reduction.

With these considerations in mind, it is possible to construct a model of budgetary trade-offs in Pakistan.[13] Clearly, before any assessment can be made of the country's ability (and willingness) to maintain or even improve its stock of physical capital, some idea must be gained about the factors affecting the government's expenditure decisions. To what extent have increasing budgetary deficits and debt levels affected infrastructural allocations? Have deficits and debt impacted only in the short run, or have longer term adjustments been associated with these variables? Must infrastructure compete with defense for funding?

On the surface Pakistan does not appear to be following very closely the international budgetary norm for low income countries. Its defense budget appears much less vulnerable than is the case in other countries, and its allocations to social sectors considerably lower than countries at similar levels of income. This might suggest that defense and social allocations are in direct competition for funds, with defense expanding at the expense of these programs.

However, part of the problem in drawing conclusions of this sort lies in the fact that, for the most part, Pakistan has been able to avoid major cuts in programs—its austerity programs in recent years have simply reduced the rate of expenditure increases.[14] Earlier, we suggested that the defense/ socio-economic trade-off is likely to be complex, and may be affected by several factors including austerity measures, budget deficits debt constraints, and foreign exchange shortages.[15] It should be noted also that the government's budgetary deficits and debt, while high by Pakistan's standards, are still considerably below that of many other developing countries. This means that debt and deficits have not necessarily forced reductions in any particular budgetary categories. Their increases may have actually aided in expanding allocations to certain programs.

---

13. Also see David Winterford and Robert E. Looney, "Public Sector Investment in Energy: Budgetary Constraints and Tradeoffs in Pakistan," *Resources Policy,* June 1993, pp. 98-105. In that article, Winterford and Looney develop a model of government budget allocations to energy. In applying the model to Pakistan, they analyze the impact of fiscal pressures, unanticipated government expenditure, and competing priorities.

14. Winterford and Looney, "Public Sector Investment in Energy: Budgetary Constraints and Tradeoffs in Pakistan."

15. See above, Chapter 7. In Pakistan's case, preliminary analysis indicated that regime changes during the period since 1972 have not played a major role in affecting budgetary priorities.

Operational Definitions

Based on the discussion above, it is clear three factors need to be included in a complete analysis of Pakistan's budgetary trade-offs.

Government Fiscal Deficit. This factor could work in either direction, depending in part on the priorities of the government toward infrastructure investment. Larger deficits may have occurred to maintain infrastructure or larger deficits to finance other expenditures may have forced the government to reduce allocations to infrastructure as part of an austerity program. For purposes of estimation the fiscal deficit is defined as expenditures minus revenues. It is lagged one year on the assumption that the extent of the current deficit may not be known with enough certainty to affect expenditure decisions significantly in the current fiscal year. That is, unanticipated revenue windfalls or shortfalls may come too late in the fiscal year to be reflected in significant shifts in expenditures.

The Debt Burden. This factor can also work both ways. Higher debt levels may reflect the high borrowing needs imposed by infrastructure investment or a high level of debt may have discouraged the government from committing itself to additional high cost physical capital investments. For purposes of estimation, the debt burden is defined as the percentage of the resources (of the Gross Domestic Product) available to service the debt.

Sectoral Priorities. This factor includes the guns-versus-butter analogy. Admittedly, infrastructure investment could be affected (positively or negatively) by movements in any of the other major budgetary categories. However, given the pervasiveness of defense expenditures, this relationship is undoubtedly the most significant budgetary category accounting for movements in infrastructural investment. The relationship between a sector's budgetary share and the government's fiscal position (here defined as expenditures minus revenues) in any year also should be indicative of the priority accorded that sector. Sectors with a relative high priority would be protected during periods of budgetary deficit—their budgetary shares should increase during periods of growing budgetary deficits. Similarly, their budgetary shares should decrease during periods of growing budgetary surplus, that is, during times when the government has ample funds to allocate to lower priority activities.

Incorporating these elements, the general form of the equation used for examining the determinants of Pakistan's budgetary shares in the short-run over the 1973-86 period was:[16]

---

16. The period for which consistent data is available. Budgetary data is from the IMF, *Government Finance Statistics Yearbook* (Washington D.C.: International Monetary Fund) various issues. Economic and debt data are from IMF, *International Financial Statistics Yearbook, 1990* (Washington D.C.: International Monetary Fund, 1990).

SHAREt = [GDEFt-1, MILXt, DEBTt]

Where:

SHAREt = the share of government expenditures accounted for the budgetary item

GDEFt-1 = the fiscal position (expenditures minus revenues in the previous year

MILXt = the share of defense expenditures in total government expenditures

DEBTt = total government debt as a share of Gross Domestic Product.

Results

Short-Run Impacts

The results of the budgetary analysis produced several distinct patterns (Tables 11.3 and 11.4). As Table 11.3 indicates, economic services as a whole were adversely affected by military expenditures. These expenditures were also retarded somewhat by the overall government debt. However they were not significantly affected by the government's fiscal position. Nevertheless great diversity occurred between the various types of economic services. Agriculture was largely complementary with military expenditures, but the budgetary shares of mining and other economic services were significantly reduced by increases in the military budget. In the aggregate infrastructure (transportation/communications) appeared to be reduced with increased military expenditures. Of note, further analysis indicated that this was only the case with regard to communications. Transportation (including road and rail) appears to be unaffected by movements in the defense budget. Also, increased indebtedness retarded allocations to economic services in general, yet infrastructure (with the notable exceptions of communications and energy) appears to have been largely expanded through increased indebtedness. Finally, in terms of budgetary priorities, agriculture, energy, and infrastructure (again with the exception of communications) did not have their budgetary shares reduced during periods of deteriorating budgetary positions, in fact, these categories had their shares expanded.

In sum, the picture that emerges from the analysis of economic allocations is one of perhaps conflicting government priorities. On the one hand, economic activities generally have a lower (often much lower) priority than military expenditures. On the other hand, the government appears willing to offset this bias, especially against infrastructure, through running higher deficits and increasing its overall debt burden.

A much different pattern characterizes the administrative/social categories of the budget (Table 11.4). Looking at Table 11.4, it is evident that, in

TABLE 11.3 Pakistan: Short-Run Budgetary Trade-offs Associated with Military Expenditures, 1973-1986 (standardized regression coefficients)

Budgetary Category

Total Economic Services (ES)
$ESt = $ 0.14 GDEFt-1 - 1.12 MILXt - 0.32 DEBTt
(1.54)   (-11.71)***   (-2.28)**
r^2(adj) = 0.727; F = 9.90; SE = 1.85

Agriculture (AG)
$AGt = $ 1.05 GDEFt-1 + 0.30 MILXt - 0.15 DEBTt
(32.07)***   (8.79)***   (-3.31)**
r^2(adj) = 0.976; F = 132.99; SE = 0.17

Mining (MIN)
$MINt = $ 0.19 GDEFt-1 - 0.81 MILXt - 0.36 DEBTt
(1.46)   (-5.96)***   (-1.80)
r^2(adj) = 0.423; F = 3.44; SE = 1.12

Energy (ENG)
$ENGt = $ 0.33 GDEFt-1 + 0.11 MILXt - 0.86 DEBTt
(5.55)***   (1.74)   (-9.27)***
r^2(adj) = 0.868; F = 22.92; SE = 0.27

Transportation/Communication (TC)
$TCt = $ 0.21 GDEFt-1 - 0.75 MILXt + 0.41 DEBTt
(2.18)*   (-7.07)***   (3.20)**
r^2(adj) = 0.799; F = 14.25; SE = 0.70

Transportation (TR)
$TRt = $ 0.64 GDEFt-1 - 0.13 MILXt + 0.59 DEBTt
(6.09)***   (-1.18)   (4.54)***
r^2(adj) = 0.779; F = 12.76; SE = 0.48

Roads (RD)
$RDt = $ 0.52 GDEFt-1 - 0.19 MILXt + 0.48 DEBTt
(3.23)**   (-1.11)   (2.52)**
r^2(adj) = 0.450; F = 3.72; SE = 0.26

Railroads (RA)
$RAt = $ 0.62 GDEFt-1 - 0.02 MILXt + 0.52 DEBTt
(7.66)***   (-0.27)   (4.55)***
r^2(adj) = 0.799; F = 14.25; SE = 0.35

Communications (COM)
$COMt = $ - 0.14 GDEFt-1 - 1.01 MILXt - 0.68 DEBTt
(-1.42)   (-9.63)***   (-4.41)***
r^2(adj) = 0.423; F = 3.44; SE = 1.12

Other Economic Services (OES)
$OESt = $ - 0.64 GDEFt-1 - 0.76 MILXt - 0.02 DEBTt
(-5.99)***   (-6.64)***   (-0.15)
r^2(adj) = 0.733; F = 10.14; SE = 1.31

Other Expenditures (OE)
$OEt = $ 0.10 GDEFt-1 - 0.59 MILXt - 0.18 DEBTt
(0.38)   (-2.15)*   (-0.66)
r^2(adj) = 0.323; F = 2.59; SE = 1.29

Equations estimated with SORITEC Statistical Analysis System Version 6.5 (Springfield, Virginia: Sorites group, 1990). Estimation method = ordinary least squares with a Cochrane-Orcutt iterative autocorrelation procedure to correct for first and second degree autocorrelation in the disturbances. r^2 = coefficient of determination from the differenced model; F = F statistic; SE = standard error of the regression; ( ) = t statistic of significance; *** significant at the 99th level of confidence; ** significant at the 95th level of confidence; * significant at the 90th level of confidence; t = current time period t-1 = previous time period. All variables except debt are defined in terms of their share of total government expenditures. Debt is defined in terms of its share of Gross Domestic Product.

general, when the administrative/social categories were affected by increased shares of the budget allocated to defense, it was in a positive manner. Specifically, public services, social security, welfare, housing and recreational/religious activities all had increases in their budgetaryshares simultaneously with defense.

Education appears little affected by defense and the debt. All levels of education appear unaffected by movements in the share of resources allocated to the military. Also, the government has not increased its debt to fund increased educational shares (nor has the debt burden resulted in austerity cuts in schools). On the other hand, the generally low priority afforded education is clearly evidenced by the negative sign on the deficit term—the austerity response stemming from increasing deficits has been concentrated in the country's educational programs, especially tertiary education, (however, the funding of "other" education was facilitated with increased levels of government deficits).

The other major budgetary category, health, did receive a high budgetary priority as evidenced by the positive sign on the deficit variable. However this bias was limited largely to "other" health, that is, health expenditures not associated with hospitals and clinics. Overall, one of the government's responses to rising debt burdens was to constrain allocations to the health sector.

As noted, the administrative/social sectors appear to come under a different set of budgetary rules than that experienced by the economic sectors, particularly infrastructure. While the economic activities clearly have a lower priority than the military, several of the social sectors, especially social security, welfare, recreation and housing, appear to be quite complementary with defense—their allocations expand (and contract) along with those of the military. Nevertheless, the government does not appear willing to accrue significantly higher levels of debt to maintain the shares of these sectors. Furthermore the government appears willing in some cases to direct the brunt of its austerity measures to particular sectors (for example, education and welfare).

Long-Run Impacts

Longer run budgetary trade-offs may have played a more significant role in reducing the share of resources allocated to the nation's capital stock. As a general proposition we hypothesize that individual budgetary allocations in Pakistan adjust over time to bridge the gap between what the country's authorities consider to be the optimal level of services, and that which exists at any point in time.

Obviously the factors determining the optimal level will vary considerably from program to program. For infrastructure it may be the level of economic activity, while for education it may be international comparisons

TABLE 11.4 Pakistan: Short-Run Administrative and Social Budgetary Trade-offs Associated with Military Expenditures, 1973–1986 (standardized regression coefficients)

Budgetary Category

Public Services (PS)
$RDt = $ 0.90 GDEFt-1 + 0.59 MILXt - 0.18 DEBTt
(8.54)*** (5.24)*** (-1.22)
r^2(adj) = 0.680; F = 8.09; SE = 0.81

Total Education (EDT)
$EDTt = $ - 0.68 GDEFt-1 - 0.10 MILXt - 0.06 DEBTt
(-2.76)** (-0.40) (-0.19)**
r^2(adj) = 0.101; F = 1.17; SE = 0.29

Primary and Secondary Education (EPS)
$EPSt = $ - 0.63 GDEFt-1 - 0.26 MILXt - 0.15 DEBTt
(-2.79)** (-1.18) (-0.67)
r^2(adj) = 0.571; F = 5.43; SE = 0.07

Tertiary Education (ET)
$ETt = $ - 1.07 GDEFt-1 - 0.12 MILXt - 0.10 DEBTt
(-8.90)*** (-0.92) (-0.74)
r^2(adj) = 0.770; F = 12.14; SE = 0.13

Other Education (EDO)
$EDOt = $ 0.56 GDEFt-1 + 0.16 MILXt + 0.12 DEBTt
(3.73)*** (1.02) (0.62)
r^2(adj) = 0.510; F = 4.47; SE = 0.27

Health (HE)
$HEt = $ 0.91 GDEFt-1 - 0.08 MILXt - 0.57 DEBTt
(11.27)*** (-0.91) (-5.57)***
r^2(adj) = 0.881; F = 25.75; SE = 0.10

Hospitals (HOS)
$HOSt = $ - 0.40 GDEFt-1 - 0.36 MILXt - 0.26 DEBTt
(-1.86) (-1.58) (-0.98)
r^2(adj) = 0.292; F = 2.38; SE = 0.06

Budgetary Category

Clinics (CLN)
$CLNt = $ - 0.61 GDEFt-1 - 0.32 MILXt - 0.21 DEBTt
(-2.64)** (-1.34) (-0.81)
r^2(adj) = 0.323; F = 2.59; SE = 0.01

Other Health (OHE)
$OHEt = $ 0.89 GDEFt-1 + 0.01 MILXt - 0.44 DEBTt
(7.18)*** (0.02) (-3.03)**
r^2(adj) = 0.787; F = 13.30; SE = 0.16

Social Security and Welfare (SSW)
$SSWt = $ - 0.95 GDEFt-1 + 0.31 MILXt + 0.30 DEBTt
(-6.92)*** (2.23)** (2.02)*
r^2(adj) = 0.800; F = 14.35; SE = 0.92

Social Security (SS)
$SSt = $ 0.65 GDEFt-1 + 0.87 MILXt + 0.22 DEBTt
(2.15)* (3.21)** (0.81)
r^2(adj) = 0.386; F = 3.10; SE = 0.02

Welfare (WEL)
$WELt = $ - 0.95 GDEFt-1 + 0.31 MILXt + 0.30 DEBTt
(-7.06)*** (2.21)* (2.03)*
r^2(adj) = 0.802; F = 14.50; SE = 0.91

Housing (HOS)
$HOSt = $ 0.86 GDEFt-1 + 0.54 MILXt + 0.39 DEBTt
(11.64)*** (6.97)*** (3.38)**
r^2(adj) = 0.745; F = 10.75; SE = 0.34

Recreation, Religious Activity (RRA)
$RRAt = $ 0.09 GDEFt-1 + 0.73 MILXt - 0.29 DEBTt
(0.27) (2.56)** (-1.00)
r^2(adj) = 0.314; F = 2.52; SE = 0.22

For a complete definition of terms and statistics, see Table 11.3

TABLE 11.5 Pakistan: Long-Run Economic Budgetary Trade-offs Associated with Military Expenditures, 1973-1986 (standardized regression coefficients)

Budgetary Category

Total Economic Services (ES)
ESt =   0.49 ESt-1 + 0.29 GDEFt - 0.78 MILXt
            (3.28)**   (2.76)1)**   (-5.32)***
r^2(adj) = 0.778; F = 12.67; SE = 1.67; Durbins h = - 2.62

Agriculture (AG)
AGt =   0.87 AGt-1 + 0.08 GDEFt + 0.32 MILXt
            (3.43)**   (0.03)   (1.84)
r^2(adj) = 0.732; F = 10.12; SE = 0.56; Durbins h = - 2.17

Mining (MIN)
MINt =   0.39 MINt-1 + 0.21 GDEFt - 0.60 MILXt
            (1.07)   (1.10)   (-1.98)*
r^2(adj) = 0.214; F = 1.91; SE = 1.31; Durbins h = - 2.13

Energy (ENG)
ENGt=   0.03 ENGt-1 + 0.23 GDEFt + 0.35 MILXt
            (0.16)   (1.10)   (2.22)*
r^2(adj) = 0.440; F = 3.61; SE = 0.55; Durbins h = - 2.11

Transportation/Communications (TC)
TCt =   - 0.12 TCt-1 + 0.23 GDEFt - 0.98 MILXt
            (-0.62)   (1.90)*   (-4.16)***
r^2(adj) = 0.613; F = 6.28; SE = 0.97; Durbins h = - 2.87

Transportation (TR)
TRt =   - 0.22 TRt-1 + 0.86 GDEFt - 0.54 MILXt
            (-0.67)   (3.16)**   (-1.93)*
r^2(adj) = 0.443; F = 3.65; SE = 0.76; Durbins h = - 2.14

Roads (RD)
RDt =   - 0.12 RDt-1 + 0.63 GDEFt - 0.51 MILXt
            (-0.06)   (4.24)****   (-2.47)**
r^2(adj) = 0.509; F = 4.46; SE = 0.25; Durbins h = - 1.93

Railroads (RA)
RAt =   - 0.44 RAt-1 + 0.99 GDEFt - 0.54 MILXt
            (-1.58)   (4.51)***   (-2.79)**
r^2(adj) = 0.801; F = 9.37; SE = 0.42; Durbins h = - 2.13

Communications (COM)
COMt=   1.04 COMt-1 + 0.46 GDEFt - 0.35 MILXt
            (3.30)**   (1.84)   (-1.64)
r^2(adj) = 0.557; F = 5.18; SE = 0.67; Durbins h = - 0.97

Other Economic Services (OES)
OESt =   - 0.03 OESt-1 - 0.64 GDEFt - 0.60 MILXt
            (-0.11)   (-2.24)   (-5.76)
r^2(adj) = 0.758; F = 11.45; SE = 1.25; Durbins h = - 2.02

Other Expenditures(OE)
OEt =   - 0.03 OEt-1 + 0.21 GDEFt - 0.49 MILXt
            (-0.08)   (0.75)   (-1.65)
r^2(adj) = 0.520; F = 2.52; SE = 1.30; Durbins h = - 2.43

For a complete definition of terms and statistics see Table 11.3.

TABLE 11.6 Pakistan: Long-Run Administrative and Social Budgetary Trade-offs Associated with Military Expenditures, 1973-1986 (standardized regression coefficients)

Budgetary Category

Public Services (PS)
$PS_t = 0.54\ PS_{t-1} + 0.36\ GDEF_t + 0.39\ MILX_t$
 $(2.09)^{**}$ (1.64) $(2.86)^{**}$
$r^2(adj) = 0.754;\ F = 11.21;\ SE = 0.71;\ Durbins\ h = 1.05$

Total Educational (EDT)
$EDT_t = 0.65\ EDT_{t-1} - 0.26\ GDEF_t + 0.17\ MILX_t$
 (1.77) (-0.88) (0.61)
$r^2(adj) = 0.092;\ F = 0.71;\ SE = 0.32;\ Durbins\ h = -1.77$

Primary/Secondary Education (EPS)
$EPS_t = 0.98\ EPS_{t-1} - 0.03\ GDEF_t - 0.04\ MILX_t$
 $(2.38)^{**}$ (-0.09) (-0.16)
$r^2(adj) = 0.449;\ F = 3.71;\ SE = 0.07;\ Durbins\ h = -2.68$

Tertiary Education (ET)
$ET_t = 0.57\ ET_{t-1} - 0.52\ GDEF_t - 0.06\ MILX_t$
 (7.74) (-6.69) (-1.12)
$r^2(adj) = 0.964;\ F = 91.01;\ SE = 0.05;\ Durbins\ h = -1.16$

Other Education (EDO)
$EDO_t = - 0.70\ EDO_{t-1} + 0.71\ GDEF_t - 0.26\ MILX_t$
 (-4.16) (5.27) (-1.53)
$r^2(adj) = 0.729;\ F = 9.97;\ SE = 0.20;\ Durbins\ h = -0.08$

Health (HE)
$HE_t = 0.74\ HE_{t-1} + 0.30\ GDEF_t + 0.09\ MILX_t$
 $(3.71)^{***}$ (1.78) (0.45)
$r^2(adj) = 0.521;\ F = 4.62;\ SE = 0.21;\ Durbins\ h = -0.95$

Hospitals (HOS)
$HOS_t = 0.18\ HOS_{t-1} - 0.33\ GDEF_t - 0.29\ MILX_t$
 (0.37) (-0.94) (-1.22)
$r^2(adj) = 0.483;\ F = 2.18;\ SE = 0.07;\ Durbins\ h = -1.98$

Budgetary Category

Clinics (CLIN)
$CLN_t = - 0.06\ CLN_{t-1} - 0.73\ GDEF_t - 0.13\ MILX_t$
 (-0.23) $(-3.02)^{**}$ (-0.59)
$r^2(adj) = 0.476;\ F = 4.03;\ SE = 0.01;\ Durbins\ h = 0.94$

Other Health (OHE)
$OHE_t = 0.67\ OHE_{t-1} + 0.30\ GDEF_t + 0.07\ MILX_t$
 $(2.80)^{**}$ (1.48) (0.36)
$r^2(adj) = 0.455;\ F = 3.78;\ SE = 0.25;\ Durbins\ h = -1.36$

Social Security/Welfare (SSW)
$SSW_t = 0.65\ SSW_{t-1} - 0.48\ GDEF_t + 0.42\ MILX_t$
 $(6.44)^{***}$ $(-4.79)^{***}$ $(4.02)^{***}$
$r^2(adj) = 0.906;\ F = 22.43;\ SE = 0.75;\ Durbins\ h = -2.13$

Social Security (SS)
$SS_t = 1.09\ SS_{t-1} + 0.04\ GDEF_t + 0.70\ MILX_t$
 $(5.18)^{***}$ (0.26) $(2.92)^{**}$
$r^2(adj) = 0.273;\ F = 2.25;\ SE = 0.02;\ Durbins\ h = -0.30$

Welfare (WEL)
$WEL_t = 0.66\ WEL_{t-1} - 0.46\ GDEF_t + 0.33\ MILX_t$
 $(7.38)^{***}$ $(-5.22)^{***}$ (3.44)
$r^2(adj) = 0.883;\ F = 26.04;\ SE = 0.70;\ Durbins\ h = -0.41$

Housing (HOS)
$HOS_t = - 0.13\ HOS_{t-1} + 0.99\ GDEF_t + 0.11\ MILX_t$
 (-0.69) $(6.10)^{***}$ (0.94)
$r^2(adj) = 0.803;\ F = 14.62;\ SE = 0.30;\ Durbins\ h = -1.10$

Recreation/Religious Affairs (RRA)
$RRA_t = - 0.19\ RRA_{t-1} - 0.63\ GDEF_t + 0.69\ MILX_t$
 (-0.73) (-2.14) (3.84)
$r^2(adj) = 0.701;\ F = 8.83;\ SE = 0.15;\ Durbins\ h = 0.24$

For a complete definition of terms and statistics see Table 11.3.

of literacy and so on. The speed at which the gap between actual and optimal levels is bridged is not only a function of inertia in the federal allocation process but also conditioned by budgetary constraints and preemption of funds by the military.

Operationally these factors can be modeled by utilizing a distributed lag estimating system along the lines originally suggested by Koyc.[17] Operationally this involves introducing the lagged value of the respective budgetary share in the regression equation:[18]

SHAREt = [SHAREt-1, GDEF, MILXt]

Where:[19]

SHAREt = the share of government expenditures accounted for the budgetary item

SHAREt-1 = the share of government expenditures accounted for the budgetary item in the previous year

GDEFt = the fiscal position (expenditures minus revenues)

MILXt = the share of defense expenditures in total government expenditures.

In this structural form, the budgetary share will not only be affected in the current time period but it will also continue to be affected over time. In other words, the effect of reduced resource availability is not a year-to-year reaction but is spread out and "decays" over time.

The results of this analysis again produced some interesting findings (Tables 11.5 and 11.6). Looking at Table 11.5, impacts for economic allocations are largely confined to the short run (as evidenced by the generally statistically insignificant values for the lagged budgetary share). On the other hand, the general negative trade-off with defense expenditures (with the exception of energy) is still in evidence. The defense impact was offset somewhat by the generally positive sign of the budgetary deficit. That is, despite having a distinctly lower priority than defense, the government was unwilling to further reduce allocations to infrastructure as part of a general austerity program.

The results for administrative/social expenditures (Table 11.6) were roughly equivalent to those obtained in the short-run analysis. The results in Table 11.6 again reveal that the military (when significant) is comple-

---

17. L. M. Koyc, *Distributed Lags and Investment Analysis* (Amsterdam: North-Holland, 1954).

18. For a discussion of distributed lag equations see Potluri Rao and Roger Miller, *Applied Econometrics* (Belmont, California, 1971), p. 165.

19. To maintain comparable degrees of freedom with the short run analysis, the debt burden was omitted from this analysis. In any case preliminary investigations indicated that this variable had minimal longer term influence over most expenditure categories.

mentary with social/administrative activities. However, these programs do not fare particularly well during periods of austerity (with the notable exception of other education, and housing). It should be noted, however, that budgetary impacts appear to last (the generally statistical significance of the lagged budgetary share term) over a longer time period than in the case of economic services.

Conclusions

For most of the 1980s Pakistan's economy grew at a high rate of 6.5 percent per annum in real terms. Despite this rapid growth and some reform initiatives, the economy showed a number of structural weaknesses. These included a weak public resource position due to a narrow and inelastic revenue base; high consumption expenditure, particularly defense, resulting in excessive budget deficits; and a high and growing debt service burden resulting from the country's heavy reliance on external borrowing to finance its economic growth in the 1980s.[20] Our analysis has shown that these factors are often interrelated, but in a complex manner. That is, their impact on any specific government program is difficult to predict *a priori*.

Although in general most types of infrastructure investment should increase with possible defense cutbacks, the same cannot be said for social expenditures. On the other hand, movements in defense allocations appear to have only a transitory affect on the share of government expenditures directed towards physical capital formation. Instead, the willingness and ability of the government to borrow will largely condition the share of resources devoted to the nation's infrastructural investments.

Social programs are even more difficult to forecast. Part of the problem lies in the fact that the Federal government has effectively vested itself with full power both with regard to revenue collection and expenditure. This situation could well be workable except for the fact that key programs—education, health and housing—are with the provinces and the provinces do not have the revenue resources to do justice to this responsibility.[21] This situation may change significantly, however, following the central government's decision to share an increased proportion of revenues with the provinces.[22]

20. The World Bank, *Pakistan: Current Economic Situation and Prospects*, p. i.
21. Hamid et al., *Financing Public Sector Development Expenditure*, p. 24.
22. See Looney and Winterford, "Infrastructure and Regional Development in Pakistan," pp. 95-114.

Defense Expenditures in the Middle East and South Asia: Sustainability and Projections

12

Thresholds and Forecasts for Defense Expenditures in the Middle East and South Asia

Overall, our analysis in the preceding chapters of the economic causes and consequences of defense spending in the Middle East and South Asia indicates that shifts in resource allocation associated with defense spending may significantly alter overall economic performance. Whether this alteration is positive or negative is subject to wide variation among countries. These variations reflect the underlying economic health of the individual countries and their relative ability to minimize potential adverse effects associated with increased defense burdens.

Economic performance has strongly influenced defense spending patterns in the Middle East and South Asia. In the period immediately following the 1973/74 oil price increases, when the region as a whole and the Middle East in particular experienced unprecedented growth in economic output and exports, defense spending increased dramatically. In the 1980s, defense spending in the Middle East declined sharply due to slumping oil revenues and sluggish economic growth. In South Asia, more buoyant growth permitted a steady rise in defense spending during the 1980s. The early 1990s have confronted regional decision-makers with a troubling combination of lower oil prices and enduring security concerns. The decade began with the unprecedented–and costly–display of coalition warfare in the Middle East during the Gulf War. It has continued to be marked by ongoing rivalries for regional dominance in the Middle East and South Asia, recurring problems with internal stability in several sample countries, and declining oil prices.

Over the long-term, defense spending has not hindered growth in most of the sample countries. This finding indicates that the average share of GDP to defense has probably remained within economically sustainable limits. From 1960 to 1987, India, Egypt, Syria, Algeria and Saudi Arabia all experienced substantial periods of positive net economic benefits from defense expenditures. The positive effects of defense spending were more pronounced in the wealthier, less resource-constrained countries. In Saudi Arabia, for example, increased defense spending has stimulated higher demand for goods and services, public and private investment, and increased spending on education. In arms producing countries such as India, modest levels of defense spending have actually stimulated growth.

In contrast, defense expenditures in Israel have stimulated investment, but their longer run impact on growth appears neutral. Pakistan has been less successful in deriving economic benefits from its military expenditures, and at times defense has impacted negatively on the economy. Egypt has also experienced periods of negative economic impacts stemming from defense expenditures.

Although the long-term effect of defense spending on the economic performance of the most of the sample countries has not been negative, neither has the near term impact been entirely positive. Increased defense spending has, in some countries, fueled imports, spurred inflation, raised foreign debt levels and reduced budgetary allocations to important developmental activities. For example, in India, Pakistan, Algeria and Syria, defense spending has increased the foreign debt levels. In Saudi Arabia, the non-oil economy seems to have become increasingly dependent on heavy military spending, thus hampering efforts toward economic diversification. In Egypt, India, Pakistan and Algeria, military spending appears to have diverted significant resources from areas such as human and physical capital formation. When defense spending absorbs an increasing share of government budgets, it usually does so at the expense of agriculture, economic services and health care.

In certain countries, in particular Egypt and Pakistan, surges in defense spending associated with arms races and intra-regional conflicts have slowed short-term economic growth. Apparently, these countries attempted to expand defense to levels inconsistent with productive absorption into the domestic economy.

As for the future, it is likely that key countries will continue to stimulate defense spending in the 1990s. The result may be a deterioration in economic performance in these countries, particularly if they are simultaneously confronted with foreign exchange scarcity. External debt from both development and commercial sources has been used to support military spending in the region. In large part, these funds have helped to neutralize many of the adverse effects associated with defense spending. The inability of countries such as Algeria, Pakistan, Egypt, and Syria to increase their external borrowing increases the likelihood that defense expenditures will cease to have positive economic impacts. In the case of Pakistan, limited access to external financing may result in defense expenditures retarding overall economic growth. It is also likely that key rivalries in the region and problems with internal security will continue to stimulate defense spending in the 1990s. This may result in deteriorating economic performance in the sample countries, particularly if they are simultaneously confronted with foreign exchange scarcity.

The findings presented in this study represent an initial step toward identifying the impact of defense expenditures on the more important economies in the Middle East and South Asia. It is important to emphasize that our analysis found that for most of the sample countries defense expenditures have not had the adverse effects often ascribed to them, except in situations where arms races or warfare accelerated military spending to levels which the domestic economy could not efficiently absorb. This suggests that a threshold exists beyond which defense expenditure becomes detrimental to overall economic performance. These thresholds would, of course, vary by country and over time, but barring sudden and dramatic political or economic change, they can be forecast at least for the short term. Consequently, drawing on the analysis presented in this book, we conclude our assessment by forecasting defense expenditure thresholds and short-term defense expenditure patterns for the individual countries in our sample.

Defense Expenditures in the Middle East and South Asia: Thresholds and Short-Term Projections

Saudi Arabia

As a result of the 1990-1991 Gulf War, concern over Iran's regional ambitions, the uncertain Middle East peace process, and increasing worries about internal security, defense spending will likely continue to have a high priority in Saudi Arabia and will likely increase over the next several years. In time, such a trend could have negative consequences for the Saudi Arabian economy, which appears to be at its military expenditure threshold.

Defense expenditures in Saudi Arabia cease to have a positive impact on the non-oil economy when they grow at a rate of over 25 percent per annum and/or average over 44 percent of non-oil GDP for a decade or more. In the decade 1978-88, defense expenditures comprised 44% of non-oil GDP.

With the prospect of lower oil revenues through the mid-1990s, together with the higher rates of increase in defense expenditures since the Gulf War, the Kingdom may have difficulties expanding defense expenditures further without appreciable negative effects on the domestic economy.

One possible factor limiting the potential negative impact of defense expenditures on the economy stems from the slowdown in investment in infrastructure in recent years to facilitate defense expenditures. However, if the resulting infrastructure deficiencies limit the expansion of the non-oil economy, then this too increases the prospect that defense expenditures may provide an increasingly negative stimulus to the economy.

Algeria

Allocations to the military will cease to have a positive stimulus on the economy if they are sustained at a level of over 3.5 percent of Gross Domestic Product. In the decade 1978-1988 they accounted for 3.2% of GDP. Since the early 1990s, Algerian authorities have confronted a significant internal security threat arising from new Islamic forces seeking power. Consequently, defense spending has risen as the authorities use the Algerian military to maintain internal order. Whatever the political or military merits of the option being pursued by Algerian authorities in addressing severe internal instability, our *economic* analysis indicates a negative impact on the economy if Algeria continues its recent pattern of relatively heavy defense spending.

In the years since the oil price declines in 1982 and during the resulting Third World debt crisis, Algeria was one of the few less developed countries to maintain access to substantial commercial credits. Committed to avoiding a rescheduling that would limit its access to international financial markets, the country borrowed from commercial banks through its most difficult years of economic crisis. The country has made every effort to avoid rescheduling its debt, and, assuming the significant internal threat is managed, Algeria should be able to meet its debt obligations without rescheduling. However, given the relatively high impact of defense expenditures on imports, the authorities need to monitor defense expenditures very carefully in the short term if they are to avoid jeopardizing the country's credit worthiness. Given this situation, if defense expenditures return to somewhat below their threshold level they should provide a positive, albeit weak stimulus to the country's economic expansion.

Egypt

Egyptian allocations to defense will have a negative impact on the economy if they grow at rates over 9 percent per annum for an extended period. The Gulf War and efforts to combat an internal Islamic threat have led to an expansion in Egyptian defense expenditures. However, given the below average rates of expansion in military expenditures during the last decade, the economy should receive a slight stimulus from these allocations (historically, defense expenditures have had a positive impact on the economy when they average rates of growth of less than 6.0 percent per annum).

On the other hand, the Gulf crisis cost the country an estimated $2 billion per year in lost remittances during the early 1990s. If the United States were to forgive Egyptian military debt and/or wave servicing of the debt, the balance of payments effect of defense expansion will not put a severe strain on the country's foreign exchange reserves. Cancellation of Egyptian military debt by the United States would also enable the country to move towards the more technical end of the spectrum of production through the acquisition of foreign designs, parts and production technology.

Syria

Iraqi aggression against Kuwait caused repercussions in Syria as elsewhere in the region. In the early 1990s, Damascus was forced to increase its military spending given the Gulf War, persistent regional instability and continuing Israeli rearming. In this regard, Syrian defense expenditures will cease to produce a positive stimulus to the economy if they grow at over 14 percent per annum for a decade.

The country's debt service problems have become more severe in recent years and lower oil prices have added further pressure. While no negative impacts from defense are likely, given the already precarious state of the Syrian economy, a sudden surge in defense spending may not produce many positive benefits. In contrast, a moderate step-up in Syrian military spending brought on by the Gulf crisis should not place severe strains on the economy. These expenditures might even provide a mild stimulus to growth.

Israel

As a result of the Gulf War, Israel will almost certainly increase its defense spending over the next several years. There is no real evidence that Israeli defense expenditures have either diverted resources away from capital formation or reduced other major sources of growth, as long as growth in defense spending was confined to under 18 percent per annum over a decade. The negative 4.3 percent per annum contraction in defense expenditures over the last ten years should leave considerable scope for a military buildup without adverse effects on the economy.

This assessment must be qualified, however, by the fact that grants from the United States have helped neutralize any latent negative effects that might otherwise have been associated with the country's heavy defense burden. Given current US budgetary conservatism Israel's defense burden may begin to contribute to the country's economic deterioration before rates of growth in the 18 percent range are reached.

Pakistan

Defense expenditures in Pakistan have a negative impact on GDP when they increase to over 6.5 percent of GDP for a decade or more. During the 1978-88 decade, this threshold had already been crossed with defense expenditures averaging 6.8%.

Defense spending in Pakistan appears to be fixed and it is unlikely to be cut during periods of austerity. Past defense spending has already inflicted a large debt burden on the country. Continued spending at recent high levels or an increase in military expenditures will put severe strains on an already struggling economy.

India

Defense expenditures in India cease to have a positive impact when they grow at rates greater than 3.0 percent per annum for a decade or more. They averaged 6.8 percent during the 1977-87 decade, well beyond this threshold. Recently, Indian defense spending has not grown much faster than the economy as a whole. Instead, defense expenditures have fluctuated between 2 and 3.5 percent of GNP. It may be that during the 1990s India will manage to be below the constraints that hamper the relationship between economic growth on the one hand and government purchases of military services on the other. However, if the conflict with Pakistan over Kashmir means a resumption of high military spending, then it is unlikely that defense spending (including spin-offs from Indian defense industries) will contribute to India's economic growth.

Conclusion

While many other observers have examined the political and security implications of military expenditures and the acquisition of advanced weapons in the Middle East and South Asia, we have attempted in this book to provide an economic assessment of the causes and consequences of regional defense expenditures. It is vital that political leaders, military specialists, and economic planners understand the economic dynamics of defense expenditures in the Middle East and South Asia. Our analysis has sought to provide a greater appreciation of key economic issues central to defense spending, namely, the economic dimensions underlining regional arms races, the impact of defense expenditures on economic growth, the linkages between defense expenditures and human capital development, and the budgetary impacts of defense expenditures. It is our hope that a greater appreciation of the economic dimensions of defense expenditures in the Middle East and South Asia will provide another basis enhancing prospects for regional peace, stability, and prosperity.

Selected Bibliography

Ahrari, M.E., "Arms Race in the Persian Gulf: The Post-Cold War Dynamics," in M.E. Ahrari and James H. Noyes, eds.,*The Persian Gulf After the Cold War*. Westport, CT: Praeger, 1993, pp. 188-192.

———, "Iran in the Post-Cold War Persian Gulf Order," in M.E. Ahrari and James H. Noyes, eds., *The Persian Gulf After the Cold War*. Westport, CT: Praeger, 1993, pp. 81-98.

——— and James H. Noyes, eds., *The Persian Gulf After the Cold War*. Westport, CT: Praeger, 1993.

Alnasrawi, Abbas, "Economic Consequence of the Iraq-Iran War," *Third World Quarterly*, 8, 3 (July 1986), p. 872.

Ames, Barry and Ed Goff, "Education and Defense Expenditures in Latin America: 1948-68," in Craig Liske, William Loehr, and John McCamant, eds, *Comparative Public Policy: Issues, Theories and Methods*. New York: John Wiley and Sons, 1975.

Amirahmadi, Hooshang, *Revolution and Economic Transition: The Iranian Experience*. Albany, New York: The State University of New York Press, 1990.

Babin, Nehma, "Military Spending, Economic Growth, and the Time Factor," *Armed Forces and Society* 15, 2 (Winter 1989), pp. 249-262.

Benoit, Emile, "Growth and Defense in Developing Countries," *Economic Development and Cultural Change* 26, 2 (January 1978), pp. 271-280.

Biswas, B. and R. Ram, "Military Expenditures and Economic Growth in Less Developed Countries: An Augmented Model and Further Evidence," *Economic Development and Cultural Change* 4, 2 (January 1986), pp. 361-72.

Blejer, Mario and Moshin Khan, "Public Investment and Crowding Out in the Caribbean Basin Countries," in Michael Connolly and John McDermott, eds., *The Economicsof the Caribbean Basin*.New York: Praeger Publishers, 1985, pp. 219-236.

Caiden, N. and A. Wildavsky, *Planning and Budgeting in Poor Countries*. New York: John Wiley, 1974.

Chan, Steven, "Military Expenditures and Economic Performance," in United States Arms Control and Disarmament Agency, *World Military Expenditures and Arms Transfers*, 1986. Washington D.C.: USACDA, 1987, pp. 29-38.

Chatterji, Manas, "A Model of Resolution of Conflict Between India and Pakistan," *Peace Research Society Papers XII* (1969).

Chubin, Shahram, "Iran and the Lessons of the War with Iraq: Implications for Future Defense Policies," in Shelley A. Stahl and Geoffrey Kemp, eds., *Arms Control and Weapons Proliferation in the Middle East and South Asia*. New York: St. Martin's Press, 1992, pp. 95-119.

Clawson, Patrick "Islamic Iran's Economic Politics and Prospects," *Middle East Journal* 42, 3 (Summer 1988), p. 371.

Cummings, John, Hossein Askari, and Michael Skinner, "Military Expenditures and Manpower Requirements in the Arabian Peninsula," *Arab Studies Quarterly* 2, 1 (Winter 1980), pp. 38-49.

Daneshku, Scheherazade, "Iran in No Position to Fill Oil Supply Gap," *Financial Times* (August 30, 1990), p. 23.

———, "Iranian Exiles Returning to the Economic Fold," *Financial Times* (May 3, 1990), p. 5.

———, "Frail Economic Underpinning," *The Middle East* 194 (December 1990), p. 8.

de Masi, Paula and Henri Lorie, "How Resilient are Military Expenditures?" *International Monetary Fund Staff Papers* (March 1989), pp. 130-165.

Deger, Saadet and Somnath Sen, "Military Expenditure, Spin-off and Economic Development," *Journal of Development Economics* 13, 1-2 (August-October 1983), pp. 67-83.

Deger, Saadat, "Human Resources, Government Education Expenditure and the Military Burden in Less Developed Countries," *Journal of Developing Areas* 20, 1 (October 1985), pp. 37-48.

——— and Robert West, "Introduction: Defense Expenditure, National Security and Economic Development in the Third World," in Saadat Deger and Robert West, *Defense, Security and Development*. London: Francis Pinter, 1987, pp. 1-16.

——— and Robert West, *Defense, Security and Development*. London: Francis Pinter, 1987.

Economist Intelligence Unit, *Iran: Country Profile*. London: Economist Intelligence Unit, various issues.

———, *Iran: Quarterly Review*. London: Economist Intelligence Unit, various issues.

———, *Pakistan, Afghanistan: Country Report*. London: Economist Intelligence Unit, various issues.

———, *Saudi Arabia: Country Report*. London: Economist Intelligence Unit, various issues.

El Mallakh, Ragaei and Jacob K. Atta, *The Absorptive Capacity of Iraq*. Lexington, Mass: Lexington Books, 1981.

Emile, Benoit, "Growth and Defense in Developing Countries," *Economic Development and Cultural Change* 26, 2 (January 1978), 271-280.

Encarnacion, J., "Some Implications of Lexicographic Utility in Development Planning," *The Philippine Economic Journal* IX, 2 (Second Semester, 1970), pp. 231-240.

Faini, Riccardo, Patricia Annez, and Lance Taylor, "Defense Spending, Economic Structure, and Growth: Evidence Among Countries and Over Time," *Economic Development and Cultural Change* 32, 3 (April 1984), pp. 487-498.

Frederiksen, Peter C. and Robert E. Looney, "Defense Expenditures and Growth in Developing Countries," *Journal of Economic Development* (July 1982), pp. 113-126.

———, "Defense Expenditures and Economic Growth in Developing Countries," *Armed Forces and Society* 9, 4 (Summer 1983), pp. 633-646.

———, "Another Look at the Defense Spending and Development Hypothesis," *Defense Analysis* 1, 3 (September 1985), pp. 205-210.

Frederiksen, P.C. and C.J. LaCivita, "Defense Spending and Economic Growth: Time Series Evidence on Causality for the Philippines, 1956-1982," *Journal of*

Philippine Development, 14 (Second Semester 1987), pp. 354-60.

Granger, C.W.J., "Investigating Causal Relations by Econometric Models and Cross-Spectral Methods," *Econometrica* 37, 3 (July 1969), pp. 424-438.

Grobar, Lisa M. and Richard C. Porter, "Benoit Revisited: Defense Spending and Economic Growth in LDCs," *Journal of Conflict Resolution* 33, 2 (June 1989), pp. 318-345.

Halliday, Fred, "The Revolution's First Decade," *Middle East Report* 19, 1 (January-February 1989), p. 19.

Hamid, Javed, et al., *Financing Public Sector Development Expenditure in Selected Countries: Pakistan*. Manila: Asian Development Bank, June 1988.

Harris, Geoffrey, "The Determinants of Defence Expenditure in the ASEAN Region," *Journal of Peace Research* 23, 1 (March l986), pp. 41-49.

———, "Economic Aspects of Military Expenditure in Developing Countries: A Survey Article," *Contemporary Southeast Asia* 10, 1 (June 1988), pp. 82-102.

——— and Newman Kusi, "The Impact of the IMF on Government Expenditures: A Study of African LDCs," *Journal of International Development* (1992), pp. 73-85.

———, Mark Kelly and Pranowo, "Trade-offs Between Defense and Education/Health Expenditures in Developing Countries," *Journal of Peace Research* 25, 2 (June 1988), pp. 165-177.

Hashim, Ahmad, "Iraq and the Post-Cold War Order," in M.E. Ahrari and James H. Noyes, eds., *The Persian Gulf After the Cold War*. Westport: Praeger, 1993, pp. 99-124.

Hess, Peter and Brendan Mullan, "The Military Burden and Public Education Expenditures in Contemporary Developing Nations: Is There a Trade-off? *Journal of Developing Areas* 22, 4 (July 1988) pp. 497-514.

Hicks, Norman and Anne Kubisch, "Cutting Government Expenditure in LDCs," *Finance and Development* 21, 3 (September 1984), pp. 37-40.

Hill, Kim Quail, "Domestic Politics, International Linkages, and Military Expenditures," *Studies in Comparative International Development* 13, 1 (Spring 1978) pp. 38-59.

Hsiao, C., "Autoregressive Modeling and Money Income Causality Detection," *Journal of Monetary Economics* 7 (1981), pp. 85-106.

———, "Causality Tests in Econometrics" *Journal of Economic Dynamics and Control* (1979), pp. 321-346.

Hyman, Anthony, "Iran," in *The Middle East Review, 1990*. Saffron Walden: World of Information, 1990, p. 69.

International Institute for Strategic Studies, *The Military Balance 1993-94*. London: Brassey's for the International Institute for Strategic Studies, October 1993.

International Monetary Fund, *Government Finance Statistics Yearbook*. Washington, D. C.: International Monetary Fund, various issues.

———, *International Finance Statistics Yearbook* Washington, D. C.: International Monetary Fund, various issues.

Joffe, George and Keith McLachlan, *Iran and Iraq: Building on the Stalemate*, Special Report No 1164. London: the Economist Intelligence Unit, November 1988.

———, *Iran and Iraq: the Next Five Years*. London: Economist Intelligence Unit, 1987.

Judge, G.G., W. Hill, H. Griffiths, H. Lutkephol, and T.C. Lee, *Introduction to the Theory and Practice of Econometrics*. New York: John Wiley and Sons, 1982.

Kick, Edward and Bam Dev Sharda, "Third World Militarization and Development," *Journal of Developing Societies* II, 1 (April 1986), pp. 49-67.

Koyc, L.M, *Distributed Lags and Investment Analysis*. Amsterdam: NorthHolland, 1954.

LaCivita, Charles J. and Peter C. Frederiksen "Defense Spending and Economic Growth: An Alternative Approach to the Causality Issue" *Journal of Development Economics*, 35, 1 (January, 1991).

Lambelet, Jean-Christian, "The Formal 'Economic' Analysis of Arms Races: What—If Anything—Have We Learned Since Richardson?" *Conflict Management and Peace Science*, 9, 2 (Spring 1986), pp. 1-18.

Lebovic, James and Ashafaq Ishaq, "Military Burden, Security Needs, and Economic Growth in the Middle East," *Journal of Conflict Resolution* 31, 1 (March 1987), p. 107-138.

Leontief, W. and F. Duchin, *Military Spending: Facts and Figures*. New York: Oxford University Press, 1983.

Lim, David, "Another Look at Growth and Defense in Less Developed Countries," *Economic Development and Cultural Change* 31, 2 (January 1983), pp. 377-84.

Looney Robert E., *Economic Origins of the Iranian Revolution*. New York: Pergamon Press, 1982.

———, *Third World Military Expenditure and Arms Production*. London: Macmillan, 1988.

———, *Economic Development in Saudi Arabia: Consequences of the Oil Price Decline*. Greenwich, Connecticut: JAI Press, 1990.

———, "Military Expenditures in Latin America: Patterns of Budgetary Trade-offs," *Journal of Economic Development* (July 1986), pp. 69-103.

———, "Austerity and Military Expenditure in Developing Contraries: The Case of Venezuela," *Socio-Economic Planning Sciences* 20, 3 (1986), pp. 161-64.

——— and P.C. Frederiksen "Defense Expenditures, External Public Debt, and Growth in Developing Countries," *Journal of Peace Research* 23, 4 (December 1986), pp. 329-338.

———, "The Impact of Political Change, Debt Servicing and Fiscal Deficits on Argentinean Budgetary Priorities," *Journal of Economic Studies* 14, 3 (1987), pp. 25-39.

———, "Impact of Military Expenditures on Third World Debt," *Canadian Journal of Development Studies* VII, 1 (1987), pp. 7-26.

——— and P.C. Frederiksen, "Impact of Latin American Arms Production on Economic Performance," *Journal of Social, Political and Economic Studies* 2, 3 (Fall 1987), pp. 309-320.

———, "The Impact of Defense Expenditures on the Saudi Arabian Private Sector, *Journal of Arab Affairs* 7, 1 (Fall 1987), pp. 198-229.

——— and Peter C. Frederiksen, "Economic Determinants of Latin American Defense Expenditures," *Armed Forces and Society* 14, 4 (Spring l988), pp. 49-471.

———, "Political Economy of Third World Military Expenditures: The Impact of the Regime Type on the Defense Allocation Process," *Journal of Political and Military Sociology* 16, 1 (Spring 1988), pp. 21-30.

———, "Defense Budgetary Process in the Third World: Does Regime Type Make A Difference?" *Arms Control* 9 (1988), pp. 186-202.

—— and P.C. Frederiksen, "The Iranian Economy in the 1970s: Examination of the Nugent Thesis," *Middle Eastern Studies* 24, 4 (October 1988), p. 492.

——, "The Role of Military Expenditures in Pre-Revolutionary Iran's Economic Decline," *Iranian Studies* XXI, 3-4 (1988), pp. 52-81.

——, "Economic Impact of Rent Seeking and Military Expenditures in Third World Military and Civilian Regimes," *American Journal of Economics and Sociology* 48, 1 (January 1989), pp. 11-30.

——, "Internal and External Factors in Effecting Third World Military Expenditures," *Journal of Peace Research* 26, 1 (February 1989), pp 33-46.

——, "Military Keynesianism in the Third World: An Assessment of Non-Military Motivations for Arms Production," *Journal of Political and Military Sociology* 17, 1 (1989), pp. 43-64.

——, "Impact of Arms Production on Third World Distribution and Growth in the Third World," *Economic Development and Cultural Change* 38, 1 (October 1989), pp. 145-154.

——, "The Role of Military Expenditures in the African Economic Crisis," *Jerusalem Journal of International Relations* 12, 1 (January 1990), pp. 76-101.

—— and P.C. Frederiksen, "The Economic Determinants of Military Expenditure in Selected East Asian Countries" *Contemporary Southeast Asia* 11, 4 (March 1990), pp. 265-277.

——, "Militarization, Military Regimes and The General Quality of Life in the Third World," *Armed Forces and Society* 17, 1 (Fall, 1990) pp. 127-139.

——, "Budgetary Priorities in Saudi Arabia: The Impact of Relative Austerity Measures on Human Capital Formation," *OPEC Review* XV, 2 (Summer 1991), pp. 133-152.

——, "Deducing Budgetary Priorities in Saudi Arabia: The Impact of Defense Expenditures on Allocations to Socio-Economic Programs," *Public Budgeting and Financial Management* (1992), pp. 311-326.

——, "Human Capital Development in the UAE: An Analysis of Budgetary Conflicts in an Era of Relative Austerity," *Public Budgeting and Financial Management* (1992).

—— and David Winterford, "Patterns of Arab Gulf Exports: Implications for Industrial Diversification of Increased Inter-Arab Trade," *Orient*, 33, 4 (December 1992), pp. 579-597.

—— and David Winterford, "Infrastructure and Regional Development in Pakistan," *Review of Urban and Regional Development Studies*, Vol. 5 (1993) pp. 95-114.

—— and David Winterford, "The Environmental Consequences of Third World Military Expenditures and Arms Production: The Latin American Case," *Rivista Internazionale di Scienze Economich e Commerciali* 40, 9, (1993) pp. 769-786.

Maizels, Alfred and Machiko K. Nissanke, "The Determinants of Military Expenditures in Developing Countries," *World Development* 14, 9 (Spring 1986) pp. 1125-1140.

——, "The Causes of Military Expenditure in Developing Countries," in Saadat Deger and Robert West, *Defence, Security and Development*. London: Francis Pinter, 1987, pp. 129-139.

McGuire, Martin C., "Foreign Assistance, Investment, and Defense: A Methodological Study with an Application to Israel, 1960-1979," *Economic Development and Cultural Change* 35, 4 (July 1987), pp. 847-873.

McKinlay, Robert, *Third World Military Expenditure: Determinants and Implications.* London: Frances Pinter, 1989.

Mehdi, Abbas Salih and Olive Robinson, "Economic Development and the Labor Market in Iraq," *International Journal of Manpower* (1983), pp. 3-39.

Mousad, Mohammed Raief, "Human Resources, Government Education Expenditure and the Military Burden in Less Developed Countries: With Special Reference to Arab Countries," *Bulletin of Arab Research and Studies* (Number 11, 1984), pp. 35-55.

Nerlove, M., "Lags in Economic Behavior" *Econometrica* 40, 2 (March, 1972) pp. 221-251.

Neuman, Stephanie, "Security, Military Expenditures and Socioeconomic Development: Reflections on Iran," *Orbis* 22, (Fall 1978), pp. 569-594.

————,"International Stratification and Third World Military Industries," *International Organization* 38, 1 (Winter 1984), pp. 167-197.

Nugent, Jeffrey, "Momentum for Development and Development Disequilibria," *Journal of Economic Development* (July 1977).

O'Leary, Michael K. and William D. Coplin, *Quantitative Techniques in Foreign Policy Analysis and Forecasting.* New York: Praeger Publishers, 1975.

Petrossian, Vahe, "Iran's Changing State," *Middle East Economic Journal* (February 10, 1989).

Rao, Potluri and Roger Miller, *Applied Econometrics.* Belmont, California, 1971.

Richards, Alan and John Waterbury, *A Political Economy of the Middle East: State, Class and Economic Development.* Boulder, CO: Westview Press, 1990.

Richie, Michael, "Saudi Arabia," in *The Middle East Review, 1987.* London: World of Information, 1987, pp. 167-83.

Rothschild, K.W., "Military Expenditure, Exports and Growth," *Kyklos* 30, (1977), pp. 804-13.

Rummel, R.J., *Applied Factor Analysis.* Evanston, Illinois: Northwestern University Press, 1970.

Saudi Arabian Monetary Agency, *Annual Report*, various issues.

Scoville, James, "The Labor Market in Prerevolutionary Iran," *Economic Development and Cultural Change* 24, 1 (October 1985), pp. 143-155.

Semple, Alison, "When the Baby Boom Explodes," *The Middle East* 168 (June 1990), p. 27.

Sivard, Ruth Leger, *World Military and Social Expenditures.* Washington: World Priorities, various issues.

Stahl, Shelley A. and Geoffrey Kemp, eds., *Arms Control and Weapons Proliferation in the Middle East and South Asia.* New York: St. Martin's Press, 1992.

Stockholm International Peace Research Institute, *SIPRI Yearbook, World Armaments and Disarmament.* SIPRI, various issues.

Stork, Joe, "Iraq: The War in the Gulf," *MERIP Reports*, 9, 7 (June 1981), pp. 16-17.

Terhal, Peter, "Foreign Exchange Costs of the Indian Military, 1950-1972," *Journal of Peace Research* XIX, 3 (1982), pp. 251-260.

Thomas, Raju G.C., "Defense Planning in India," in Stephanie G.Neuman, ed., *Defense Planning in Less-Industrialized States.* Lexington, MA: Lexington Books, 1984.

Thornton, D.L. and D.S. Batten, "Lag-length Selection and Tests of Granger Causality Between Money and Income," *Journal of Money, Credit and Banking* 17, 2 (May 1985), pp. 164-78.

Twinam, Joseph, "The Saudi Role in the New Middle East Order," in M.E. Ahrari and James H. Noyes, eds., *The Persian Gulf After the Cold War*. Westport: Praeger, 1993, pp. 125-146.

United States, *World Military Expenditures and Arms Transfers*. Washington D.C.: United States Arms Control and Disarmament Agency, various issues.

————, Congressional Budget Office, *Limiting Arms Exports to the Middle East*. Washington D.C.: Congressional Budget Office, September 1992.

Verner, Joel, "Budgetary Trade-offs between Education and Defense in Latin America: A Research Note," *Journal of Developing Areas* 18, 1 (October 1983), pp. 77-92.

Ward, Michael D., et al., "Economic Growth, Investment, and Military Spending in India, 1948-1988," Working Paper, Research Program On Political and Economic Change, Institute of Behavioral Science University of Colorado (March 15, 1990).

Weede, Erich, "Military Participation Ratios, Human Capital Formation, and Economic Growth: A Cross-National Analysis," *Journal of Political and Military Sociology* 11, 1 (Spring 1983), pp. 11-20.

Westing, Arthur H., "Military Expenditures and their Reduction," *Bulletin of Peace Proposals* 9, (1978), pp. 24-29.

Winterford, David, "Security, Sovereignty and Economics: Armaments Limitation in Asia," *Pacific Focus*, 11, 1 (Spring 1987) pp. 135-164.

———— and Robert E. Looney, "Gulf Oil: Geo-Economic and Geo-Strategic Realities in the Post-Cold War and Post-Gulf War Era," in M.E. Ahrari and James H. Noyes, eds., *The Persian Gulf After the Cold War*. Westport: Praeger, 1993, pp. 149-171.

————, "Public Sector Investment in Energy: Budgetary Constraints and Tradeoffs in Pakistan," *Resources Policy*, June 1993, pp. 98-105.

————, "The Industrialization Challenge Confronting Small, Resource-Rich Third World States," *Orient*, 34, 2, June 1993, pp. 231-244.

Wolf, Charles, "Economic Success, Stability, and the 'Old' International Order," *International Security* 6, 1 (Summer 1981), pp. 75-92.

World Bank, Focus on Poverty, 1983. Washington D.C.: World Bank, 1983.

————, *IDA in Retrospect*. Washington D.C.: World Bank, 1983.

————, *Sub-Saharan Africa: Progress Report on Development Prospects and Programs*. Washington D.C.: World Bank, 1983.

————, *Syria: Recent Economic Developments and Prospects*. Washington: World Bank, Report No. 5563-SYR, May 1986.

————, *Pakistan: Current Economic Situation and Prospects*. Washington: The World Bank, Report No. 9283-PAK, March 22, 1991.

————, *Social Indicators of Development, 1988*. Washington D.C.: World Bank, various issues.

————, *World Development Report*. New York: Oxford University Press, various issues.

Index